The

Writings

of

J.

Frank

Dobie:

A Bibliography

Christianson-Leberman

The

Writings

of

J.

Frank

Dobie:

A Bibliography

By Mary Louise McVicker

Introduction by
Harry H. Ransom

Museum of the Great Plains, Lawton

GREAT PLAINS HISTORICAL ASSOCIATION

AT THE MUSEUM OF THE GREAT PLAINS • P. O. BOX 1122
LAWTON, OKLAHOMA 73501

The Museum of the Great Plains is, in part, dedicated:

To gather information that will better enable present and future inhabitants of the Great Plains to understand the vivid contrast of the land, climate, and people of the region. To enrich the future, to promote appreciation of beauty, and to serve as the voice of history in the Great Plains.

Marvin E. Tong, Jr.
Director
Museum of the
Great Plains

 *Preface*

his bibliography attempts a comprehensive listing of all of the works of J. Frank Dobie for the use of all who are interested in his writing. It grew from a list of his periodical publications compiled from his collection for his own use. I have enjoyed the exceptional opportunity of using Mr. Dobie's collection, now at the University of Texas, the excellent collection of the Texas Collection of the University of Texas and those of a number of other Texas and California libraries.

Books, the first of five sections, provides a full description of the editions and variant issues of those books entirely by Mr. Dobie. Titles are arranged in chronological order of publication and sub-arranged chronologically by editions and variant issues.

Contributions to the Books of Others, section B, lists in brief form all other books containing any writing by Mr. Dobie. His contributions vary greatly in length and scope; here are books he edited and compiled, those with his prefaces and introductions, anthologies containing reprints of articles and stories written by him, etc. These items are arranged chronologically by year of publication, alphabetically by author or editor within each year followed by later editions.

Magazine Articles and Stories, section C, lists work which appeared in periodical publications. Items are arranged chronologically by year, alphabetically by title, each followed by any reprints. When a reprint notation does not appear, Mr. Dobie is the authority; editors change titles, cut and rearrange material to such an extent that it is often most difficult to know whether an article or story is a reprint or a new work on the subject. Since magazine covers often are not bound in, varying dates found on the covers of certain magazines are not given.

Pamphlets, Reprints, etc., section D, contains items published in pamphlet form, written by Mr. Dobie or containing some contribution of his. A slightly fuller description is provided for his own works. Since the word pamphlet has not been strictly defined, some of these might have been listed in sections A or B. The arrangement is that of section B.

Sunday Newspaper Column, section E, lists the pieces by the author's titles, except for the year 1964 and a few omitted on his lists. The arrangement is chronological by the dates he expected them to be published. Frequently these pieces were published with varying captions in the different papers, and often they were edited. On a few occasions a paper would publish an article on a later date.

It has been a pleasure to collect and collate this information and a great privilege to know Mr. Dobie. I cannot acknowledge all of the most generous help I have received from other librarians, scholars, students and friends of Mr. Dobie's. He himself gave much of his time to answer my many questions and supplied information that could have been obtained from no other source. In spite of the assistance I have been given, I have been unable to find several items I know of and there probably are others; I shall be grateful to receive any corrections or additions.

Mary Louise McVicker

Introduction

THE WORK OF J. FRANK DOBIE

By Harry E. Ransom
Chancellor of the University of Texas

Frank Dobie and his literary career have been described in many generalizations. Each is true in part—but only in part. Each will deserve restatement as Dobie, the writer and the man, becomes a permanent figure in the history which he helped to make.

Dobie's earliest public and academic reputation acquired the misleading label of "folklorist." As a matter of fact, folklore—which he constantly redefined for himself and his readers—was only a point of departure. Among sundry intellectual specialties and academic moated towers, the term gave him a small, habitable fort. From its hand-hewn battlements he took occasional potshots at the stiff educational formalities, empty ceremonies, and stuffed vanities of the academic world. Within its walls, which opened wide gates of access to him by all kinds of unarmed honest folk, he maintained the essence of his selfhood. He refused to form a troop of little admiring defenders within this free stockade. The only "Dobie School" which appeared from 1920 to 1964 was a wide and friendly company of all sorts of estates, ages and attitudes, a company in fact and in spirit schooled by his example. About one of the University's proudest and most ambiguous mottoes, he once said, "Truth can't be institutionalized. It can be learned and it can be spread, but there is no curriculum for intellectual honesty."

In his lifetime, Dobie became one of the legends of Texas. Yet his is a legend too large to fit into future editions of his early book by that title.

As an author of books, essays, and stories; as editor, talker, teacher, newspaper columnist, letter writer, epigrammatist, and genius in the rare art of eloquent silence, Dobie was an individualist. On occasion, his individualism appeared to be Texan and sounded American. Its literary origins, however, were in the elder idiom of the English language. More than once he said that the piece of writing which had influenced him most was Hazlitt's "On the Feeling of Immortality in Youth." His works shows the influence of no "Western" writer. He collected Hudson. He adapted John Stuart Mill. He admired White of Selborne (and every other man who not only looked into nature but really saw it and felt it and joined it to living belief).

In the formal sense, Dobie was never a student of literary classics; but he had a profound knowledge of Biblical and Shakespearean text and remembered words of men as different as Walton, Burton, Lamb, Carlyle, and Thoreau. He taught literature not according to period, theme, circle, or critical theory. He simply laid open for his students a wealth of durable ideas, transient opinions, and fleeting impressions with great clarity and deep conviction, but without dogmatism. His literal summary of his pedagogy: every teacher should have many sadde bags crammed with facts, fancies, impressions, and opinions for his own campfires and his own forced marches. But no student should be harnessed in the trappings of any teacher.

As a stylist, Dobie developed his own ways of writing. The process was less deliberate than that of most authors and less conscious, except for the long and profound influence of Bertha Dobie. His memory resorted to the melodies of the best English and American writers. Yet his tongue and his pen were often tuned to the Texas range, the Mexican talemaker, and rhythms in his own head. By these means he brought sense and substance into what might otherwise have been pages of borrowed provincialism smeared with local color.

A reader of Dobie's bibliography will find both depth and breadth. Concerning plans for the volume, he was sometimes dubious and only reluctantly cooperative. He kept saying: "Let's wait until something better comes. I don't want a bibliography deposited until I'm deposited."

Nothing except her own insight, perseverance, and taste recommends Mary Louise McVicker's work more highly than the fact that Dobie himself helped her carry it forward. She has done so with a real sense of time and proportion and value.

The process and terminology of bibliographical record are confusing because the circumstances of composition and printing and publication which they report are often muddled. In Dobie's work, the muddlement was neither accidental nor biographically insignificant. He made a point of not paying much attention to a book "finally published." Yet his whole process of authorship was complicated by verbal rumination, reworking, refinement, and republication.

As a result of his method, the printed trails to his most memorable books can be found in newspapers, magazines, pamphlets, and occasional volumes. Conversely, some of the best short things he wrote were left in newsprint, not quite forgotten but not easily visible. The gathering and publication of those words which should not be lost will be a major task of his literary executors.

For the best spirit of his best work, students will do well to look to Dobie's correspondence, out of which he brought many of his most vital ideas; they will do equally well to listen to the fading echoes of his conversation, through which flashed and crackled much of his liveliest expression.

Future scholars must arrange and keep rearranging the categories of Dobie's writing. Despite his own disclaimers and those of his most attentive readers, one section will surely be "Folklore"—the lore of the Southwest and Mexico, which he recorded after immeasurable travel, wide reading, wider correspondence, and careful listening. Among his earlier works are legendary treasure, folk custom, folk language, tales and anecdotes in motion, and lost anecdotes and tales to which he gave new impetus. His earliest devotion was to the range as part of American history, an unspoiled and undefensive loyalty to the ranch and ranch life; to people, animals, plants, seasons—a calendar which cannot be turned back and a compass of hard times, good times, courage, failure, joy, companionship in an unstaked, unfenced world.

Dobie's earliest impact upon academic study and writing (and the periodic shock waves which he generated in academic circles) have caused many of his strongest admirers to forget one of his great intellectual strengths. There are those who cherish the Dobie "position" only because of the intransigence with which he invariably confronted the organized intransigence of regulations on which he thought the regulators set too much stock. When such a regulation in any realm of life, traffic law or academic administration, seemed to him to be a device—even a reasonable device—he refused to erect it into a philosophy or a way of life.

Among many shifting positions in these external matters, Dobie never hesitated on any given day to proclaim, "Here I stand." Yet he was never satisfied with merely standing pat or staying put. Unlike many writers and teachers who discover a good thing and convert it into an insurance policy, Dobie kept changing his points of view, his willing exceptions, his keen interests. In a dozen ways, he wrote and said, "I am busy becoming contemporary with myself." His joy in that process is a sensation which no close-minded writer—radical, liberal, conservative, reactionary, or narcissistic—can ever share.

In the future of criticism now beginning, Dobie's volumes on the longhorn, the coyote, and the mustang are likely to attract most attention and gain highest praise. His lyrical passage on the mustang will be quoted more often—at least in classrooms and on official occasions—than anything else he wrote.

This likelihood is double irony, good and bad. Good because in the broadest sense, Dobie was a poet. Bad because this memorable manifesto on freedom may be mistaken for sentimental devotion, nostalgia, or prescriptive doctrine. The real mind and spirit of Frank Dobie as a man are reflected better in *The Mustangs* as a whole, in the companion books, and throughout a life of talk and written words not yet in print. By all of these Dobie expressed his aspiration to freedom for himself and for every other human being. He attained that freedom in his thinking, maintained it, sometimes against formidable odds, in his living, and defended it unforgettably as the essential condition of all men who would stay fully alive.

Books

A VAQUERO OF THE BRUSH COUNTRY

A1 a(1)   A VAQUERO of the / BRUSH COUNTRY / BY /
J. FRANK DOBIE / Partly from the Reminiscences
of John Young / [device] / ILLUSTRATED BY /
JUSTIN C. GRUELLE / THE SOUTHWEST
PRESS / DALLAS :: :: :: TEXAS / 1929

Collation: colored frontispiece; title as above within
ornamental border; verso *Copyright 1929 / BY / THE
SOUTHWEST PRESS / Printed in the United States of
America;* dedication *To / George W. Saunders . . . / . . . /
and / To the memory of my uncle, James M. (Jim) / Dobie
. . .;* verso blank; *CONTENTS* p. v; verso blank; *LIST OF
ILLUSTRATIONS* p. vii; verso blank; *A NECESSARY EX-
PLANATION* pp. ix-xv; verso blank; text pp. 1-297; verso
blank; *APPENDIX A* pp. 299-301; *APPENDIX B* pp. 302-
303; verso blank; *INDEX* pp. 305-314.

Running titles: *A Necessary Explanation, Appendix A,
Appendix B* and *Index* on rectos and versos; chapter titles
on rectos, title on versos.

Illustrations: colored photograph frontispiece; four
photographs on each of the plates facing pp. 6, 144, 198,
290; and a facsimile facing p. 110. Tailpieces, pen and
ink sketches, at end of each chapter. Title within ornamental line border.

Maps of Texas, with *RIO GRANDE RIVER*, on lining-
papers.

Bound in black and white snake skin pattern boards,
with tan cloth backstrip and tan label on front, stamped
in brown. Label on front: within ornamental border,
*A VAQUERO OF THE / BRUSH COUNTRY / [line] / J.
FRANK DOBIE.* Spine: *A VAQUERO / of the / BRUSH /*

A VAQUERO *of the* BRUSH COUNTRY

BY

J. FRANK DOBIE

Partly from the Reminiscences of John Young

ILLUSTRATED BY

JUSTIN C. GRUELLE

THE SOUTHWEST PRESS

DALLAS :: :: :: TEXAS

1929

COUNTRY / [type ornament] / *DOBIE* / *SOUTHWEST PRESS.*

Uncut. 24 x 16½ cm.

A1 a(2) ⸺ ⸺

Collation: . . . verso of title-page . . . *SOUTHWEST PRESS* / *SECOND EDITION* [i.e. second issue] / *Printed in the United States of America* . . .

Maps of Texas, with *RIO GRANDE RIVER,* on lining-papers.

After the first issue, Mr. Dobie requested that the word *RIVER* be deleted from *RIO GRANDE RIVER* on the lining-paper maps. Since there has been general agreement that this was done in the second and later printings, it is probable that there are copies of the second issue with the corrected map; however those examined were not corrected.

A1 a(3) ⸺ ⸺

Later printings have *RIO GRANDE* on the lining-paper map.

A1 b(1) A VAQUERO / of the / BRUSH COUNTRY / BY / J. FRANK DOBIE / Partly from the Reminiscences of John Young / [star] / ILLUSTRATED BY / JUSTIN C. GRUELLE / GROSSET & DUNLAP / PUBLISHERS · NEW YORK [1936]

Collation: half-title: *A VAQUERO OF THE BRUSH COUNTRY;* verso blank; frontispiece in black and white; title as above within ornamental border; verso *Copyright, 1929* / *BY* / *THE SOUTHWEST PRESS* / *Manufactured in the United States of America* / *by H. Wolff Book Mfg. Co., Inc., New York City;* dedication; verso blank; *CONTENTS;* verso blank; *A NECESSARY EXPLANATION* pp. xi-xvi; half-title: *A VAQUERO OF THE BRUSH COUNTRY;* verso blank; text pp. 3-279; verso blank; half-title: *APPENDICES;* verso blank; *APPENDIX A* pp. 283-285; *APPENDIX B* pp. 286-287; verso blank; half-title: *INDEX;* verso blank; *INDEX* pp. 291-302.

Running titles: *A NECESSARY EXPLANATION, APPENDIX A, APPENDIX B* and *INDEX* on both rectos and versos; chapter titles on rectos, title on versos.

Illustrations: frontispiece in black and white; tailpieces at the end of chapters I-III, V-XI, XIV-XXI. Without the plates. Title-page border, a decorative rope design, differs from that of the first edition.

Maps on lining papers, with *RIO GRANDE.*

Bound in tan cloth stamped in dark blue. Front: [5 lines] / *A* / *VAQUERO* / *OF THE* / *BRUSH* / *COUNTRY* / [star] / *J. FRANK DOBIE* / [5 lines]. Spine: [5 lines] / *A* / *VAQUERO* / *OF THE* / *BRUSH* / *COUNTRY* / [star] / *DOBIE* / [5 lines] / *GROSSET* / *& DUNLAP.*

Uncut, except top edge cut and blue. 22 x 15cm.

Type reset, printed on a smaller page.

A1 b(2) . . . GRUELLE / BOSTON / LITTLE, BROWN AND COMPANY / 1943

Collation: half-title: *A VAQUERO OF THE BRUSH COUNTRY;* verso *BOOKS BY / J. FRANK DOBIE;* frontispiece in black and white; title as above within ornamental border; verso *COPYRIGHT 1929, BY J. FRANK DOBIE / . . . / New Edition Published February 1943 / PRINTED IN THE UNITED STATES OF AMERICA;* dedication . . .

Illustrations and title-page border are those of the Grosset & Dunlap edition.

Maps on lining-papers, with RIO GRANDE.

Bound in rust cloth stamped in dark blue, with the ornaments and type of the Grosset & Dunlap edition except for the publisher's name on spine, ... lines] / *LITTLE, BROWN / AND COMPANY.*

Uncut, except top edge cut and blue. 21 ½ x 15cm.

Printed from the Grosset & Dunlap plates.

A1 b(3) . . . GRUELLE / PREFACE BY / LAWRENCE CLARK POWELL / BOSTON / LITTLE, BROWN AND COMPANY

Collation: half-title: **A VAQUERO OF THE BRUSH COUNTRY;** verso *Books by J. Frank Dobie;* frontispiece in black and white; title as above within ornamental border; verso *COPYRIGHT 1929 BY J. FRANK DOBIE / . . . / New Edition Published February 1943 / Sixth Printing / PRINTED IN THE UNITED STATES OF AMERICA;* dedication; verso blank; *CONTENTS;* verso blank; *PREFACE / THE TIME, THE PLACE, AND THE BOOK* pp. vii-ix; verso blank; *A NECESSARY EXPLANATION* pp. xi-xvi . . .

Running titles: *THE TIME, THE PLACE, AND THE BOOK, A NECESSARY EXPLANATION, APPENDIX A, APPENDIX B,* and *INDEX* . . .

Illustrations and title-page border are those of the Grosset & Dunlap edition. Facsimile facing p. 206.

Maps on lining-papers, with *RIO GRANDE.*

Bound in rust stamped in dark blue . . .

Fore-edge uncut, top and bottom edges cut, 22 x 15cm.

A1 c J. FRANK DOBIE / A VAQUERO OF THE / BRUSH COUNTRY / PARTLY FROM THE REMINISCENCES OF JOHN YOUNG / LONDON / HAMMOND. HAMMOND & CO., LTD. / 87 GOWER STREET, W. C. I ⌈1949]

Collation: half-title: *A VAQUERO OF / THE BRUSH COUNTRY;* verso *Other books by / J. FRANK DOBIE;* frontispiece; title as above; verso *Copyright 1949 by J. Frank Dobie, / first published in the British Empire / by Hammond, Hammond & Co., Ltd., 1949 / With Illustrations by / Justin C. Gruelle / Printed in Great Britain by / The Camelot Press Ltd., London and Southampton / 6.49;* dedication; verso blank; *CONTENTS;* verso *ILLUSTRA-*

TIONS; A NECESSARY EXPLANATION pp. [9]-14; text pp. [15]-262; *Appendix A* pp. [263]-265; *Appendix B* pp. 265-266; *INDEX* pp. [267]-274; notes on the author and his works [2] pp. of advertising.

Running titles: *A NECESSARY EXPLANATION,* chapter titles, and *APPENDICES* on rectos; title on versos; except *INDEX* on both rectos and versos.

Illustrations of the American edition; tailpieces at end of Chapters I-IV, VI-XII, XIV-XX.

Bound in rust cloth stamped in gold. Spine *A / Vaquero / of the / Brush / Country /* [star] */ J. FRANK / DOBIE /* [device] */ HAMMOND / HAMMOND*

Type reset.

Cut. 22 x 15cm.

A1 d A VAQUERO / OF THE / BRUSH COUNTRY / (CONDENSED EDITION) / By J. FRANK DOBIE / Partly from / the Reminiscences / of John Young / Pennant / Books / NEW YORK / [1954]

Collation: publisher's blurb p. [i]; verso blank; title as above; verso *A VAQUERO . . . / PRINTING HISTORY / Originally Published by Southwest Press, 1929 / Little, Brown Edition Published February 1943 / 1st Printing January, 1943 / 2nd Printing January, 1946 / 3rd Printing November, 1949 / 4th Printing March, 1952 / Pennant Edition Published November, 1954 / 1st Printing October, 1954 / Copyright, 1929, by J. Frank Dobie / . . . / Pennant Books are published by / Bantam Books, Inc., 25 W. 45th St., New York 36, N. Y. CONTENTS;* verso blank; dedication; verso blank; text pp. 1-184.

Without illustrations.

Bound in illustrated paper covers. Numbered P51 on front and spine.

Type reset.

Cut. 18 x 11cm.

CORONADO'S CHILDREN

A2 a(1) CORONADO'S CHILDREN / Tales of Lost Mines and / Buried Treasures / of the Southwest / BY / J. FRANK DOBIE / Author of "A Vaquero of the Brush Country" / ILLUSTRATED BY / BEN CARLTON MEAD / [device] / THE SOUTHWEST PRESS / DALLAS   TEXAS [1931]

Collation: frontispiece; title as above within border of type ornaments between double lines; verso *Copyright, 1930, by / THE SOUTHWEST PRESS / PRINTED IN THE UNITED STATES OF AMERICA;* dedication *To / MY MOTHER / ELLA BYLER DOBIE / . . . / AND / TO THE MEMORY OF MY FATHER / R. J. DOBIE / A COWMAN OF THE / TEXAS SOIL;* verso blank; *IN THE BEGINNING* pp. v-xii; *CONTENTS* pp. xiii-xiv; *LIST OF ILLUSTRATIONS* [and] *MAPS AND CHARTS* p. xv; verso blank; text pp. 1-341; verso blank; *NOTES* pp. 343-359; verso

CORONADO'S CHILDREN

Tales of Lost Mines and
Buried Treasures
of the Southwest

BY

J. FRANK DOBIE

Author of "A Vaquero of the Brush Country"

ILLUSTRATED BY

BEN CARLTON MEAD

THE SOUTHWEST PRESS

DALLAS   TEXAS

blank; *GLOSSARY OF MEXICAN AND OTHER LOCAL-ISMS / OF THE SOUTHWEST* pp. 361-367.

Running titles: *In the Beginning* and chapter titles on rectos, title on versos; *Contents, Notes* and *Glossary* on both rectos and versos.

Illustrations: in a true black, frontispiece; plates facing pp. 114, 170, 194, 260, 330; maps and charts on pp. 35, 47, 55; illustration p. 234; signs pp. 334-337; full page facsimile p. 339. Tailpieces, pen and ink sketches, at end of each chapter; tailpiece of Chapter XI, a skull and cross; Chapter XIX, characters.

Map on lining papers, red on yellow.

Bound in black cloth stamped in gold. Front, within vignette of treasure chest, *CORONADO'S / CHILDREN / By J. FRANK DOBIE*. Spine: *CORONADO'S / CHILDREN /* [short line] */ DOBIE /* [vignette, a cross] */ SOUTHWEST PRESS*

Uncut, except top edge cut and red. 24 x 16 ½cm.

First printing has the word "clean" omitted from the dedication. This was restored in the second and subsequent printings.

First printing October, 1930, published March, 1931.

" . . . members who paid their dues for 1929 will receive about December a copy of *Coronado's Children,* a book made up of tales about lost mines and buried treasures of the Southwest. While not a regularly numbered publication of the Society *Coronado's Children* . . ." cf. Dobie, J. Frank, editor. Man, Bird, and Beast. Austin, Texas Folk-lore Society, 1930. p. [v]

A2 a(2)   . . . MEAD / 1931 / THE LITERARY GUILD OF AMERICA / NEW YORK

Collation . . . verse of title-page *Copyright, 1930, by / THE SOUTHWEST PRESS / Printed in U. S. A. / PRESS OF / BRAUNSWORTH & CO., INC. / BOOK MANUFAC-TURERS / BROOKLYN, NEW YORK;* dedication . . . *R. J. DOBIE / A CLEAN COWMAN OF THE / TEXAS SOIL . . .*

Illustrations in brownish black. Variant tailpieces at end of Chapter XII, *PECOS MISSION,* and Chapter XIX, a fenceline scene.

Bound in yellow cloth stamped in gold, with the ornaments and type of the first issue except for the publisher's name on spine, . . . cross] / LITERARY / GUILD.

Text printed from the original plates.

A2 a(3)   —— ——

The second printing of The Southwest Press April, 1931.

Collation: . . . verso of title-page *Copyright, 1930, by / THE SOUTHWEST PRESS / Printed in U. S. A. / PRESS OF / BRAUNSWORTH & CO., INC. / BOOK MANUFAC-TURERS / BROOKLYN, NEW YORK;* dedication . . . *R. J. DOBIE / A CLEAN COWMAN OF THE / TEXAS SOIL . . .*

Illustrations in a brownish black. Variant tailpieces at end of Chapters XII and XIX.

Text printed from the original plates; *GLOSSARY* . . . reset with additional words.

A2 a(4)   Coronado's Children / TALES OF LOST MINES AND BURIED / TREASURES OF THE SOUTH-WEST / BY / J. FRANK DOBIE / Author of "A Vaquero of the Brush Country" / "On the Open Range" / ILLUSTRATED BY / BEN CARLTON MEAD / [device] / GARDEN CITY PUBLISHING COMPANY, INC. / GARDEN CITY NEW YORK [1934]

Collation: . . . verso of title-page *Copyright* 1930, *by / THE SOUTHWEST PRESS / Printed in U. S. A.;* dedication . . . *R. J. DOBIE / A CLEAN COWMAN OF THE / TEXAS SOIL* . . . P. xv deleted.

Illustrations, in a true black, the same plates but bound in following pp. 112, 168, 192, 264, and 328. With the variant tailpieces of Chapters XII and XIX.

Printed from the original plates, published 1934.

A2 a(5)   A Grosset & Dunlap edition, printed from the original plates.

1st printing April 1939, published May 1939.

A2 a(6)   Coronado's Children / TALES OF LOST MINES AND BURIED / TREASURES OF THE SOUTH-WEST / BY / J. FRANK DOBIE / Author of "A Vaquero of the Brush Country" / ILLUSTRATED BY / BEN CARLTON MEAD / This book, while produced under / wartime conditions, in full com- / pliance with government regula- / tions for the conservation of paper / and other materials, is / COM-PLETE AND UNABRIDGED / GROSSET & DUN-LAP / Publishers NEW YORK

Collation: half-title: *CORONADO'S CHILDREN;* verso blank; title as above; verso *Copyright,* 1930, *by / THE SOUTHWEST PRESS / Printed in U. S. A.;* dedication . . . *R. J. DOBIE / A CLEAN COWMAN OF THE / TEXAS SOIL;* verso blank; *IN THE BEGINNING* pp. v-[xii]; *CON-TENTS* pp. xiii-xiv; text . . .

Illustrations on pages of the text are those of the earlier issues, with the variant tailpieces. Frontispiece, plates, and lining paper map deleted.

Bound in tan cloth stamped in maroon, with the orna-ments and type of the first issue, except for the pub-lisher's name on spine . . . a cross] / *GROSSET / & DUN-LAP*

Fore edge uncut, top edge cut and dark blue. 21x14½cm.

Text printed from the plates of the first issue, a smaller paper edition, with p. xv deleted, and with a third print-ing of the glossary.

A2 a(7) Coronado's Children / TALES OF LOST MINES AND BURIED / TREASURES OF THE SOUTHWEST / BY / J. FRANK DOBIE / Author of "A Vaquero of the Brush Country" / ILLUSTRATED BY / BEN CARLTON MEAD / GROSSET & DUNLAP / Publishers   New York

> Collation: half-title: *CORONADO'S CHILDREN;* verso blank; title as above within border; verso *Copyright,* 1930, *by / J. FRANK DOBIE / Printed in U.S.A.;* dedication . . . *R. J. DOBIE / A CLEAN COWMAN OF THE / TEXAS SOIL* . . .
>
> Illustrations on pages of the text are those of the earlier issues, with the variant tailpieces. Frontispiece, plates, and lining paper map deleted.
>
> Bound in peach cloth stamped in black, with the ornaments and type of the first issue, except for the publisher's name on spine, . . . cross] / GROSSET / & DUNLAP
>
> Fore edge uncut, top edge cut and dark blue. 21 x 14 ½cm.
>
> Text printed from the plates of the first issue, a smaller paper edition, with p. xv deleted, and with a third printing of the glossary.

A2 b CORONADO'S CHILDREN / Tales of Lost Mines and Buried / Treasures of the Southwest / By / J. FRANK DOBIE / Embossed in 5 Volumes / VOLUME I[-V] / Copyright, 1930, by The Southwest Press / Printed for the Library of Congress / Washington, D. C. / By Permission of the Author / PRINTED AT THE / American Printing House for the Blind / LOUISVILLE, KENTUCKY / 1949

> Collation. Vol. I: printed title as above; verso blank preliminary material in Braille [17] pp.; verso blank; text in Braille pp. 1-135, [1]. Vol. II: printed title; verso blank; title in Braille; verso blank; contents in Braille [2] pp.; text in Braille pp. 137-299, [1]. Vol. III: printed title; verso blank; title in Braille; verso blank; contents in Braille; verso blank; text in Braille pp. 301-435, [1]. Vol. IV: printed title; verso blank; title in Braille; verso blank; contents in Braille [2] pp.; text in Braille pp. 437-577, [1]. Vol. V: printed title; verso blank; title in Braille; verso blank; contents in Braille [2] pp.; text in Braille pp. 579-743, [1]
>
> Bound in green cloth stamped in silver. Front has title in Braille stamped in upper left corner. Spine: *CORONADO'S / CHILDREN / [short line] / DOBIE / [short line] / IN 5 VOLS. / Vol. I[-V] / [line] / BRAILLE / GRADE 2 / PRINTED FOR / THE LIBRARY / OF CONGRESS / U. S. A. / American Printing / House / for the Blind / Louisville, Ky. / 1949 / [line]*
>
> Cut. 29½ x 28½ cm.

A2 c   [Type ornament opposite the first three lines of title] Tales of Lost Mines / and Buried Treasures / of the Southwest / [ornamental line] / CORO-NADO'S CHILDREN / [ornamental line] / by J. Frank Dobie / [device] BANTAM BOOKS New York [1953]

> Collation: publisher's blurb p. [i]; title as above pp. [ii-iii]; dedication: . . . *R. J. DOBIE / A CLEAN COWMAN OF THE / TEXAS SOIL /* [double, heavy and light, line] / *CORONADO'S CHILDREN / A BANTAM BOOK Published by arrangement with / Little, Brown & Company, Inc. / Printing History / . . . / Bantam Edition Published March,* 1953 / 1*st Printing* . . . . . *February,* 1953 / . . . p. [iv]; *In The Beginning* pp. [v-xii]; text pp. 1-344, NOTES pp. 345-361; verso blank; *Glossary* . . . pp. 363-371; verso advertisement.
>
> Running titles: chapter titles, *Notes, Glossary* on rectos; title on versos.
>
> Without the illustrations, except the signs on pp. 339-342.
>
> Without the maps on lining papers.
>
> Bound in illustrated paper covers.
>
> Type reset.
>
> Cut, all edges orange. 16 x 11cm.

A2 d   J. FRANK DOBIE / LOST MINES / OF THE OLD WEST / Coronado's Children / Illustrated by / BEN CARLTON MEAD / Hammond, Hammond and Company : London [1960]

> Collation: half-title; verso *Other books by J. Frank Dobie;* title as above; verso *First published in Great Britain* 1960 / *Originally published in the United States under / the title Coronado's Children /* © *Copyright* 1930, *by the Southwest Press / Printed in Great Britain / for Hammond, Hammond & Co. Ltd.,* 87 *Gower Street, W. C. I. / by Lowe & Brydone (Printers) Ltd., London, N. W.* 10 / 460; dedication; verso blank; *CONTENTS* pp. vii-viii; *IN THE BE-GINNING* pp. ix-[xvi]; text pp. 1-341; verso blank; *NOTES* pp. 343-359; verso blank; *GLOSSARY OF MEXICAN AND OTHER LOCALISMS / OF THE SOUTHWEST* pp. 361-367.
>
> Without running titles.
>
> Illustrations. Frontispiece, plates, and map on lining papers deleted. Other illustrations are those of the first American edition.
>
> Bound in tan cloth stamped in rust. Spine: *Lost / Mines / of the / Old West /* [asterisk] / *J. FRANK / DOBIE /* [device] / *HAMMOND / HAMMOND*
>
> Cut, all edges white. 22 x 14cm.
>
> A line by line reprint from the Southwest Press trade edition.

ON THE OPEN RANGE

A3 a(1)   ON THE / OPEN RANGE / BY / J. FRANK
DOBIE / Author of Coronado's Children and A
Vaquero / of the Brush Country / Illustrated by /
BEN CARLTON MEAD / [device] / THE SOUTH-
WEST PRESS / DALLAS - - - - - TEXAS [1931]

Collation: colored frontispiece; recto blank; title as
above; verso *Copyright, 1931, by* / *THE SOUTHWEST
PRESS* / *PRINTED IN U. S. A.* / *PRESS OF* / *BRAUN-
WORTH & CO., INC.* / *BOOK MANUFACTURERS* /
BROOKLYN, NEW YORK; dedication *For* / *The Children
of the Southwest* / . . . / *and especially for* / *Richard,
Ray Pearl, Edgar, Patty,* / *Bertha Lucile, and Emily;* verso
blank; *CONTENTS* pp. v-vi; *LIST OF ILLUSTRATIONS*
p. vii; verso blank; *PREFACE* pp. ix-xii; text pp. 1-296;
SUGGESTED READINGS pp. 297-302; *WORDS, NAMES,
AND PHRASES PECULIAR* / *TO THE OPEN RANGE
COUNTRY* pp. 303-312.

Running titles: *Contents,* and *Preface* on both rectos
and versos; chapter titles, *Suggested Readings,* and *Words,
Phrases and Names* on rectos, title on versos.

Illustrations: colored frontispiece; colored plates facing
pp. 22, 98, and 292; full page black and white illustrations
on pp. 35, 60, 71, 106, 111, 138, 151, 172, 197, 223, 239, 257,
and 273; and a black and white chart on p. 288. Title
within ornamental frame border. Tailpieces at end of
chapters I-IV, VI-VII, and X.

Two of the three vignettes used for tailpieces on the
lining papers.

Printed on rag paper.

Bound in bright blue cloth stamped in orange. Front
[three vignettes within rope triangles, title within a square
of rope border with a vignette at end] *On the Open
Range* / *By* / *J. Frank Dobie.* Spine: *On* / *the* / *Open* /
Range / • / *Dobie* / *SOUTHWEST* / *PRESS*

Cut. 20 x 13cm.

With the last paragraph p. [xii] beginning *"Had it not
been for P. L. Turner* . . .

Variant binding. Spine: . . . *SOUTHWEST* / *PRESS* /
[three lines]

Variant binding. Spine: . . . *SOUTH* / *WEST* / *PRESS*

A3 a(2)   —— ——

A school edition printed from the original plates on
thin glazed paper.

Bound in darker blue cloth.

A3 a(3)   . . . Mead / [device] / DALLAS / BANKS UPSHAW
AND COMPANY

Collation: . . . title as above; verso *Copyright, 1931, by* /
THE SOUTHWEST PRESS / *Fifth Printing, March, 1940* /

BANKS UPSHAW AND COMPANY / Copyright, 1940, by / J. FRANK DOBIE / Printed in the United States of America; . . .

The last paragraph of the Preface, p. [xii] omitted.

Bound in dark blue cloth. Spine: . . . *Dobie / BANKS / UPSHAW / AND / COMPANY*

Printed from the original plates.

Cut. 20½ x 14cm.

A3 a(4) —— ——

The original plates were stolen from Banks Upshaw and Company; reprinted by offset process.

A3 b ON THE OPEN RANGE / [line] / BY / J. FRANK DOBIE / Author of / The Longhorns, Coronado's Children / etc. / Illustrated by / BEN C. MEAD / [vignette] / LONDON / SIR ISAAC PITMAN & SONS, LTD. / 1946

Collation: half title: *ON THE OPEN RANGE;* verso blank; title as above; verso *First Published in Great Britain by / Sir Isaac Pitman & Sons, Ltd., 1946 / . . . / MADE IN GREAT BRITAIN AT THE PITMAN PRESS, BATH / . . .; PREFACE* pp. v-vii; *CONTENTS* pp. viii-ix, verso *LIST OF ILLUSTRATIONS;* text pp. 1-206; *WORDS, NAMES, AND PHRASES PECULIAR / TO THE OPEN RANGE COUNTRY* pp. 207-214; *A FEW SUGGESTED BOOKS FOR FURTHER READING* at foot of p. 214.

Running titles: chapter and section titles on rectos; title on versos.

Illustrations: plates. Vignettes on half-title and title pages and tailpieces at end of Contents and chapters 2 and 13. Illustrations are those of the American edition.

Bound in tan paper stamped in green. Vignette as on title-page on the lower outside corner of the front cover. Spine, reading from bottom to top, *ON THE OPEN RANGE* [ornament] *DOBIE*, and across at foot *PITMAN*.

Cut. 19 x 12½cm.

A new revised edition with a new preface substituted, chapters rearranged, and part of the original text omitted. Type reset.

TONGUES OF THE MONTE

A4 a(1) J. FRANK DOBIE / TONGUES / OF THE / MONTE / [vignette, national seal of Mexico / line, white diamonds on black] / DOUBLEDAY, DORAN & COMPANY, INC. / Garden City, New York / 1935

Collation: half-title: *TONGUES OF THE MONTE /* [line of white diamonds on black] verso *BOOKS BY / J. FRANK DOBIE;* title as above; verso *PRINTED AT THE Country*

J. FRANK DOBIE

TONGUES

OF THE

MONTE

DOUBLEDAY, DORAN & COMPANY, INC.

Garden City, New York

1935

Life Press, GARDEN CITY, N. Y., U. S. A. / COPYRIGHT, 1935 / *BY J. FRANK DOBIE / ALL RIGHTS RESERVED / FIRST EDITION; The Things Which Are Caesar's* pp. v-vi; *CONTENTS* p. vii; verso blank; half-title: *TONGUES OF THE MONTE* / [line of white diamonds on black] verso blank; text pp. 1-301.

Running titles: *THE THINGS WHICH ARE CAESAR'S* on verso; chapter titles on rectos, title on versos.

Illustrations: two lines of music on p. 10, signs and diagrams on p. 248, 257, 285, 286, and 291.

Tan lining-papers.

Bound in yellow cloth with red and dark blue decorations including the national seal of Mexico. Front, title in yellow on dark blue, *TONGUES / OF THE MONTE / J. FRANK DOBIE.* Spine, yellow on dark blue, *TONGUES / OF THE / MONTE / J. FRANK / DOBIE,* and red on yellow, *DOUBLEDAY / DORAN*

Uncut, except top edge cut and red. 24 x 16cm.

This was announced, before publication, with the title: Hacienda of the Five Wounds.

A4 a(2)   J. FRANK DOBIE / THE MEXICO / I LIKE / [device] / UNIVERSITY PRESS IN DALLAS / Southern Methodist University / 1942

Collation: half-title: *THE MEXICO I LIKE / Published as / TONGUES OF THE MONTE / Republished with a new / introduction and new title;* verso *Books by / J. FRANK DOBIE;* title as above; verso *Copyright,* 1935 / *AS / TONGUES OF THE MONTE / By J. Frank Dobie / First Printing / AS / THE MEXICO I LIKE; The Trail to Mexico* pp. v-xii; *CONTENTS;* verso blank; half-title: *THE MEXICO . . .;* verso blank; text pp. 1-301.

Without running titles.

Preface, p. xii, signed: *Austin, Texas, / November* 10, 1942.

Bound in green cloth, stamped in silver. Spine: *THE / MEXICO / I LIKE / BY / J. FRANK DOBIE / UNIVERSITY / PRESS / IN DALLAS.*

Cut, all edges white. White lining-papers. 22½ x 15½cm.

Printed from the original plates, with running titles removed, and a new preface added.

A4 a(3)   J. FRANK DOBIE / TONGUES / OF THE / MONTE / [vignette, national seal of Mexico / line, white diamonds on black] / LITTLE, BROWN AND COMPANY · BOSTON / 1947

Collation: blank page; verso *BOOKS BY / J. FRANK DOBIE;* half-title *TONGUES OF THE MONTE / [line, white diamonds on black] verso blank; title as above; verso *COPYRIGHT BY J. FRANK DOBIE,* 1935, 1947 / *. . . / Published November* 1947 / *PRINTED IN THE UNITED*

STATES OF AMERICA; Preface: The Trail to Mexico pp. vii-xiv; *CONTENTS;* verso blank; half-title: *TONGUES OF THE MONTE /* [line, white diamonds on black]; verso blank; text pp. 1-301.

Without running titles.

Text printed from the original plates, with the preface, p. xiv, signed: *Austin, Texas / March,* 1947. This preface is that of the 1942 edition except for the last paragraph which has been rewritten; completely reset.

Bound in tan cloth, with decorations of the 1935 edition.

Cut, all edges white. White lining-papers. 23 x 15cm.

A4 b   J. FRANK DOBIE / TONGUES OF THE MONTE / THE MEXICO I LIKE / [vignette black and white drawing] / With Wood Engravings by / ERIC KING / LONDON / HAMMOND, HAMMOND & CO., LTD. / 87 GOWER STREET W. C. I. [1938]

Collation: half-title: [star] / *TONGUES OF THE MONTE / THE MEXICO I LIKE /* [star], verso *Other books by / J. FRANK DOBIE*; title as above; verso *First published in the British Empire / by Hammond, Hammond & Co., Ltd.,* 1938 / *Printed in Great Britain by / Latimer, Trend & Co., Ltd., Plymouth /* 1.49; *PREFACE / The Trail to Mexico* pp. 5-10; *Contents* p. 11; verso blank; text pp. 13-219; *Index* pp. 220-224.

Running titles: *Preface* and *Index* on both rectos and versos; chapter titles on rectos, title on versos.

Illustrations: wood engravings at head of Preface and each chapter. Illustrations of the American edition: two lines of music on p. 10, signs and diagrams on p. 182, 189, 208, 209, 213.

Bound in green cloth stamped in gold. Vignette, drawing of a hat on front cover. Spine: *Tongues / of the / Monte /* [star] / *J. FRANK / DOBIE /* [device] / *HAMMOND / HAMMOND*

Cut. 22½ x 14½cm.

Type reset, with an index added.

THE FLAVOR OF TEXAS

A5   THE FLAVOR / OF TEXAS / By J. FRANK DOBIE / [star] / With Illustration by / ALEXANDRE HOGUE / [line] / Dealey and Lowe 1936 Dallas / [line]

Collation: frontispiece; title as above; verso *COPYRIGHT,* 1936, *BY J. FRANK DOBIE / PRINTED IN THE UNITED STATES OF AMERICA;* dedication *To / MR. and MRS. O. J. SHEERAN;* verso *BOOKS BY J. FRANK DOBIE;* two quotations from *Sam Houston* and *Brit Bailey;* verso *ACKNOWLEDGEMENTS;* table of contents THE

FLAVOR OF TEXAS; verso blank; *ILLUSTRATIONS;* verso blank; half-title; verso blank; text pp. [1]-282; tail-piece; verso blank; *INDEX* pp. [285]-287.

Running titles: chapter titles on rectos, title on versos.

Illustrations: frontispiece, full page illustrations on pp. [11], [33], [63], [85], [121], [157], [247], and [283]

Bound in printed cloth, salmon on tan, stamped in black. Front: *The FLAVOR / OF TEXAS / J. Frank Dobie.* Spine: *THE / FLAVOR / OF / TEXAS /* [star] */ DOBIE / DEALEY / AND / LOWE*

Cut. 22½ x 14½cm.

TALES OF THE MUSTANG

A6   Tales of the / Mustang / [tan line] / BY J. FRANK DOBIE / ILLUSTRATIONS BY JERRY BY-WATERS / [vignette in tan, horse] / 1936 / THE BOOK CLUB OF TEXAS / DALLAS

Collation: half title: *Tales of the Mustang;* verso blank; title as above; verso *COPYRIGHT* 1936 *BY / J. FRANK DOBIE;* dedication *TO / . . . / John H. McGinnis;* verso quotation from *Hoermann, The Daughter of Tehuan;* Contents; verso blank; *The Pedigree of a Horse-Tale* pp. 11-12; text pp. [13]-89; verso Colophon] [number in red ink] */ OF THIS EDITION / THREE HUNDRED COPIES HAVE BEEN PRINTED / BY THE REIN COMPANY / FOR / THE BOOK CLUB OF TEXAS /* [tan ornament]

There are no running titles.

Illustrations: vignette and tailpiece; initial in various colors at beginning of the preface and each chapter. Black and white headpiece with top part in the color of the initial, at head of each chapter.

Bound in gray boards with a black paper label on front [cactus plant on line in green] */ Tales of the Mustang* [in white]

Uncut. 20½ x 15cm.

APACHE GOLD & YAQUI SILVER

A7 a(1)   [Brown oramental line] / Apache Gold & / Yaqui Silver / [vignette in brown, an Indian head] / By J. Frank Dobie • Illustrated by Tom Lea / Boston • Little, Brown and Company • 1939 / [brown ornamental line]

Collation: blank page: verso *Books by / J. Frank Dobie;* half-title: *Apache Gold and Yaqui Silver*: verso blank; colored frontispiece; title as above; verso *COPYRIGHT* 1928, 1931, 1938, 1939 *BY J. FRANK DOBIE / . . . / FIRST EDITION / Published March* 1939 */ PRINTED IN THE*

Apache Gold & Yaqui Silver

By J. Frank Dobie · Illustrated by Tom Lea

Boston · Little, Brown and Company · 1939

UNITED STATES OF AMERICA; extra leaf *Two hundred and sixty-five numbered copies of this / SIERRA MADRE EDITION / have been printed on rag paper, / bound in buckram and boards / and autographed by the author and by the artist. / This is Number* [number] */ J. Frank Dobie* [autograph] */ Tom Lea* [autograph]; verso blank; dedication *To Raymond Dickson, Joe and Dub Evans, / Charlie Newman, Cole Railston, Kelly Simmons / . . .;* verso blank; *THE TRAIL OF A STORY / HUNTER* pp. ix-xv; verso blank; *Contents* p. xvii; verso blank; text pp. [1]-[356]; *APPENDIX / I. Where I Dug for Adams / Gold* pp. 357-362; *II. A Note on Scalp Hunters / in Mexico* pp. 363-366.

Running titles: *The Trail of a Story Hunter* and *Appendix* on both rectos and versos; chapter titles on rectos, title on versos.

Illustrations: full page plates with section half-title at the foot of the page on pp. [1], [149], [183], [261], [287], [309], [327], and [341]. Colored frontispiece and colored plates following pp. 16, 82, 190, and 306. Full page black and white illustrations on pp. [21], [53], [70], [95], [98], [116], [133], [146], [156], [158], [180], [219] a map, [247], and [268]. Small black and white illustrations on pp. 7, 10, 19, 26, 31, 43, 63, 65, 88, 103, 165, 188, 190, 208, 213, 234, 239, 255, 279, 316, 339, and [356]

Bound in tan gold flecked paper with tan cloth back strip, with silver label stamped in brown on spine: [ornamental line] */ Apache / Gold / & / Yaqui / Silver /* [short ornamental line] */ J. Frank / Dobie /* [ornamental line]. In a box case of black silver flecked paper with salmon colored paper label: [ornamental line] */ Apache / Gold / & / Yaqui / Silver /* [short ornamental line] */ J. Frank / Dobie / SIERRA MADRE / EDITION / No. . . . . . . /* [ornamental line]. An additional silver label, as on spine, tipped in at end of the book.

Uncut. 23 x 15cm.

First Printing, Limited Edition, February 1939.

A7 a(2)   —— ——

Trade edition published March 1939.

The words *FIRST EDITION* deleted from the verso of the title-page. Without the extra leaf following the title-page.

Bound in tan cloth, with the title-page vignette in dark blue within ornamental border in gold stamped on front. Spine stamped in gold: *Apache / Gold / & / Yaqui / Silver /* [ornamental line] */ J. Frank / Dobie / Little, Brown.*

Cut. 23 x 15cm.

A7 a(3)   . . . / Boston • Little, Brown and Company • 1945 / [brown ornamental line]

Collation . . . title as above; verso . . . / *Reprinted April 1945 / PRINTED IN THE UNITED STATES* . . .

Without the frontispiece and colored plates.

Binding same as the first trade edition, except for smaller type used on the spine.

Reprinted from the original plates on thin paper.

A7 b [ornamental line] / APACHE GOLD / and Yaqui Silver / by J. FRANK DOBIE / [device] / BANTAM BOOKS • NEW YORK / [ornamental line • [1951]

Collation: publisher's blurb; verso blank; title as above; verso *APACHE GOLD AND YAQUI SILVER / A BANTAM BOOK published by arrangement with / Little, Brown & Company / Printing History / Little, Brown Edition Published March,* 1939 / . . . / *Bantam Edition Published November,* 1951 / 1st Printing . . . . . . October, 1951 / . . .; *Contents;* verso dedication; *THE TRAIL OF A STORY HUNTER* pp. [vii-xi]; verso blank; text pp. 1-204; *APPENDIX* pp. 204-212; *Note* of advertising at foot of p. 212.

Without running titles.

Without illustrations.

Bound in illustrated paper covers. Numbered: 940, on front and spine.

Type reset.

Cut. 16½ x 11cm.

1st Printing, October, 1951.

A7 c APACHE GOLD / AND YAQUI SILVER / by / J. FRANK DOBIE / [vignette] / ILLUSTRATED BY TOM LEA / LONDON / HAMMOND, HAMMOND & COMPANY [1956]

Collation: half-title; APACHE GOLD AND YAQUI SILVER; verso *Books by J. Frank Dobie;* title as above; verso *COPYRIGHT BY J. FRANK DOBIE / First published in Great Britain* 1956 / *Printed in Great Britain by / Latimer, Trend & Co. Ltd., Plymouth / for Hammond, Hammond & Co., Ltd. / 87 Gower Street, W. C. I* / 956; *CONTENTS;* verso dedication; *THE TRAIL OF A STORY HUNTER* pp. 7-11; verso first illustrated half title; text pp. 13-247; verso illustration; *Appendix I* . . . pp. 249-252; *Appendix* 2 . . . pp. 253-255; verso quotations from reviews of the 6 books by J. Frank Dobie.

Running titles: *The TRAIL OF A STORY HUNTER* and chapter titles on rectos, title on versos; *APPENDIX* on both rectos and versos.

Illustrations are those of the American edition. Full page plates with section half-title at the foot of the page on pp. [12], [112], [134], [186], [202], [216], [228], and [238]. Full page black and white illustrations on pp. [26], [59], [75], [79], [90], [102], [110], [119], [132], [157] a map, [177], and [248]. Smaller black and white illustrations on pp. 17, 18, 24, 30, 33, 41, 47, 53, 56, 71, 82, 117, 123, 137, 139, 150, 154, 168, 171, 183, 191, 197, 220, and 235.

Bound in maroon cloth stamped in gold. Spine: *Apache /
Gold / and / Yaqui / Silver / J. Frank / Dobie /* [device] /
HAMMOND / HAMMOND
Cut. 22 x 14cm.
Type reset.

A7 d   J. FRANK DOBIE / [line] / APACHE GOLD /
AND / YAQUI SILVER / [line / device] / *TRANS-
WORLD* PUBLISHERS / LONDON [1957]

Collation: publisher's blurb; verso blank; title as above;
verso *APACHE GOLD AND YAQUI SILVER / A CORGI
BOOK / Originally published in England by / Hammond,
Hammond & Company. / Printing History / Hammond,
Hammond Edition published* 1956 / *Corgi Edition published* 1957 / ... / *Made and printed in Great Britain by /
Love & Malcomson Ltd., Redhill; Contents;* verso dedication; *THE TRAIL OF A STORY HUNTER* [5] pp.; verso
blank; text pp. 1-204; *APPENDIX* pp. 204-[212]; advertisement at foot of p. [212]

Without running titles.

Without illustrations.

Bound in illustrated paper covers. Numbered on spine:
T484.

Cut. 16½ x 11cm.

Printed from the plates of the Bantam edition, with a
new title leaf and advertisements at front and end replaced.

JOHN C. DUVAL

A8 a(1)   JOHN C. DUVAL / FIRST TEXAS MAN OF
LETTERS / His Life and / Some of His Unpublished
Writings / [line] / By J. FRANK DOBIE / With
Sketches by TO LEA / [vignette / line] / DALLAS /
SOUTHWEST REVIEW / 1939

Collation: half-title: *JOHN C. DUVAL / FIRST TEXAS
MAN OF LETTERS;* verso colored frontispiece; title as
above; verso *Copyright,* 1939 / *BY THE / SOUTHWEST
REVIEW; CONTENTS;* verso blank; *PREFACE;* verso
blank *JOHN C. DUVAL* pp. 9-40; half-title: *DUVAL'S /
UNPUBLISHED WRITINGS /* [star]; verso blank; the un-
published writings pp. 43-105; verso *THIS EDITION IS
LIMITED TO / ONE THOUSAND COPIES / OF WHICH /
NINE HUNDRED AND FIFTY / ARE FOR SALE / PRINT-
ED BY / BENNETT PRINTING COMPANY / DALLAS.*

Without running titles.

Illustrations: colored frontispiece; vignette on title-
page; full page illustrations on pp. 52, 64, 76, 86; smaller
illustrations on pp. 58, 70, 80. All illustrations are drawings in black on tan and white background. Title is within
a tan line border with tan lines.

Bound in tan cloth stamped in brown, with rust colored back strip stamped in gold. Front: *JOHN C. DUVAL / FIRST TEXAS MAN OF LETTERS /* [star] */ By J. FRANK DOBIE / Illustrations by TOM LEA.* Spine, reading from top to bottom *JOHN C. DUVAL* [star] *By J. FRANK DOBIE.*

Cut. 22½ x 16cm.

A8 a(2) JOHN C. DUVAL / FIRST TEXAS MAN OF LETTERS / HIS LIFE AND / SOME OF HIS UNPUBLISHED WRITINGS / J. FRANK DOBIE / WITH SKETCHES BY / TOM LEA / [vignette] / DALLAS / SOUTHERN METHODIST UNIVERSITY PRESS / [1965]

Collation: half title . . .; verso black and white frontispiece; title as above; verso © 1939 */ BY SOUTHWEST REVIEW / SOUTHERN METHODIST UNIVERSITY PRESS / Second edition,* 1965 */ PRINTED IN THE UNITED STATES OF AMERICA / BY THE / SOUTHERN METHODIST UNIVERSITY PRINTING DEPARTMENT / AT DALLAS, TEXAS; CONTENTS* . . . pp. 43-105; verso blank.

Illustrations are the drawings in black and white. Title is in rust and black on white.

Bound in tan cloth stamped in gold. Spine reading from top to bottom *J. FRANK DOBIE* [star] *JOHN C. DUVAL* [star] *SMU PRESS.*

Cut. 23½ x 16cm.

THE LONGHORNS

A9 a(1) [Colored frontispiece extends across the top of the title-page] / THE LONGHORNS / BY J. FRANK DOBIE / [ornament in red] / ILLUSTRATED BY TOM LEA / LITTLE, BROWN AND COMPANY • BOSTON / 1941.

Collation: blank page; verso *Books by J. FRANK DOBIE;* half-title: *THE LONGHORNS;* verso blank; blank page; verso colored frontispiece extending across the top of this page and of the title-page following; title as above; verso *COPYRIGHT* 1941, *BY J. FRANK DOBIE / . . . / FIRST EDITION / Published March* 1941 */ PRINTED IN THE UNITED STATES OF AMERICA;* [leaf of heavy rough tan paper] 265 *NUMBERED COPIES OF THIS / RAWHIDE EDITION / HAVE BEEN PRINTED, ROPED / AND TALLIED. THEY HAVE / BEEN BRANDED BY THE / AUTHOR AND BY / THE ARTIST. THIS IS NUMBER* [number in manuscript */ vignette portraits of author and artist /* autographed] *Frank Dobie* and [autographed] *Tom Lea;* verso blank; dedication *TO / SID W. RICHARDSON /* . . . *Chapter by chapter, I make particular / dedications to some of these friends;* verso blank; *CONTENTS;* verso blank; *INTRODUCTORY: MAKERS OF HISTORY* pp. xiii-xxiii / verso blank; half-title; THE LONGHORNS; verso

THE LONGHORNS

BY J. FRANK DOBIE

ILLUSTRATED BY TOM LEA

LITTLE, BROWN AND COMPANY · BOSTON
1941

blank; text pp. 3-346. *PHOTOGRAPHIC RECORD / OF THE LONGHORNS;* verso description of following illustration; 48 illustrations on 16 leaves with descriptions of each on verso of preceding illustration, verso of last leaf blank; *NOTES* pp. 347-379; verso blank; *INDEX* pp. 381-388.

Without running titles.

Illustrations: frontispiece in color across top half of title-page and preceding page; vignette portraits on leaf of heavy paper following title-page; full page illustrations on pp. [19], [31], [65], [67], [79], [93], [113], [137], [157], [173], [185], [197], [219], [227], [253], [265], [271], [291], [313], [325] and [345]; 48 illustrations on 16 leaves with descriptive letterpress on verso of preceding; and headpieces at beginning of introduction and each chapter.

Bound in calfskin stamped in brown; ornament of title-page stamped in center of front cover. Spine: [2 chain line between two lines] / *THE / LONG- / HORNS* / [chain line between two lines] / *DOBIE* / [3 chain line between two lines] / *LITTLE, BROWN / AND COMPANY* / [chain line between two lines] In box case of gray cloth with colored illustration of the frontispiece across the top of the back, spine, and front; ornament of title-page stamped in black on foot of front. Spine, stamped in black *Dobie* / [colored illustration] / *The / Longhorns / No.* / [number] / *Little, Brown / and Company*

Cut. 22 x 14½cm.

Printed February 1941, published March 1941.

A9 a(2) —— ——

Trade edition issued at the same time.

FIRST EDITION deleted from verso of the title-page.

Without the extra leaf following the title-page.

Bound in grey cloth, binding same as the box case of the limited edition.

A9 a(3) J. FRANK DOBIE / The Longhorns / ILLUSTRATED BY TOM LEA / Grosset's UNIVERSAL Library / GROSSET & DUNLAP / NEW YORK [July 1957]

Collation: *Grosset's UNIVERSAL Library;* verso blank; title as above; verso *COPYRIGHT 1941, BY J. FRANK DOBIE / . . . ,/ BY ARRANGEMENT WITH LITTLE BROWN AND COMPANY / PRINTED IN THE UNITED STATES OF AMERICA; CONTENTS; verso blank; INTRODUCTORY: MAKERS OF HISTORY* pp. xiii-xxiii; verso blank; half-title; verso blank; text pp. 3-346; *NOTES* pp. 347-379; verso blank; *INDEX* pp. 381-387, [1]

Printed from the original plates. Without the frontispiece and Photographic Record.

Bound in illustrated paper covers. Numbered: UL-25 on front and spine.

Cut. 20½ x 13½cm.

A9 a (4)   [Colored frontispiece extends across the top of the title-page] / THE LONGHORNS / BY J. FRANK DOBIE / [ornament in red] / ILLUSTRATED BY TOM LEA / BRAMHALL HOUSE · NEW YORK

Collation: blank page, verso *Books by J. Frank Dobie;* half title: *THE LONGHORNS;* verso blank; blank page; verso colored frontispiece extending across the top of this page and of the title-page; title as above; verso © *COPYRIGHT MCMXLI, BY J. FRANK DOBIE / . . . / BY ARRANGEMENT WITH LITTLE, BROWN AND COMPANY / This edition published by Bramhall House, / a division of Clarkson N. Potter, Inc., by / arrangement with Little, Brown & Company / (B) / PRINTED IN THE UNITED STATES OF AMERICA; CONTENTS;* verso blank; *INTRODUCTORY: MAKERS OF HISTORY* pp. xiii-xxiii; verso blank; full page illustration [i.e. p. 345]; verso blank; half-title; verso blank; text pp. 3-344, [1]; verso blank; *PHOTOGRAPHIC RECORD / OF THE LONGHORNS* [33] pp.; verso blank; NOTES pp. 347-379; verso blank; *INDEX* pp. 381-387, [1]

Printed from the Little, Brown edition, without the dedication. The photographic record is omitted from the contents and the illustrations following the descriptions *ON THE TRAIL AND RANGE* and *BATTLE OF THE BULLS* incorrectly reversed.

Bound in lighter cloth, without the illustration of the Little, Brown copies, stamped in dark brown; ornament of title-page stamped on foot of front. Spine *Dobie / The / Longhorns / Bramhall / House.*

Cut. 21½ x 14½cm.

A9 b   THE LONGHORNS / By / J. FRANK DOBIE / Embossed in 4 Volumes / VOLUME I[-IV] / Copyright, 1941, by J. Frank Dobie / All rights reserved, including the right to reproduce / this book or portions thereof in any form. / Embossed and Printed for the / LIBRARY OF CONGRESS / 1941 / By Permission of the Publisher / LITTLE, BROWN & COMPANY / BOSTON / PRINTED AT THE / American Printing House for the Blind / LOUISVILLE, KENTUCKY

Collation. Vol. I: printed title as above; verso blank; preliminary material in Braille 3 leaves, [19] pp.; verso blank; text in Braille pp. 1-143 [1]. Vol. II: printed title; verso blank; 2 preliminary leaves in Braille; text in Braille pp. 145-291 [1]. Vol. III: printed title; verso blank; 2 preliminary leaves in Braille; text in Braille pp. 293-443. Vol. IV: printed title; verso blank; 2 preliminary leaves in Braille; text in Braille pp. 445-575 [1]

Bound in blue cloth stamped in silver. Front has title in Braille stamped in upper left corner. Spine *THE / LONG-*

HORNS / [short line] / *DOBIE* / [short line] / (*IN* 4
VOLS.) / *VOL.* 1[-IV] / [line] / *BRAILLE* / *GRADE* 2 /
PRINTED FOR / *THE LIBRARY* / *OF CONGRESS* /
U. S. A. / *American Printing* / *House* / *for the Blind* /
Louisville, Ky. / 1941 / [line]

> Cut. 29½ x 28½cm.

A9 c   [Colored frontispiece] / J. FRANK DOBIE / THE
LONGHORNS / Illustrated by Tom Lea / LONDON /
NICHOLSON & WATSON [1943]

> Collation: half-title *THE LONGHORNS;* verso and fol-
> lowing recto, frontispiece and title as above as in the
> American edition; verso . . . / *Published in* 1943. / *By
> Nicholson & Watson,* / 26, *Manchester Sq., London, W. I.* /
> *Printed at Redhill, Surrey.* / *By Love and Malcolmson;*
> publisher's blurb; verso blank; *CONTENTS;* verso blank;
> *INTRODUCTORY: MAKERS OF HISTORY* pp. ix-xvi;
> half-title *THE LONGHORNS* verso blank; text pp. 19-292;
> 48 photographs on recto of 16 leaves, descriptive letter-
> press for each on verso of preceding, letterpress for first
> photograph deleted, verso of last leaf blank.

> Running titles: introduction and chapter titles on rectos,
> title on versos.

> Illustrations are those of the American edition. The full
> page illustrations are on pp. [31], [41], [67], [69], [81],
> [91], [107], [125], [141], [155], [165], [175], [191], [199],
> [219], [227], [233], [249], [265], [275], and [291]

> Bound in red cloth. Spine *The* / *LONG-* / *HORNS* / *J.
> FRANK* / *DOBIE* / *NICHOLSON* / *&* / *WATSON*

> Cut. 22 x 14cm.

> Type reset.

GUIDE TO LIFE AND LITERATURE
OF THE SOUTHWEST

A10 a(1) Guide to / LIFE AND LITERATURE / of the /
SOUTHWEST / WITH A FEW OBSERVATIONS /
By J. FRANK DOBIE / ILLUSTRATED / The Uni-
versity of Texas Press / AUSTIN, TEXAS / 1943

> Collation: frontispiece; title as above; verso Not Copy-
> righted / *Anybody is welcome to help himself to* / *any
> of it in any way; Contents;* verso *ILLUSTRATIONS;* text
> pp. [7]-111.

> Running titles: chapter titles on rectos, *Life and Litera-
> ture of the Southwest* on versos.

> Illustrations: frontispiece; plate facing p. 92; full page
> illustrations on pp. 20 and 36; small illustrations on pp.
> 24, 43, 50, 53, 59, 63, 69, 71, music 72, 73, 75, 76, 77, 81, 82,
> 86, 90, 94, 96, and 111.

> Bound in grey paper stamped in black. Front: *Guide
> to* / *LIFE AND LITERATURE* / *of the* / *SOUTHWEST* /
> *By J. Frank Dobie.*

Cut. 23 x 15cm.

This annotated bibliography was first compiled for the use of the author's class in Life and Literature of the Southwest at the University of Texas.

See also B14, B39, B44, B46, B54 and D14.

A10 a(2) —— ——

Interleaved. Variant binding.

Bound in green cloth stamped in black. Front: *Guide to / LIFE AND LITERATURE / of the / SOUTHWEST / By J. Frank Dobie /* [vignette]

A10 a(3) . . . ILLUSTRATED / Published by / The University of Texas Press, Austin / Special printing for / University Press in Dallas / Southern Methodist University / 1943

Bound in yellow cloth stamped in brown. Front: *J. Frank Dobie /* [vignette] */ Guide to / LIFE AND LITERATURE / OF THE / SOUTHWEST*

Printed from the original plates, with a new title-page.

A10 a(4) . . . ILLUSTRATED / [short line] / University Press in Dallas / Southern Methodist University / 1943

Collation: frontispiece; title as above; verso blank; *Contents* . . .

Bound in blue paper stamped in black. Front: *J. Frank Dobie /* [vignette] */ Guide to / LIFE AND LITERATURE / OF THE / SOUTHWEST*

Printed from the original plates, with a new title-page.

A10 a(5) —— ——

Reprinted by the University Press in Dallas, Southern Methodist University, 1950, by offset process.

A10 b   Guide to Life and Literature / of the / Southwest / REVISED AND ENLARGED IN BOTH KNOWLEDGE AND WISDOM / J. FRANK DOBIE / DALLAS · 1952 SOUTHERN METHODIST UNIVERSITY PRESS

Collation: half-title: *LIFE AND LITERATURE OF THE SOUTHWEST;* verso and following page, double title-page, with title as above; verso *Not copyrighted in* 1942 */ Again not copyrighted in* 1952 */ Anybody* . . .; *Contents* pp. v-vi; *Illustrations* pp. vii-viii; *A Preface With Some Revised Ideas* pp. 1-8; text pp. 9-195; verso blank; *Index* pp. 197-222.

Running titles: preface and chapter titles on rectos; *LIFE AND LITERATURE OF THE SOUTHWEST* on versos; *INDEX* on both rectos and versos.

Illustrations: full page illustration on pp. 41, 91, 133, and [138] Smaller illustrations on pp. 31, 33, 37, 49, 57, 81, 103, 121, 128 music, 135, 145, 153, 158, 163, 169, and 175.

Bound in tan cloth stamped in black. Front: *J. Frank*

Dobie Spine: *DOBIE* / [reading from top to bottom] *Life and Literature of the Southwest* / [at foot] *S M U.*

Cut. 23½ x 15½cm.

A TEXAN IN ENGLAND

A11 a   J. Frank Dobie / [ornamental line] / A TEXAN / IN / ENGLAND / [ornamental line] / LITTLE, BROWN AND COMPANY · BOSTON / 1945

Collation: half-title *A TEXAN IN ENGLAND;* verso *Books by J. Frank Dobie;* title as above; verso *COPYRIGHT* 1944, *BY THE CURTIS PUBLISHING COMPANY / COPYRIGHT* 1944, 1945, *BY J. FRANK DOBIE / . . . / FIRST EDITION / Published May* 1945 / *PRINTED IN THE UNITED STATES OF AMERICA; DEDICATION / At the English-Speaking Union in Cam-* / *bridge, Mrs. Belinda Norman-Butler . . .;* verso *Acknowledgments; P for Preface* pp. [vii]-xiii; verso blank; *Contents;* verso blank; half-title: *A TEXAN IN ENGLAND;* verso blank; text pp. [3]-279; verso blank; *Index* pp. [281]-285.

Running titles: *P FOR PREFACE* and *INDEX* on both rectos and versos; chapter titles on rectos, title on versos.

Without illustrations.

Bound in tan cloth stamped in red. Vignette on front. Spine, at top *Dobie;* reading from top to bottom *A TEXAN In England;* at foot *LITTLE,* / *BROWN.*

Cut. 19½ x 13½cm.

Printed March 1945, published May 1945.

Published simultaneously in Canada by McClelland and Stewart Limited.

A11 b   J. FRANK DOBIE / [line] / A Texan in / England / [line] / LONDON / HAMMOND, HAMMOND & CO. LTD. / 87 GOWER STREET, W. C. I. / [1946]

Collation: half-title: *A TEXAN IN ENGLAND ;* verso blank; frontispiece, portrait of the author; title as above; verso *Copyright throughout the / British Empire (excluding Canada) by / Hammond, Hammond & Co., Ltd. / PRINTED IN GREAT BRITIAN / AT THE BAYNARD PRESS BY / SANDERS PHILLIPS & CO., LTD., / CHRYSSELL ROAD, LONDON S. W. 9; DEDICATION;* verso *ACKNOWLEDGEMENTS; Contents;* verso *ILLUSTRATIONS; P for Preface* pp. [9]-12; text pp. [13]-192.

Running titles: *P FOR PREFACE* on both rectos and versos; chapter titles on rectos, title on versos.

Illustrations: photographs A-G, including the frontispiece, plates printed on both sides following pp. 14, 80, and 96.

Bound in tan cloth stamped in dark blue. Spine: *A TEXAN / IN / ENGLAND / J. FRANK / DOBIE / [device] / HAMMOND / HAMMOND*

Cut. 22 x 14½cm.

Type reset.

J. Frank Dobie

A TEXAN
IN
ENGLAND

LITTLE, BROWN AND COMPANY · BOSTON

1945

THE VOICE OF THE COYOTE

A12 a(1) The Voice of the Coyote / BY J. FRANK DOBIE / [vignette, three coyotes] / ILLUSTRATED BY OLAUS J. MURIE / Little, Brown and Company • Boston • 1949

Collation: blank page; verso *Books by J. Frank Dobie;* half title: *THE VOICE OF THE COYOTE;* verso frontispiece, black on tan; title as above, black on tan; verso *COPYRIGHT* 1947, 1949, *BY THE CURTIS PUBLISHING COMPANY / COPYRIGHT* 1949, *BY J. FRANK DOBIE / . . . / FIRST EDITION / Published May* 1949 */ . . . / Published simultaneously / in Canada by McClelland and Stewart Limited / PRINTED IN THE UNITED STATES OF AMERICA;* extra blank leaf autographed by the author; dedication *TO / BERTHA McKEE DOBIE / . . . ;* verso blank; *INTRODUCTION: COYOTE AND MAN* pp. ix-xvii; verso blank; *CONTENTS* pp. xix-xx; half title: *THE VOICE OF THE COYOTE;* verso blank; text pp. 3-[351]; verso blank; *NOTES* pp. 353-368; *MY CREDITORS: BOOKS AND PEOPLE* pp. 369-376; half title: *INDEX;* verso blank; *INDEX* pp. 379-386.

Without running titles.

Illustrations: frontispiece and title vignette. Full page plates, including in the paging, pp. [5], [13], [57], [61], [67], [75], [103], [111], [141], [199], [231], [243], [281], [291], [303], and [327]. Small illustrations on pp. 43, 70, 90, 97, 164, 250 music, 254, 255, 259, 260, and 276. Headpieces at the beginning of the Introduction and each chapter; tailpieces at the end of the Introduction and chapters XIV and XVII.

Bound in rust cloth with vignette, coyote head, stamped in gold on front. Spine, rust with blue painted label, stamped in gold; on rust [vignette / heavy line]; on blue [2 heavy, 1 light, lines] / THE / Voice / *OF THE / Coyote / J. Frank / Dobie* / [1 light, 2 heavy, lines]; on rust [heavy line / vignette] / *Little, Brown / and Company.*

Cut. 22 x 14½cm.

Printed March 1949, published May 1949.

Final paragraph on page [351] beginning: *"In the mountains Jeff Milton . . .*

A12 a(2) —— ——

Trade edition, without the extra blank leaf with the author's autograph, issued at the same time.

FIRST EDITION / Published May 1949.

A12 a(3) —— ——

Reprinted March, 1949, for the Natural History Book Club.

A12 b J. FRANK DOBIE / THE VOICE OF THE / COYOTE / [vignette] / LONDON / HAMMOND, HAMMOND & CO., LTD. / 87, GOWER STREET, W. C. I [1950]

The Voice of the Coyote

BY J. FRANK DOBIE

ILLUSTRATED BY OLAUS J. MURIE

Little, Brown and Company · Boston · 1949

Collation: half title; verso *Other books by* / *J. FRANK DOBIE;* title as above; verso *Copyright by J. FRANK DOBIE* / *First published in the British Empire* / *by Hammond, Hammond & Co., Ltd.,* 1950 / *With Illustrations by* / *OLAUS J. MURIE* / *Printed in Great Britain by* / *Butler & Tanner Ltd., Frome and London* / 7.50; *INTRODUCTION* pp. v-xiii; verso dedication; *CONTENTS* pp. [1-2]; text pp. 3-350, [1]; verso blank; *NOTES* pp. 353-368; *MY CREDITORS*: *BOOKS AND PEOPLE* pp. 369-376; *ACKNOWLEDGMENTS;* verso blank; *INDEX* pp. 379-386.

Bound in aqua cloth stamped in gold. Spine *The* / *Voice* / *of the* / *Coyote* / *J. FRANK* / *DOBIE* / [device] / *HAMMOND* / *HAMMOND*

Cut. 21 x 14cm.

A line by line reprint of the American edition, without corrections and including the last paragraph on page [351]

A12 c   THE VOICE OF THE COYOTE / BY / J. Frank Dobie / Embossed in Three Volumes / VOLUME I[-III] / Printed by Permission / of the Publishers / Little, Brown and Company, Boston / Copyright, 1949, by J. Frank Dobie / Printed for / The Library of Congress / Washington, D. C. / Howe Memorial Press / Perkins Institution and / Massachusetts School / for the Blind / Watertown, Mass. / 1950

Collation. Vol. I: embossed title as above; verso blank; preliminary material in Braille [19] pp.; verso blank; text in Braille pp. [1-2] 3-179 [1] Vol. II: embossed title; verso blank; preliminary material in Braille [2] leaves; text in Braille pp. [181-182] 183-389 [1] Vol. III] embossed title; verso blank; preliminary material in Braille [1] leaf [2] pp.; text in Braille; [391-392] 393-607 [1]

Bound in dark green cloth stamped in gold. Front has title in Braille stamped in upper left corner. Spine: *THE* / *VOICE* / *OF THE* / *COYOTE* / [short line] / *DOBIE* / *IN THREE* / *VOLUMES* / *VOL. I[-III]* / *BRAILLE* / *GRADE 2* / *PRINTED FOR* / *THE LIBRARY* / *OF CONGRESS* / 599.74 / *HOWE* / *MEMORIAL* / *PRESS* / *WATERTOWN,* / *MASS.*

Cut. 29½ x 28½cm.

A12 d   THE VOICE OF THE COYOTE / by J. FRANK DOBIE / Illustrated by / Olaus J. Murie / A Bison Book / University of Nebraska Press / 1961 / [device]

Collation: blank page; verso *A NOTE ABOUT THE AUTHOR; half title*: *THE VOICE OF THE COYOTE;* verso blank; title as above; verso *Copyright* 1947, 1949, *by the Curtis Publishing Company* / *Copyright* 1949, *by J. Frank Dobie* / . . . / *Bison Book edition, reproduced from the Sixth printing, pub-* / *lished by arrangement with Little, Brown and Company;* dedication; verso blank; *INTRODUCTION*: *COYOTE AND MAN* pp. ix-xvii; verso blank;

THE
Ben Lilly Legend

by J. FRANK DOBIE

BOSTON
LITTLE, BROWN AND COMPANY
1950

CONTENTS pp. xix-xx; half-title: *THE VOICE OF THE COYOTE;* verso blank; text pp. 3-[351]; verso blank; *NOTES* pp. 353-368; *MY CREDITORS: BOOKS AND PEO-PLE* pp. 369-376; half title; *INDEX;* verso blank; *INDEX* pp. 379-386.

Bound in illustrated paper covers. Numbered on spine: BB 109.

Printed from the original plates with type corrections and with last paragraph deleted from p. [351]

Cut. 20 x 13cm.

THE BEN LILLY LEGEND

A13 a(1) THE / Ben Lilly Legend / by J. FRANK DOBIE / [device] / BOSTON / LITTLE, BROWN AND COMPANY / 1950

Collation: blank page: verso *Books by J. Frank Dobie;* half-title: *The Ben Lilly Legend;* verso blank; colored frontispiece; *Ben Lilly, interpreted by Tom Lea;* title as above; verso COPYRIGHT 1950, *BY THE CURTIS PUB-LISHING COMPANY / COPYRIGHT 1950, BY J. FRANK DOBIE / . . . / FIRST EDITION / Published May 1950 / . . . / Published simultaneously / in Canada by McClel-land and Stewart Limited / PRINTED IN THE UNITED STATES OF AMERICA;* blank leaf; *DEDICATION* [to] *T. Y. Harp . . .;* verso blank; *Esau the Hunter* pp. ix-xiv; *Contents* p. xv; verso blank; *Illustrations;* verso blank half-title: *The Ben Lilly Legend;* verso blank; text pp. 3-219; verso blank; *Sources: People and Print* pp. 221-229; verso blank; half-title: *Index;* verso blank; *Index* pp. 233-237.

Running titles: *ESAU THE HUNTER, SOURCES: PEO-PLE AND PRINT,* and *INDEX* on both rectos and versos; chapter titles on rectos, title on versos.

Illustrations: colored frontispiece; 9 black and white illustrations (including photographs) on 6 plates of slick paper facing pp. 30, 46, 94, 142, 158, and 190; 1 black and white plate on the paper of the text p. [59] verso blank.

Bound in tan cloth stamped in maroon. Vignette on front. Label on spine, maroon stamped in tan, *The / Ben / Lilly / Legend / • / J. FRANK / DOBIE;* and maroon on tan *Little, Brown*

Cut. 21 x 14cm.

A13 a(2) Reprinted ca. August 1950, for the Natural History Book Club.

A13 b THE / Ben Lilly Legend / by / J. FRANK DOBIE / LONDON / HAMMOND, HAMMOND & CO., LTD. / 87, GOWER STREET, W. C. I. [1952]

Collation: blank page; verso *Books by J. Frank Dobie;* half-title: *The Ben Lilly Legend;* verso blank; title as above; verso *Copyright by J. FRANK DOBIE / First pub-*

lished in Great Britain 1952 / . . . / *Printed in Great Britain by D. R. Hillman & Sons, Ltd. Frome* / 0.2952; *DEDICATION* . . .

Illustrations: the black and white plates of the American edition. Without the colored frontispiece.

Bound in maroon cloth stamped in gold. Spine: *The / BEN / LILLY / Legend / J. FRANK / DOBIE* / [device] / *HAMMOND / HAMMOND*

Cut. 20½ x 14cm.

Printed from the plates of the American edition on thinner paper. Without the colored frontispiece and with the title of the frontispiece deleted from the list of illustrations.

THE MUSTANGS

A14 a(1) THE MUSTANGS / by J. Frank Dobie / [vignette] / ILLUSTRATED BY CHARLES BANKS WILSON / Little, Brown and Company • Boston [1952]

Collation: blank page; verso *Books by J. Frank Dobie;* half-title: THE MUSTANGS; verso blank; colored frontispeace; title as above; verso *COPYRIGHT* 1934, 1951, 1952 *BY THE CURTIS PUBLISHING COMPANY / COPYRIGHT* 1936, 1949, 1950, 1951, 1952 *BY J. FRANK DOBIE* / . . . / *FIRST EDTION* / . . . / *Published simultaneously / in Canada by McClelland and Stewart Limited / PRINTED IN THE UNITED STATES OF AMERICA;* blank page; verso mounted *ORIGINAL DRAWING BY THE ARTIST; One hundred numbered copies of this / Pinto Edition / have been branded by the / author and by the artist. / This is number* . . . . . . / [autographed] *J. Frank Dobie* / [autographed] *Charles Banks Wilson;* verso blank; dedication to the . . . *R. J. Dobie ranch* . . .; verso blank; *CONTENTS* p. ix; verso blank; *A PERSONAL INTRODUC-TION* pp. xi-xvii; verso blank; half-title: *THE MUS-TANGS* / [vignette / quotation from]—*The Merchant of Venice.* p. [1]; text pp. [2]-331; verso blank; *NOTES* pp. 333-364; half-title: *INDEX;* verso blank; *INDEX* pp. 367-376.

Without running titles.

Illustrations: colored frontispiece. Full page illustrations on pp. [19], [33], [49], [69], [85], [123] [129], [187], [203] and [309]; double page illustration at top of pp. 152-153; small illustrations on pp. 45, 107, 179, 185, 223, 237, 263, and 293. Headpieces at beginning of each chapter, including double ones at beginning of chapters I, VI, and XII. Vignette on title-page and half-title on p. [1]

Illustrated lining-papers, brown on tan.

Bound in red and white colt skin; with label of brown leather stamped in gold on the spine [ornamental line] / *THE / MUSTANGS* / [short line] / *J. FRANK DOBIE* / [ornamental line] In box case, tan stamped in brown, front [vignette] / *THE MUSTANGS / J. Frank Dobie.* Spine

THE MUSTANGS

by J. Frank Dobie

ILLUSTRATED BY CHARLES BANKS WILSON

Little, Brown and Company · Boston

THE / MUSTANGS / [vignette] / J. Frank / Dobie / LIT-TLE, BROWN

Cut. 22 x 15cm.

Printed August 1952, published September 1952.

A14 a(2) —— ——

First edition, variant. The two leaves following the title-page replaced by a single blank leaf autographed: *J. Frank Dobie.*

Bound in half tan cloth stamped in rust and half dark blue stamped in gold. Front, rust on tan vignette, and gold on dark blue, *THE MUSTANGS / J. Frank Dobie.* Spine, rust on tan, *THE / MUSTANGS / [vignette] / and gold on dark blue, J. Frank / Dobie / LITTLE, BROWN.*

A14 a(3) —— ——

First edition, variant, trade edition. Without the two leaves following the title-page of the limited edition. With the cloth binding of the variant autographed edition.

A14 a(4) —— ——

Reprinted November 1952, for the Natural History Book Club.

A14 a(5) —— ——

A paperback edition, March 1964, reproduced photographically, slightly reduced, without the frontispiece or illustrated lining papers, with slight changes on verso of title-page: ... *Published simultaneously in Canada / by Little, Brown & Company (Canada) Limited / PRINTED IN THE UNITED STATES OF AMERICA.*

Bound in illustrated paper covers. Numbered 35 on front and spine.

Cut, all white edges. 20 x 13cm.

A14 b   [star / quotation] / —The Merchant of Venice. / [star] / THE / Mustangs / [star] / by / J. FRANK DOBIE / [star] / BANTAM BOOKS · NEW YORK [device. 1954]

Collation: publisher's blurb; verso and following page title as above; verso *THE MUSTANGS / A BANTAM BOOK published by arrangement with / Little, Brown & Company, Inc. / Printing History / Lillle, Brown Edition Published September, 1952 / 1st Printing . . . . . . August, 1952 / 2nd Printing . . . . . . November, 1952 / 3rd Printing . . . . . . November, 1952 / 4th Printing . . . . . . December, 1952 / Little, Brown Limited Edition Published September, 1952 / 1st Printing . . . . . . August, 1952 / History Book Club Selection for November, 1952 / Bantam Edition Published February, 1954 / 1st Printing . . . . . . January, 1954 / ... / PRINTED IN THE UNITED STATES OF AMERICA / Bantam Books, 25 West 45th Street, New York 36, N. Y.;* CONTENTS; verso dedication; *A PERSONAL INTRODUCTION* pp. [vii-xiii]; verso blank; text pp. 1-274; *NOTES* pp. 275-304; advertisement; verso publisher's note.

Without illustrations.

Bound in illustrated paper covers. Nombered A1212 on front and spine.

Cut, buff edges. 18 x 11cm.

A14 c THE MUSTANGS / by J. Frank Dobie / [vignette] / ILLUSTRATED BY CHARLES BANKS WILSON / LONDON / HAMMOND, HAMMOND & COMPANY [1954]

Collation: half-title: *THE MUSTANGS;* verso *Books by J. Frank Dobie;* colored frontispiece; title as above; verso *COPYRIGHT BY J. FRANK DOBIE / First published in Great Britain 1954 / . . . / Printed in Great Britain by / Billing and Sons Ltd., Guildford and London / for Hammond, Hammond and Co. Ltd. / 87 Gower Street, W. C. I. / 654; dedication;* verso blank; *CONTENTS* p. vii; verso blank; *A PERSONAL INTRODUCTION* p. ix-xiv; half-title: *THE MUSTANGS p.* [1]; text pp. [2]-331; verso blank; half-title: *INDEX: INDEX* pp. 334-343; advertisements pp. 344-346.

Illustrations are those of the American first edition.

Without the illustrated lining-papers.

Bound in red cloth stamped in gold. Spine: *The / Mustangs / [star] / J. FRANK / DOBIE / [device] / HAMMOND / HAMMOND*

Cut, top edge maroon. 22 x 14½cm.

A line by line reprint of the first American edition, probably by offset process, with the page numbers of the introduction and index changed, several paragraphs added at end of A Personal Introduction, and the notes omitted.

A14 d J. FRANK DOBIE / GROSSE WILDE FREIHEIT / DIE GESCHICHTE DER MUSTANGS / [short line] / MIT ZAHLREICHEN ABBILDUNGEN / UND ZWEI KARTEN / DEUTSCHE VERLAGS-ANSTALT / STUTTGART

Collation: half-title: *GROSSE WILDE FREIHEIT;* verso blank; title as above; verso *Ins Deutsche übertragen von / FELIX BERNER / Titel der amerikanischen Ausgabe: "The Mustangs" / (Little, Brown and Company, Boston), Copyright by / the Curtis Publishing Company and by J. Frank Dobie / 1956 / Alle deutschen Rechte bei der Deutschen Verlags-Anstalt CmbH., Stuttgart. / Umschlag und Einband von Willy Widmann. Klischees: Willy Berger, Stutt- / gart. Gesetzt aus der Linotype-Baskerville. Druck der Deutschen Verlags- / Anstalt GmbH., Stuttgart. Papier von der Papierfabrik Salach in Salach, / Württemberg. Printed in Germany; Inhalt;* verso blank; [Vorrede] pp. 7-[8]; text pp. 9-249 [1]; *BEMERKUNGEN ZUR DEUTSCHEN AUSGABE;* verso *ABBILDUNGEN.*

Illustrations are not those of the American edition. Plates printed on both sides: 12 photographs on 8 pages facing pp. 32, 97, [112], 113, 176, 177, 192, and 193; 5

drawings on 4 pages facing pp. 33, 48, 49, and 96. Folded map of the West, verso map of Texas, bound in at end.

Without illustrated lining papers.

Bound in green cloth, vignette stamped in gold on front. Spine, black label stamped in gold, *DOBIE* / [line] / *GROSSE* / *WILDE* / *FREIHEIT*

Cut, top edge gold. 21 x 14cm.

Text reset and rearranged, with new illustrations.

A14 e [Vignette] / THE MUSTANGS / by / J. Frank Dobie / [quotation from] / —THE MERCHANT OF VENICE / Illustrated by Carl Pfeufer / [device] / BANTAM BOOKS · NEW YORK [1958]

Collation: publisher's blurb; verso *BANTAM FRONTIER CLASSICS;* title as above; verso *THE MUSTANGS / A Bantam Book published by arrangement with / Little, Brown & Company, Inc. / Printing History / . . . / Bantam edition published February* 1954 / *Bantam Fifty edition published July* 1958 / *Copyright*, 1934, 1951, 1952, *by The Curtis Publishing Co. / Copyright*, 1936, 1949, 1950, 1951, 1952 *by J. Frank Dobie / . . . / PRINTED IN THE UNITED STATES OF AMERICA / Bantam Books, 25 West 45th Street, New York* 36, *New York; Contents;* verso blank; dedication; verso blank; *A Personal Introduction* pp. ix-xiv; text pp. 1-278; *NOTES* pp. 279-304; advertisement; verso blank.

Running titles: *A PERSONAL INTRODUCTION* on both rectos and versos; chapter titles and *NOTES* on rectos, title on versos.

Illustrations: small black and white drawings on title-page, pp. 12, 16, 33, 35, 37, 44, 51, 53, 57, 62, 68, 75, 92, 98, 102, 111, 122, 130, 132, 138, 147, sign 167, 181, 183, 209, 222, 227, 242, and 258.

Bound in illustrated paper covers. Cover photograph by Hy Peskin of Free Lance Photographers Guild, Inc. Numbered FI778 on front and spine.

Cut, yellow edges. 18 x 10½cm.

Type reset, arrangement and content of text is that of the first American edition, with new illustrations.

TALES OF OLD-TIME TEXAS

A15 a(1) J. FRANK DOBIE / Tales of / Old-Time Texas / [device] / Illustrated by / BARBARA LATHAM / Little, Brown and Company / Boston Toronto [1955]

Collation: blank page; verso *BOOKS BY J. FRANK DOBIE;* half-title: *Tales of Old-Time Texas;* verso frontispiece; title as above; verso *COPYRIGHT* © 1928, 1930, 1931, 1943, 1955, *BY J. FRANK DOBIE / . . ./ FIRST EDITION / Published simultaneously in Canada / by Little, Brown & Company (Canada) Limited / PRINTED IN THE UNITED STATES OF AMERICA; DEDICATION / Indebted to many storytellers, I dedicate this book to certain ones / who have helped make it and have added to my life*

J. FRANK DOBIE

Tales of Old-Time Texas

Illustrated by
BARBARA LATHAM

Little, Brown and Company

Boston   *Toronto*

. . . / . . . / *Bill (W. H.) Kittrell . . . Rocky Reagan /
and Asa Jones . . . Elojio / Juarez . . . Railroad (R. R.) /
Smith and W. M. Longworth . . . / . . . Wes Burton . . . /
. . . Mrs. Bruce Reid, / . . . Jim Ballard . . . / . . . H. B. /
Parks . . . Captain / Dan Smith . . .;* verso blank; *Introduction* pp. [ix]-xiv; *Contents* pp. [xv]-xvi; half-title:
Part One; verso blank; text pp. [3]-90; half-title: *Part
Two;* verso blank; text pp. [93]-135; verso blank; half-
title: *Part Three;* verso blank; text pp. [139]-177; verso
blank; half-title: *Part Four;* verso blank; text pp. [181]-
216; half-title: *Part Five;* verso blank; text pp. [219]-
310; half-title: *Notes and Credits;* verso blank; *Notes and
Credits* pp. [313]-327; verso blank; *Index* pp. [329]-336.

Running titles: *Introduction, Contents, Notes and Credits, Index* on both rectos and versos; chapter titles on
rectos and title on versos.

Illustrations, drawings in black and white: full page
illustrations frontispiece, pp. [7], [29], [49], [153], [161],
[213], [229], [247], [255], [265], [283] and [295]; half-page
illustrations on pp. 37, 59, 82, 98, 114, 121, 129, 145, 163, 171,
176, 183, 197, 235, 277, 298, and 304; and small illustrations
on pp. 53, 55, 56, 58, 61, 68, 72, and 75.

Rust colored lining papers.

Bound in yellow paper with half rust cloth. Spine,
stamped in gold on rust, *TALES / OF / OLD- / TIME /
TEXAS / J. Frank / Dobie / LITTLE, BROWN*

Cut. 22 x 15cm.

A15 a(2) ——— ———

1963 issue in soft covers. *FIRST EDITION* deleted from
the verso of the title-page.

Bound in buff paper covers, stamped in white and
black. Front: [in white] *Tales of / Old-Time / Texas*
[in black] *J. FRANK DOBIE /* [vignette, ornamental boot]
Spine, reading from top to bottom, [in white] *DOBIE*
[in black] *Tales of Old-Time Texas* [in white] *Little,
Brown;* at foot, [in white] 33 / [and in black, device]
On the back cover, title and quotations from reviews, in
white and black.

Cut. 20 x 13cm.

A15 b   . . . Texas / Illustrated by / BARBARA LATHAM /
Hammond, Hammond and Company: London [1959]

Collation: half-title: *Tales of Old Time Texas;* verso
Other Books by J. Frank Dobie; frontispiece; title as above
verso *First published in Great Britain* 1959 / © *Copyright,*
1928, 1930, 1931, 1943, 1955, *by J. Frank Dobie / Printed in
Great Britain / for Hammond, Hammond & Co. Ltd.,* 87
*Gower Street, W. C. I / by Lowe & Brydone (Printers)
Ltd., London, N. W.* 10; *DEDICATION* . . .

Bound in tan cloth, stamped in brown. Spine: *Tales /
of / Old-Time / Texas / * / J. FRANK / DOBIE /* [device]
HAMMOND / HAMMOND

Cut. 22 x 14cm.

A line by line reprint of the American edition, probably
offset process.

UP THE TRAIL FROM TEXAS

A16 a(1) UP THE TRAIL / FROM TEXAS / [line, star, line, in tan on white] / by J. FRANK DOBIE / Illustrated by JOHN C. WONSETLER / [Landmark / BOOKS: device, in tan on white] / RANDOM HOUSE · NEW YORK [1955]

Collation: half-title: *Up the Trail from Texas;* verso blank; title as above; verso © *Copyright* 1955 *by J. Frank Dobie / . . . / Published in New York by Random House, Inc. and / simultaneously in Toronto, Canada, by Random House / of Canada, Limited / . . . / Manufactured in the United States of America;* dedication To Frank Dobie *Faulk;* verso blank; *Contents;* verso blank; half-title: *Up the Trail from Texas /* [quotation from]—*John R. Craig, Ranching with Lords and / Commons;* verso blank; text pp. 3-178; *Index* pp. 179-182; list of *LANDMARK BOOKS;* verso *Have you read these World Landmarks?,* a list.

Running titles: chapter titles on rectos, title on versos; *Index* on both rectos and versos.

Illustrations: double page map in tan and black on white pp. [56-57]; full page drawings in tan and black on white pp. [11], [21], [25], [69], [101], and [171]; half page drawings in tan and black on white pp. 17, [36], [60], [73], [81], 85, 93, [112], 121, [136], 148, and 177; double half-page drawings in tan and black on white pp. [44-45], [144-145], and [160-161]; small black and white diagram on p. 67; black and white headpieces at the beginning of each chapter.

Illustrated lining papers, blue on tan vignettes.

Bound in bright pink cloth, stamped in black and blue. Front: title within border of head of longhorn stamped in black at top of wreath of black flowers and blue leaves *UP THE / TRAIL FROM / TEXAS* Spine: [black flower with blue leaves above black line] / *DOBIE* / [title reading from top to bottom within blue line border] *UP THE TRAIL / FROM TEXAS /* [ornament as above reversed] / [*Landmark / BOOKS:* device] / *Random House*

Cut. 21½ x 15cm.

This is number 60 of the *Landmark Books,* written for young people.

A16 a(2) —— ——

Variant binding. Bound in gray cloth, stamped in white and black, *Up the Trail from Texas /* [stamped in black] *J. FRANK DOBIE /* [vignette in black, illustration of p. 10]. Spine, black on white painted label, within black border, [decorative line] / *UP THE / TRAIL / FROM / TEXAS /* [type ornament] / *Dobie /* [vignette]

I'll Tell You
a Tale

by J. Frank Dobie

*Selected and Arranged by the Author
and Isabel Gaddis*

ILLUSTRATIONS BY BEN CARLTON MEAD

LITTLE, BROWN AND COMPANY · BOSTON · TORONTO

I'LL TELL YOU A TALE

A17 a(1) I'll Tell You / a Tale / by J. Frank Dobie / Selected and Arranged by the Author / and Isabel Gaddis / [vignette, head of a longhorn] / ILLUSTRATIONS BY BEN CARLTON MEAD / LITTLE, BROWN AND COMPANY · BOSTON · TORONTO [1960]

Collation: blank page; verso *Books by J. Frank Dobie;* half-title: *I'll Tell You a Tale;* verso blank; title as above; verso *COPYRIGHT, 1931, BY THE SOUTHWEST PRESS / COPYRIGHT 1934, 1947, 1949, 1950, 1951, 1952, BY / THE CURTIS PUBLISHING COMPANY. / COPYRIGHT 1928, 1930, 1931, 1935, 1936, 1938, / 1939, 1941, 1947, 1949, 1950, 1951, 1952, / 1955.* © *1960, BY J. FRANK DOBIE. / . . . / FIRST EDITION / . . . / Published simultaneously in Canada / by Little, Brown & Company (Canada) Limited / PRINTED IN THE UNITED STATES OF AMERICA;* dedication *To the memory of my cherished friend / ROY BEDICHEK;* verso blank; *The Author's Intrusion* pp. [ix]-xiii; verso blank; *Contents* pp. [xv]-xvii; verso blank; half-title: *The / Longhorn Breed /* [vignette] verso blank; text pp. [3]-47; verso blank; half-title: *Mustangs / and Mustangers /* [vignette] verso blank; section introduction pp. [51]-52; text pp. [53]-98; half-title: *The Saga of the Saddle /* [vignette] verso blank; section introduction; verso blank; text pp. [103]-128; half-title: *Characters / and Happenings / of Long Ago /* [vignette] verso blank; text pp. [131]-181; verso blank; half-title: *Animals of the Wild /* [vignette] verso blank; text [185]-245; verso blank; half-title: *In Realms of Gold /* [vignette] verso blank; text pp. [249]-330; half-title: *Ironies /* [vignette] verso blank; text [333]-353; *Whence These Tales Have Come* pp. [355]-356; half-title: *Glossary of Spanish-Mexican Words;* verso blank; *Glossary . . .* pp. [359]-362.

Running titles: *THE AUTHOR'S INTRUSION, CONTENTS, WHENCE THESE TALES HAVE COME* and *GLOSSARY OF SPANISH-MEXICAN WORDS* on rectos and versos; section titles on rectos and title on versos.

Illustrations: the title-page vignette is repeated on each section half-title and the larger tailpiece on p. 18; cattle brands on pp. 6, 7, 9, 10, 11, [12], [30], 31, 32, 33; small illustrations on pp. 10, 33, 92, 122, 156, 165, 222, 236, 250, 255, 270, 280, 307, 317, 338 and 350; tailpieces on pp. 18, 58, 67, 79, 109, 116, 128, 137, 145, 173, 186, 195, 208, 219, 245 and 299.

Bound in tan cloth stamped in green and red, title-page vignette stamped in green on front. Spine, [in green] *I'll / TELL / YOU / A TALE /* [in red] *J. FRANK / DOBIE /* [and in green] *LITTLE, BROWN.*

Cut. 21½ x 14½cm.

Isabel Gaddis compiled these tales from earlier works; the author approved the selection and rewrote much of the material.

COW PEOPLE

J. Frank Dobie

with photos

LITTLE, BROWN AND COMPANY · BOSTON · TORONTO

A17 a(2) —— ——

Third printing.

Bound in slightly lighter tan cloth. Front: [vignette stamped in green; and stamped in red] *A SPECIAL EDITION / SOUTHWESTERN SAVINGS ASSOCIATION*. Spine . . .

An issue of 3000 copies distributed, beginning March, 1961, by The Southwestern Savings Association as "A special gift for you with your $100 or more Add-On or New Account during our 9th Anniversary celebration."

COW PEOPLE

A18 a(1) COW PEOPLE / J. Frank Dobie / [type ornament / device] / with photos / LITTLE, BROWN AND COMPANY · BOSTON · TORONTO [1964]

Collation: half title: *COW PEOPLE* / [type ornament]; verso *Books by J. Frank Dobie;* title as above; verso *COPYRIGHT* © 1964 *BY J. FRANK DOBIE* / . . . / *FIRST EDITION* / *Published simultaneously in Canada* / *by Little, Brown & Company (Canada) Limited* / *PRINTED IN THE UNITED STATES OF AMERICA;* dedication *TO* / *Walker Stone and Ralph Johnston* . . .; verso blank, *Introduction* pp. vii-x; *Contents;* verso blank; half title: *COW PEOPLE* / [type ornament]; verso blank; text pp. 3-294; *A Note on Sources* pp. 295-297; verso blank; *Index;* verso blank; index pp. 301-305.

Running titles: *Introduction* and chapter titles on rectos, title on versos; *Index* on rectos and versos.

Illustrations: full page photographs on pp. [5], [27], [54], [65], [67], [69], [71], [73], [92], [95], [99], [156], [160], [165], [167], [171], [173], [181], [186], [189], [203], [207], [217], [220], [223], [225], [228] ,[234], [243], [248], [260], [268] and [284]; full page drawing on pp. [196] and [253]; the type ornament, silhouette of a cow, also on pp. [ii], vii, xi, 7, 24, 53, 58, 91, 100, 113, 119, 120, 147, 159, 170, 185, 191, 198, 202, 205, 213, 215, 218, 222, 226, 233, 237, 242, 246, 249, 252, 261, 267, 270, and the head of each chapter; 2 brands on p. 201.

Bound in black on rust patterned boards. Device blind stamped on front cover. Spine, stamped in gold, *COW* / *PEOPLE* / [type ornament] / *Dobie* / *LITTLE,* / *BROWN*.

Cut. 21½ x 14½cm.

A18 a(2) Limited edition: 15 numbered copies, with an added leaf individually autographed bound in, and specially bound in cowhide.

A18 b . . . Dobie / [type ornament] / Illustrated / LONDON / HAMMOND, HAMMOND & COMPANY [1965]

Collation: . . . title as above; verso . . . / *FIRST EDITION* / *Published in Great Britain and the British Com-*

Rattlesnakes

J. Frank Dobie

LITTLE, BROWN AND COMPANY · BOSTON · TORONTO

monwealth / by Hammond, Hammond & Co. Ltd. / 87 Gower Street, London, W. C. I / Published simultaneously in the U.S.A. and Canada / by Little, Brown & Company (Canada) Limited / PRINTED IN THE UNITED STATES OF AMERICA; dedication . . .

Bound in tan cloth stamped in brown. Spine: *COW / PEOPLE /* [star] */ J. FRANK / DOBIE /* [device] */ HAMMOND / HAMMOND.*

This is the American edition with a new titlepage and binding.

RATTLESNAKES

A19   Rattlesnakes / J. Frank Dobie / [vignette] / LITTLE, BROWN AND COMPANY · BOSTON · TORONTO [1965]

Collation: recto blank; verso *Books by J. Frank Dobie;* half title: *Rattlesnakes;* verso blank; title as above; verso *COPYRIGHT © 1965 BY BERTHA DOBIE / .. / FIRST EDITION / Published simultaneously in Canada / by Little, Brown & Company (Canada) Limited / PRINTED IN THE UNITED STATES OF AMERICA;* two verses of poetry from */—VAIDA STEWART MONTGOMERY / "To a Rattlesnake";* verso blank; *Contents;* verso blank; half title: *Rattlesnakes;* verso blank; text pp. 3-201; verso blank.

Running titles: chapter titles on rectos, title on versos.
Without illustrations.

Bound in blue cloth. Device blind stamped, lower right, front cover. Spine, reading from top to bottom, stamped in black, *Rattlesnakes,* and in yellow *J. Frank Dobie;* at foot in black *Little, / Brown.*

Cut, top edge brown. 21½ x 14½cm.

SOME PART OF MYSELF

A20   J. FRANK DOBIE / [line] / SOME PART / OF MYSELF / [device] / with illustrations / LITTLE, BROWN AND COMPANY · BOSTON · TORONTO [1967]

Collation: blank page; verso [a list of books] *By J. Frank Dobie;* half title: *SOME PART / OF MYSELF;* verso blank; title as above; verso *COPYRIGHT 1952 BY J. FRANK DOBIE / COPYRIGHT 1953, © 1956, 1957, 1962, 1967 BY BERTHA DOBIE / ... / FIRST EDITION / ... / Published simultaneously in Canada / by Little, Brown & Company (Canada) Limited / PRINTED IN THE UNITED STATES OF AMERICA;* dedication *To / Fannie, Elrich, and Martha / and the memory of / Lee and Henry;* verso blank; quotation from *—Walt Whitmam;* verso blank; *Foreword* pp. [xi]-xiii signed *Bertha McKee Dobie;* verso blank; *Contents;* verso blank; half title: *SOME PART /*

OF MYSELF; verso blank; text pp. [3]-271; verso blank; half title: *INDEX;* verso blank; index pp. 275-282.

Running titles: *FORWORD* and *INDEX* on both rectos and versos; chapter titles on rectos, title on versos.

Illustrations: 21 photographs on both sides of 6 plates following pp. 14, 46, 110, 142, 206, and 238.

Bound in light green cloth stamped in black and red. Device blind stamped on lower right corner of front cover. *Spine*: [in black] *Some / Part of / Myself /* [in red] *J. Frank / Dobie /* [in black] *Little, Brown.*

Cut. 22 x 14½cm.

Collected and edited by Bertha McKee Dobie.

Contributions to the Books of Others

1910

B1   The Sou'wester. Vol. VII. MCMX. Georgetown, Tex.,
The Athletic Association of Southwestern University
[1910]

   Editor-in-chief, J. Frank Dobie.

1923

B2 a   Dobie, J. Frank, editor.

   Publications of the Texas Folk-lore Society, Number II. Austin, Texas Folk-lore Society, 1923.

   Weather Wisdom of the Texas-Mexican Border. By J. Frank Dobie: pp. [87]-99.

B2 b   —— ——

   Coffee in the Gourd. Austin, Texas Folk-lore Society [1935]

   Publications of the Texas Folk-lore Society. Number II. 1923. Reprint edition, 1935.

   Rebaptised in Ink: p.v. Signed: J. Frank Dobie.

   Weather Wisdom of the Texas Mexican Border. By J. Frank Dobie: pp. [87]-99.

1924

B3 a ⎯⎯ ⎯⎯

Legends of Texas. Austin, Texas Folk-lore Society, 1924.

Publications of the Texas Folk-lore Society. No. III.

Editors Preface: pp. iii-v.

An Inquiry into the Sources of Treasure Legends of Texas. By J. Frank Dobie: pp. [3]-12.

The Legend of the San Saba or Bowie Mine. By J. Frank Dobie: pp. 12-20.

Treasure Legends of McMullen County. By J. Frank Dobie: pp. 28-43.

Legendary Spanish Forts Down the Nueces. By J. Frank Dobie: pp. 43-49.

The Battlefields of Palo Alto and Resaca de la Palma in Legend. By J. Frank Dobie: pp. 51-52.

How Dollars Turned into Bumble Bees and Other Legends. By J. Frank Dobie: pp. 52-57.

The Silver Ledge on the Frio. By J. Frank Dobie: pp. 60-62.

The Nigger Gold Mine on the Big Bend. By J. Frank Dobie: pp. 64-67.

The Hold of Gold Near Wichita Falls. By J. Frank Dobie: pp. 80-81.

The Snively Legend. By J. Frank Dobie: pp 95-99.

Antonette's Leap or The Legend of Mount Bonnell. By J. Frank Dobie: pp. 171-176.

How the Brazos River Got Its Name. By J. Frank Dobie: pp. 209-217.

Lost Canyon of the Big Bend Country. By J. Frank Dobie: pp. 238-241.

B3 b ⎯⎯ ⎯⎯

.... Hatboro, Pa., Folklore Associates, 1964 [c1924]

Publications of the Texas Folklore Society. Reprint edition, No. 4.

1925

B4 a ⎯⎯ ⎯⎯

Publication of the Texas Folk-lore Society. Number IV. Austin, Texas Folk-lore Society, 1925.

Foreward Remarks by the Editor: pp. [5]-6.

Versos of the Texas Vaquero. By J. Frank Dobie: pp. [30]-43.

B4 b   —— ——

Happy Hunting Ground. Hatboro, Pa., Folklore Associates, 1964 [c1925]

Publications of the Texas Folklore Society. Reprint edition, No. 4.

1926

B5 a   —— ——

Publications of the Texas Folk-lore Society. Number V. Austin, Texas Folk-lore Society, 1926.

Remarks Necessary and Unnecessary. By the Editor: pp. [3]-4.
The Tournament in Texas. By J. Frank Dobie: pp. [93]-103.

B5 b   —— ——

Rainbow in the Morning. Hatboro, Pa., Folklore Associates, 1965 [c1926]

Publications of the Texas Folklore Society. Reprint edition, No. 5.

1927

B6   —— ——

Texas and Southwestern Lore. Austin, Texas Folk-lore Society, 1927.

Publication of the Texas Folk-lore Society, number VI.
The Editor's Prerogative: pp. [5]-6.
Ballads and Songs of the Frontier Folk. By J. Frank Dobie: pp. [121]-183.

1928

B7   —— ——

Follow de Drinkin' Gou'd. Austin, Texas Folk-lore Society, 1928.

Publications of the Texas Folk-lore Society, number VII.
Report Sir [by J. Frank Dobie] pp. [5]-6.
Pioneer Folk Tales. By Mary Jourdan Atkinson and J. Frank Dobie: pp. [69]-77.
More Ballads and Songs of the Frontier Folk. By J. Frank Dobie: pp. [155]-180.

1929

B8   The Book of Knowledge. XXI. The Book of Texas. Dallas [c1929]

Editor, Holland Thompson . . . Editor-in-chief, The Book of Knowledge, The Grolier Society.
Literature and Art in Texas [by J. Frank Dobie] pp. [265]-292.

B9   Briggs, Thomas H.; Curry, Charles M.; and Payne, L. W., Jr.

Literature for the Junior High School. Book III. Chicago, Rand McNally & Co., 1929.

The Saga of the Saddle. By J. Frank Dobie: pp. 643-652.

1930

B10   Botkin, B. A., editor.

Folk-say, a Regional Miscellany. Norman, University of Oklahoma Press, 1930.

Provincialism [by] J. Frank Dobie: p. 321.

B11 a   Dobie, J. Frank, editor.

Man, Bird, and Beast. Austin, Texas Folk-lore Society, 1930.

Publications of the Texas Folk-lore Society. Volume VIII.
Just a Word: pp. [5]-7. Signed: J. Frank Dobie.

B11 b   —— ——

. . . [Facsimile Edition] Dallas, Southern Methodist University Press [1965, c1930]

B12   Jennings, Napoleon Augustus.

A Texas Ranger. Dallas, Southwest Press [c1930]

Foreword: pp. iii-xi. Signed: J. Frank Dobie.

1931

B13 a   Dobie, J. Frank, editor.

Southwestern Lore. Austin, Texas Folk-lore Society; Dallas, The Southwest Press, 1931.

Publications of the Texas Folk-lore Society. Number IX.
Saludas!: p. v. By J. Frank Dobie.

B13 b   —— ——

　　　. . . Hatboro, Pa., Folklore Associates, 1965 [1931]

　　　Publications of the Texas Folk-lore Society. Reprint
　　　edition, No. 9.

B14   Rogers, John William.

　　　Finding Literature on the Texas Plains. Dallas, The
　　　Southwest Press [1931]

　　　Life and Literature of the Southwest. By J. Frank Dobie:
　　　pp. 31-57.

　　　Enlarged and published later as Guide to Life and
　　　Literature of the Southwest.

1932

B15 a   Dobie, J. Frank, editor.

　　　Tone the Bell Easy. Austin, Texas Folk-lore Society,
　　　1932.

　　　Publications of the Texas Folk-lore Society. Number X.
　　　Muchas Gracias: pp. [5]-7. Signed: J. F. D.

　　　Mustang Gray: Fact, Tradition, and Song. By J. Frank
　　　Dobie: pp. [109]-123.

B15 b   —— ——

　　　. . . [Facsimile Edition] Dallas, Southern Methodist
　　　University Press [1965, c1932]

1933

B16   —— ——

　　　Spur-of-the-Cock. Austin, Texas Folk-lore Society,
　　　1933.

　　　Publications of the Texas Folk-lore Society. Number XI.

B17   Pearce, T. M.; and Hendon, Telfair, compilers and
　　　editors. America in the Southwest, a Regional An-
　　　thology. Albuquerque, N. M., The University Press,
　　　1933.

　　　Points of View: pp. 119-141. From Southwest Review,
　　　Summer issue, 1929.

　　　True Culture Is Eclectic, but Provincial: pp. 128-129.
　　　Signed: J. Frank Dobie. From Southwest Review.

　　　The Saga of the Saddle. By J. Frank Dobie: pp. 262-283.
　　　From Southwest Review, Winter, 1928.

B18 a   Van Emden, Frieda W.

Sure Enough How Come? San Antonio, The Naylor Company, 1933.

Illustrated by Leslie Turner.
The Sign-post: pp. xiii-xvi. Signed: J. Frank Dobie.

B18 b   . . . The Naylor Company, 1938.

Revised and reprinted July, 1938.

1934

B19   Boatright, Mody C.

Tall Tales from Texas. Dallas, The Southwest Press [1934]

Illustrated by Elizabeth E. Keeper.
Special Edition for the Texas Folk-lore Society: on flyleaf at front. Signed: J. Frank Dobie.
A Preface on Authentic Liars: pp. vii-xvii. Signed: J. Frank Dobie.

B20   McGraw, H. Ward, editor.

Prose and Poetry of America. Syracuse, The L. W. Singer Company [1934]

The Saga of the Saddle [by] J. Frank Dobie: pp. 1097-1107.

1935

Dobie, J. Frank, editor. Coffee in the Gourd. See B2 b.

B21   Dobie, J. Frank, editor.

Puro Mexicano. Austin, Texas Folk-lore Society, 1935.

Texas Folk-lore Society Publications. Number XII.
Prefatory Wisdom by the Editor: pp. v-viii.
Catorce. By J. Frank Dobie: pp. 194-200.

B22   Pound, Louise; Stenberg, Theodore; Callahan, James P.; etc.

Ideas and Models. New York, Henry Holt and Company [1935]

Bowie and the Bowie Knife [by] J. Frank Dobie: pp. 457-471. [Reprinted from the Southwest Review, April, 1931]

B23   Thompson, Stith, editor.

Round the Levee. Austin, Texas Folk-lore Society
[1935]

Publication of the Texas Folk-lore Society. Number I.
1916. Reprint Edition, 1935.
Upon This Rock: A Reprint Notice: p. [v] Signed: J.
Frank Dobie, secretary and editor.

1936

B24   Owens, William A.

Swing and Turn: Texas Play-party Games. Dallas,
Tardy Publishing Company, 1936.

This collection . . . is not a numbered publication issued by the Texas Folk-lore Society, but by arrangement
with the publisher . . . distributed to members of the Society for the year 1936.
Special Edition for the Texas Folk-lore Society: leaf
at front, signed: J. Frank Dobie Secretary and Editor of
the Texas Folk-lore Society.

B25   Thomas, W. H.

Some Current Folk-songs of the Negro. [Austin]
Folk-lore Society of Texas [1936?]

Read before the Folk-lore Society of Texas, 1912.
Will Thomas and the Texas Folk-lore Society: p. [1]
Signed: J. Frank Dobie. Austin, Texas. April, 1936.
First published, 1912, without the introduction by Dobie.

1937

B26   Arnold, Oren, editor.

Roundup, a Collection of Western Stories, Poems,
and Articles for Young People. Dallas, Banks Upshaw and Company [c1937]

Illustrated by Creston F. Baumgartner.
When I Was a Boy on the Ranch. By J. Frank Dobie:
pp. 162-172. Reprinted by permission of the author from
the October, 1933, St. Nicholas Magazine.

B27   Dobie, J. Frank, editor; Boatright, Mody C., associate
editor.

Straight Texas. Austin, Texas Folk-lore Society,
1937.

Publications of the Texas Folk-lore Society. Number
XIII.
Taking It Straight. (Dedicated to Ab Blocker): p. [v.
Signed] J. F. D.
Stories in Texas Place Names. By J. Frank Dobie: pp.
[1]-78.

1938

B28   Clarke, Frances E., compiler.

Gallant Horses; Great Horse Stories of Our Day.
New York, The Macmillan Company, 1938.

The White Steed of the Prairies. By J. Frank Dobie:
pp. 51-73. [Reprinted from] The American Mercury.

B29 a   Dobie, J. Frank; Boatright, Mody C.; and Ransom,
Harry H., editors.

Coyote Wisdom. Austin, Texas Folk-lore Society,
1938.

Texas Folk-lore Society Publications. Number XIV.
Illustrations by Mark Storm and others.
Pertinences and Patrons. By the Editor: pp. 5-7.

B29 b   —— ——

. . . [Facsimile Edition] Dallas, Southern Methodist University Press [1965, c1938]

Van Emden, Frieda W. Sure Enough How Come?
See B18 b.

B30   Wood, Ray, compiler.

Peckerwood Rimes. [Beaumont, Tex., The Grey-
stone Press, 1938]

Illustrated by Ed Hargis.
Foreword: p. [5] Signed: J. Frank Dobie.

1939

B31   Becker, May Lamberton, editor.

Golden Tales of the Southwest. New York, Dodd,
Mead & Company, 1939.

Decoration by Lois Lenski.
The Mystery of the Palo Duro. By J. Frank Dobie. pp.
59-64.

B32   Dobie, J. Frank; Boatright, Mody C.; and Ransom, Harry H., editors.

In the Shadow of History. Austin, Texas Folk-lore Society, 1939.

Texas Folk-lore Society Publication. Number XV.
The Line That Travis Drew. By J. Frank Dobie: pp. 9-16.
The Roadrunner in Fact and Folk-Lore. By J. Frank Dobie: pp. 146-174. This essay . . . appeared, somewhat abbreviated, in the Natural History Magazine, New York, September, 1939.

B33   El Paso, Texas. Centennial Museum Gallery.

Exhibition of the Fifty Original Drawings, by Tom Lea, Illustrating the New Volume by J. Frank Dobie, Apache Gold & Yaqui Silver, April 10 to 14, 1939, Centennial Museum Gallery, El Paso, Texas. [El Paso, 1939]

List of Illustrations, with Comment by J. Frank Dobie.

B34   Potter, Jack.

Lead Steer and Other Tales. Clayton, N. M., Leader Press, 1939.

Belling the Lead Steer. By J. Frank Dobie: pp. [3]-12.

1940

B35 a   Adams, James Truslow, editor.

Dictionary of American History. New York Charles Scribner's Sons, 1940.

Volume I: "Arkansas Traveler", p. 107; Barbed Wire, p. 163; Bears, Bear Hunters and Bear Stories, pp. 171-172; Bowie Knife, p. 230; Bronco, p. 242; Cattle Brands, p. 325, Cattle Drives, pp. 325-326; Chaparral, p. 341.

Volume II: Conquistadores, p. 25; Cow Towns, p. 79; Cowpuncher, p. 81; Coyote, p. 82; Drouth, p. 170; Dust, p. 179; Entrada, p. 219; Fiddlers and Fiddle Tunes, p. 270; Green River Knife, p. 423.

Volume III: Horse: Cow Horse, p. 46; Horse Stealing, pp. 49-50; "Joe Bowers", p. 177; Longhorns, Texas, p. 300; Medicine Show, pp. 370-371; Mesas, p. 379; Mesquite, p. 379.

Volume IV: Mule-Skinner, p. 40; Mustangs, p. 49; Poker, p. 292; Ranches, pp. 414-415; Rattlesnakes, p. 417; Razorback Hogs, p. 418; Remudas, p. 448; Rodeos, p. 499.

Volume V: Sandbar Duel, p. 27; Shooting Match, p. 76; Texas Rangers, pp. 256-257; Thirst, p. 263; Trail Drivers, pp. 302-303; Windmills, pp. 470-471.

B35 b   —— ——

. . . Second Edition, Revised. New York, Scribner's Sons, 1942.

B36 a   Dobie, J. Frank; Boatright, Mody C.; and Ransom, Harry H., editors.

Mustangs and Cow Horses. Austin, Texas Folk-lore Society, 1940.

Publication Number XVI of the Texas Folk-lore Society.
The Deathless Pacing White Stallion. By J. Frank Dobie: pp. 171-183.
Cow Horse Names, Colors and Cures. By J. Frank Dobie: pp. 234-249.
Pitching Horses and Panthers. By J. Frank Dobie: pp. 291-303.
As Smart As a Cutting Horse. By J. Frank Dobie: pp. 403-413.

B36 b   —— ——

. . . [Facsimile Edition] Dallas, Southern Methodist University Press [1965, c1940]

Second Edition, 1965.

B37   Montgomery, Whitney, editor.

The Road to Texas. Dallas, The Kaleidograph Press [c1940]

Drawings by Ruth McCauley Thorne.
Vanitas. San Antonio, Summer [in verse]: p. 87. Signed: J. Frank Dobie.

B38   Taintor, Sarah Augusta; and Monro, Kate M.

English for American Youth. New York, The Macmillan Company, 1940.

When I Was a Boy on a Ranch: p. 66. Signed: J. Frank Dobie. Reprinted from St. Nicholas 1933.

B39   Texas University. Department of English.

ШЈ 342 (i.e. Lazy E. 342). A Collection of Stray Mavericks Caught, Roped, and Branded by Members of the "Big Corral" (English 342: Life and Literature of the Southwest) under the Scrutiny of the Foreman, Wm. H. Cleveland, Jr., and Containing a Few Opening Remarks by the Boss o' the Outfit, J. Frank Dobie. No. 1. Austin, University of Texas, 1940.

Mimeographed.
See also B44, B46, and B54.

1941

B40   Bradley, Ann; and Sharp, Lawrence A., editors.

Echoes of the Southland, Book Two. Austin, The Steck Company [1941]

The Saga of the Saddle: pp. 134-145.

B41   Denhardt, Robert Moorman.

The Quarter Horse. Fort Worth, The American Quarter Horse Association, 1941.

Billy Horses and Steel Dust. By J. Frank Dobie: p. 63-68.

B42   Dobie, J. Frank; Boatright, Mody C.; and Ransom, Harry H., editors.

Texian Stomping Grounds. Austin, Texas Folk-lore Society, 1941.

Texas Folk-lore Society. Publications, Number XVII.

B43   Inglis, Rewey Belle; Gehlman, John; Bowman, Mary Rives; and Foerster, Norman, editors.

Adventures in American Literature. Standard Third Edition. New York, Chicago, Harcourt, Brace and Company, 1941.

The Heraldry of the Range· pp. 177-184. By J. Frank Dobie.

B44   Texas. University. Department of English.
      ⊔ 342 [i.e. Lazy E. 342] A Collection of Stray Mavericks Caught, Roped, and Branded by Members of the "Big Corral" (English 342: Life and Literature of the Southwest) Under the Scrutiny of the Foreman, A. P. Thomason and Containing A Few Opening Remarks by the Boss of the Outfit: J. Frank Dobie. No. 2. Austin, University of Texas, 1941.

Just a Weed: leaf [ii] Signed: J. Frank Dobie.
Mimeographed.
See also B39, B46, and B54.

1942

Adams, James Truslow, editor. Dictionary of American History. See B35b.

B45   Ranch Romances.

Tops in Westerns. [n. p., 1942]

Re-issue [from the magazine Ranch Romances]
The Story under the Grasses. By J. Frank Dobie: pp.
113-117.

B46   Texas. University. Department of English.

Typically Texian. Being a Collection of "Dog-Run"
Sayings and Doings by the Lazy Easers of English
342 (Life and Literature of the Southwest) Culled
out by Lazy Listener Donald Day and Sent Stamped-
ing on Their Way by a Flash of Lightning from
Rawhide Yarner J. Frank Dobie. Volume III. Austin,
University of Texas, 1942.

One Paisano to Another: leaf [ii] Signed: J. Frank
Dobie.
Mimeographed.
See also B39, B44, and B54.

B47   Wright, Solomon Alexander.

My Rambles as East Texas Cowboy, Hunter, Fish-
erman, Tie-cutter. Austin, Texas Folk-lore Society,
1942.

Range Life Series; under the general editorship of J.
Frank Dobie.
Arranged, with introduction, by J. Frank Dobie.
Introduction: pp. xi-xii.
Illustrations by B. E. Lewis.
Printed at El Paso, by Carl Hertzog.

1943

B48   Benedict, Carl Peters.

A Tenderfoot Kid on Gyp Water. Austin, Texas
Folk-lore Society; and Dallas, University Press, 1943.

Range Life Series, under general editorship of J. Frank
Dobie.
550 copies of this book have been printed and the type
melted.
Carl Hertzog — El Paso, Texas, printer.
Introduction. By J. Frank Dobie: pp. xiii-xviii.

B49   Boatright, Mody C.; and Day, Donald, editors.

Backwoods to Border. Austin, Texas Folk-lore Society; Dallas, University Press, Southern Methodist
University, 1943.

Texas Folk-lore Society Publications, Number XVIII;
J. Frank Dobie, general editor.

Twenty Years an Editor: pp. vii-xii. Signed: J. Frank Dobie.

A Buffalo Hunter and His Song. By J. Frank Dobie: pp. [1]-10.

B50   McCauley, James Emmit.

A Stove-up Cowboy's Story. Austin, Texas Folklore Society; Dallas, University Press, 1943.

Range Life Series; under general editorship of J. Frank Dobie.
Introduction by John A. Lomax.
Drawings by Tom Lea.
700 copies of this book have been printed and the type melted.
Carl Hertzog — El Paso, Texas, printer.

B51   Nichols, Edwin S.

Ed Nichols Rode a Horse. As told to Ruby Nichols Cutbirth. [Austin] Texas Folklore Society; Dallas, University Press, 1943.

Range Life Series; under general editorship of J. Frank Dobie.
Frontispiece by Jerry Bywaters.

B52   Perry, George Sessions, editor.

Roundup Time; a Collection of Southwestern Writing. New York, London, Whittlesey House, McGraw-Hill Book Company, Inc. [c1943]

Lead Steers and Neck Oxen, by J. Frank Dobie: pp. 242-255. . . . a selection from *The Longhorns*.

B53   Simmons, Gurdon; and Meyer, Ralph Louise, compilers.

This Is Your America. Volume III. New York, Literary Classics, Inc., 1943.

Illustrated by William Sharp.
How "Old Igo" Kept Books. By J. Frank Dobie: pp. 13-[19]
A reprint of a newspaper sketch.

B54   Texas. University. Department of English.

LLJ 342 [i.e. Lazy E. 342] A Bunch of Ladinos. Rounded up and Herded into the Big Corral by the Vaqueros of Outfit 342 of the Lazy E. Range. Cut out by Inspector Frank Goodwyn; Roped, Marked and Branded by Jack Maguire, Caporal; John Deschner, Administrador; and Top Hands: Dorothy James, Etta Grace Parks, Rachael Barber; and Sent Bawling on Their Way by J. Frank Dobie, Boss of the Outfit, May, 1943. [Austin, University of Texas, 1943]

The Back-Trail also Runs Forward: leaves [iii-iv]
Signed: J. Frank Dobie.
Mimeographed.
See also B39, B44, and B46.

1944

B55   Boatright, Mody C.; and Day, Donald, editors.

From Hell to Breakfast. Austin, Texas Folk-lore Society; Dallas, University Press, Southern Methodist University, 1944.

Texas Folk-lore Society Publication, number XIX; J. Frank Dobie, general editor.
A Tale of the Two Companions. By J. Frank Dobie: pp. [36]-41.

B56   Botkin, B. A., editor.

A Treasury of American Folklore, Stories, Ballads, and Traditions of the People. New York, Crown Publishers [1944]

Foreword by Carl Sandburg.
Short excerpts from various books, stories and articles, by J. Frank Dobie: pp. [xxix], 59-60, 325-326, 396-398, 412-413, [489], 570-571, and 763-766.

1945

B57   Boatright, Mody C.

Gib Morgan, Minstrel of the Oil Fields. [Austin] Texas Folk-lore Society, 1945.

Texas Folk-lore Society, Publication, Number XX; J. Frank Dobie, general editor.
Illustrated by Betty Boatright.
Printed at El Paso by Carl Hertzog.

B58   Hoole, W. Stanley.

Sam Slick in Texas. San Antonio, The Naylor Company [c1945]

Foreword: pp. vii-x. Signed: J. Frank Dobie.

B59   Stover, Elizabeth Matchett.

Son-of-a-Gun Stew, a Sampling of the Southwest. Dallas, University Press, Southern Methodist University, 1945.

Foreword by John William Rogers.
Illustrated by Harold D. Bugbee.
The Making of a Son-of-a-Gun Stew: pp. ix-x. Signed: J. Frank Dobie.
The Longhorn Blood Call, by J. Frank Dobie: pp. 157-172. Reprinted from Southwest Review, XXIV: 4, July, 1939. [In The Longhorns]

1946

B60   Atlantic Monthly.

The Pocket Atlantic. New York, Pocket Books, Inc. [1946]

Edited and with an Introduction by Edward Weeks.
The stories and articles in this book . . . appeared originally in The Atlantic Monthly.
The Cold-Nosed Hounds. By J. Frank Dobie: pp. 215-221

B61   Boatright, Mody C., editor.

Mexican Border Ballads and Other Lore. Austin [Texas Folklore Society] 1946.

Publication of the Texas Folklore Society [No.] XXI.
Do Rattlesnakes Swallow Their Young? By J. Frank Dobie: pp. [43]-64.

B62   Pearce, Thomas Matthews, and Thomason, Alton Parker, editors.

Southwesterners Write. The American Southwest in Stories and Articles by Thirty-Two Contributors. Albuquerque, The University of New Mexico Press, 1946.

Illustrated by Helen S. Pearce.
Horns. By J. Frank Dobie: pp. 64-77. From *The Longhorns* (1941)

B63   Rhodes, Eugene Manlove.

The Little World Waddies. [El Paso, c1946]

Illustrated by Harold Bugbee.
Designed and printed at The Pass of the Rio Bravo by Carl Hertzog for William Hutchinson of Cohasset Stage, Chico, California.

1000 copies printed December, 1946.

My Salute to Gene Rhodes. By J. Frank Dobie: pp. xiii-xxi. [This, with a few changes, was used as an introduction to the Best Novels and Stories of Eugene Manlove Rhodes]

See also B73.

1947

B64   Autry, Gene, compiler.

Saddles - - - - Sagebrush - - - - Sixguns. Western Stories. New York, Dell Publishing Company [1947]

The Rider of Loma Escondida. By J. Frank Dobie: pp. [29]-35.

B65   Denhardt, Robert Moorman.

The Horse of the Americas. Norman, University of Oklahoma Press, 1947.

Foreword: pp. xv-xvii. Signed: J. Frank Dobie.

B66   Johnson, Thomas H., editor.

A Man's Reach, Some Choices Facing Youth Today. New York, G. P. Putnam's Sons [c1947]

Animal Tales of the Southwest, by J. Frank Dobie: pp. 122-143. [This transcription of a lecture, delivered at the Lawrenceville School, New Jersey, later incorporated in The Voice of the Coyote and The Mustangs]

B67   Standard Oil Company of California.

See Your West. [n. p., Standard of California, 1947]

Natural-color prints with descriptive text, by various authors, on verso of each.

Big Ben National Park: p. [106]. Signed: J. Frank Dobie.

The Guadalupe Mountains: p. [108]. Signed: J. Frank Dobie.

1948

B68   Bradley, Ann; and Sharp, Laurence A., editors.

Echoes of the Southland. Book One. Austin, The Steck Company [1948]

The Buffalo Stampede, by J. Frank Dobie: pp. 58-63. [In *On the Open Range*]

When I Was a Boy on the Range. By J. Frank Dobie: pp. 302-315. [Reprinted from St. Nicholas Oct. 1938]

B69   Lambert, Fred.

By Gone Days of the Old West. Kansas City, Missouri, Burton Publishing Company [c1938]

Illustrated by the Author.
Foreword: p. [9] Signed: J. Frank Dobie.

B70   New Mexico Magazine.

This Is New Mexico. Santa Fe, The Rydal Press [c1948]

Edited by George Fitzpatrick.
Sketches by Wilfred Stedman.
The original New Mexico Magazine publication of each article.
Don Quixote of the Six-Shooter [by] J. Frank Dobie: pp. 62-68.

1949

B71   Boatright, Mody C., editor.

The Sky Is My Tipi. Austin, The Texas Folk-lore Society; Dallas, University Press, 1949.

Publication of the Texas Folk-lore Society No. XXII.
The Apache and His Secret: pp. [142]-154. At head of title: J. Frank Dobie.

B72   Macauley, Thurston.

The Great Horse Omnibus; from Homer to Hemingway. Chicago, New York, Ziff-Davis Publishing Company [c1949]

Introduction by Bing Crosby.
Little Gretchen and the White Steed [by] J. Frank Dobie: pp. 91-95.
The Black Horse of Pancho Villa [by] J. Frank Dobie: pp. 166-167.

B73 a   Rhodes, Eugene Manlove.

The Best Novels and Stories. Boston, Houghton Mifflin Co., 1949.

Edited by Frank V. Dearing.
A Salute to Gene Rhodes: pp. xi-xxii. Signed: J. Frank Dobie. [A revision of the introduction to Rhodes' The Little World Waddies] See also B63.

B73 b   —— ——

Sunset Land; the Best Novels of Eugene Manlove Rhodes. [New York, Dell Publishing Company, Inc., c1949]

Edited by Frank V. Dearing.
A Salute to Gene Rhodes: pp. [9]-22. Signed: J. Frank Dobie.
A Dell Book. D152.

1950

B74   Russell, Charles M.

Seven Drawings by Charles M. Russell with an additional drawing by Tom Lea . . . and an Essay on These Pictures: "The Conservatism of Charles M. Russell" by J. Frank Dobie . . . El Paso, Carl Hertzog [1950]

In a portfolio of heavy rust paper.

B75   St. Nicholas.

The Second St. Nicholas Anthology. Edited by Henry Steele Commager. New York, Random House [c1950]

When I Was a Boy on the Ranch, by J. Frank Dobie: pp. 278-283.

B76 a   Siringo, Charles A.

A Texas Cowboy, or Fifteen Years on the Hurricane Deck of a Spanish Pony. New York, William Sloane Associates [c1950]

With Bibliographical Study & Introduction by J. Frank Dobie.
Drawings by Tom Lea.
Typography by Carl Hertzog.
Introduction. Charles Siringo, Writer and Man, by J. Frank Dobie: pp. ix-xxxv.
Bibliography of Siringo's Writings: pp. xxxvii-xl.

B76 b   —— ——

. . . Pony. [New York] A Signet Book Published by The New American Library [1951]

Drawings by Tom Lea.
A Note on Charlie Siringo, Writer and Man. By J. Frank Dobie: pp. 153-173.
Bibliography of Siringo's Writings [by J. Frank Dobie] pp. 174-176.

B77   Thomas Gilcrease Foundation.

An Exhibition of Paintings and Bronzes, by Frederic Remington [and] Charles M. Russell, May to October, 1950. Tulsa [1950]

Charles M. Russell, by J. Frank Dobie: unpaged.

1951

B78   Bailey, Matilda; and Leavell, Ullin.

Worlds of Adventure; the Mastery of Reading. [New York] American Book Company [c1951]

Coyote between Two Sheep [by] J. Frank Dobie: pp. 151-152. From *The Voice of the Coyote*.

B79   Botkin, B. A., editor.

A Treasury of Western Folk-lore. [Southwest Edition] New York, Crown Publishers, Inc. [1951]

Foreword by Bernard DeVoto.
This limited edition . . . is made especially for the Southwest: [4] pp. st front. Signed: J. Frank Dobie.
Short excerpts from various books, stories and articles by J. Frank Dobie: pp. 10, 90, 91-93, 100-101, 120-124, 267, 363-367, 474-475, 483-484, 491-494, 498, 512-513, 546-547, 550, 680-683, 702-703, 762, 775-776.

B80   Bushman, John G., and Mathews, Ernst G., editors.

Readings for College English. New York, American Books Co. [c1951]

The Cold-Nosed Hounds: pp. 535-540. [By] J. Frank Dobie.

B81   Evans, G. W.

Slash Ranch Hounds. Albuquerque, University of New Mexico Press, c1951.

Lion Markers. By J. Frank Dobie: pp. 107-122. From The Country Gentleman. May, 1928.

B82   Hudson, Wilson M., editor.

The Healer of Los Olmos and other Mexican Lore. Austin, Folklore Society; Dallas, Southern Methodist University Press, 1951.

Publication of Texas Folk-lore Society. Mody C. Boatright, editor. Number XXIV.
Charm of Mexican Folk Tales. By J. Frank Dobie: pp. 1-8.

B83   Latham, John H.

Lonesome Longhorn. Philadelphia, The Westminster Press [1951]

Adapted from a Longhorn tale [Sancho and Other Returners in *The Longhorns*].

Siringo, Charles A. A Texas Cowboy. See B76b.

B84   Williams, James Robert.

Cowboys Out Our Way. New York, Charles Scribner's Sons, 1951.

With an Introduction by J. Frank Dobie.
Jim Williams and Out Our Way, by J. Frank Dobie: pp. 1-6.

1952

B85   American Peoples Encyclopedia Yearbook. Events and Personalities of 1951. Franklin J. Meine, editor-in-chief. Chicago, The Spencer Press, Inc. [c1952]

Mexico: col. 748-750. Signed: J. Frank Dobie.

B86   The Glory of Our West. Foreword by Joseph Henry Jackson. Garden City, N. Y., Doubleday & Company, Inc. [c1952]

"Remember the Alamo": p. 60. Signed: J. Frank Dobie. Colored photograph by Mike Roberts: p. 61.
Big Ben National Park: p. 62. Signed: J. Frank Dobie. Colored photograph by Ansel Adams: p. 63.
The Guadalupe Mountains: p. 64. Signed: J. Frank Dobie. Colored photograph by Ansel Adams: p. 65.

B87 a   Murrow, Edward R., Editor.

This I believe: The Living Philosophies of One Hundred Thoughtful Men and Women in All Walks of Life. New York, Simon and Schuster, 1952.

Foreword by Edward R. Murrow.
Edited by Edward P. Morgan.
What Makes Me Feel Big. By J. Frank Dobie: pp. 39-40.

B87 b   —— ——

... the Personal Philosophies ... life; with a Foreword by Edward R. Murrow. London, Hamish Hamilton [1953]

J. Frank Dobie: pp. 128-129.

1953

B88   Boatright, Mody C.; Hudson, Wilson M.; and Maxwell, Allen, editors.

Folk Travelers. Ballads, Tales, and Talk. Austin, The Texas Folk-lore Society; Dallas, Southern Methodist University Press, 1953.

Publication of the Texas Folk-lore Society. Number XXV.
The Traveling Anecdote: pp. 1-17. At head of title: J. Frank Dobie.

B89   The Book of Knowledge, 1953 Annual. New York, Toronto, The Grolier Society [c1953]

Outlaws of the Old West. By J. Frank Dobie: pp. 238-242.

B90   Brewer, J. Mason.

The Word on the Brazos; Negro Preacher Tales from the Brazos Bottoms of Texas. Austin, University of Texas Press, 1953.

Illustrations by Ralph White, Jr.
A Word on The Word. By J. Frank Dobie: pp. vii-xii.

B91   Howe, Elvon L., editor.

1952 Brand Book. Sixteen Original Studies in Western History. Denver, Colorado, The Westerners [c1953]

With special sketches by H. D. Bugbee.
Posse edition of fifty copies.
Trail Driving 100 Years Ago by J. Frank Dobie: pp. [ii]-1-15.

B92   Lea, Tom.

Tom Lea, a Portfolio of Six Paintings with an Introduction by J. Frank Dobie. Austin, University of Texas Press, 1953.
Tom Lea by J. Frank Dobie: pp. 3-[8]

Murrow, Edward R., editor. This I Believe. See B87b.

1954

B93   Belcher, William Francis; Clifton, E. S.; Male, R. R., Jr.; Olive, W. J.; and Shockley, M. S., editors.

Reading and Writing. New York, Rinehart & Company, Inc. [c1954]

Midas on a Goatskin, by J. Frank Dobie: pp. 308-314.
From *Coronado's Children.*

B94   Boatright, Mody C.; Hudson, Wilson M.; Maxwell, Allen, editors.

Texas Folk and Folklore. Dallas, Southern Methodist University Press, 1954.

Publications of the Texas Folk-lore Society . . . Number XXVI.
Dedicated to J. Frank Dobie, editor for the Texas Folklore Society for twenty years, from 1923 to 1943.
Drawings by Jose Cisneros.
Treasure Legends of McMullen County [by] J. Frank Dobie: pp. 83-100.
The Deathless Pacing White Stallion [by] J. Frank Dobie: pp. 105-112.
Versos de los Bandidos [by] J. Frank Dobie: pp. 143-147.
The Paisano's Cactus Corral [by] J. Frank Dobie: pp. 289-295.

B95   Peery, William Wallace, editors.

21 Texas Short Stories. Austin, University of Texas Press, 1954.

Midas on a Goatskin: pp. 192-201. Reprinted from *Coronado's Children*.

B96   Vogue Magazine.

The Arts of Living, from the pages of Vogue Magazine. [New York] Simon and Schuster, 1954.

With biographical profiles by its editors, and a preface by Gilbert Highet.
The Art of Discovery: pp. [32]-38. At head of title: J. Frank Dobie.

1955

B97   Mohle, Eula Phares, editor.

Texas Sampler. New York, Oxford Book Company, 1955.

Treasure Tales of the Southwest [by] J. Frank Dobie: pp. 84-89. [Extract from *Coronado's Children*]

B98   Sellars, David Kelly, editor.

Texas Tales, Selected from the Best Stories Appearing in the Publications of The Texas Folklore Society and Other Sources. Dallas and New York, Noble and Noble, Publishers, Inc. [c1955]

Edited for school use.
Most of these stories are Dobie's, from *Legends of Texas*.

1956

B99   Boatright, Mody C.; and Hughes, Leo, editors.

College Prose. [Austin] The University of Texas. Boston, Houghton Mifflin Company [1956]

Midas on a Goatskin, by J. Frank Dobie: pp. 11-18.

B100   Jewett, Arno; Edman, Marion; Scannell, Ruth; and McKee, Paul.

Journey into America. Boston, Houghton Mifflin Company [c1956]

"Remember the Alamo!" A Picture Article by J. Frank Dobie: pp. [299]-302.

B101   Riders West. A Dell First Edition, an Original Book with Stories and Articles by Luke Short, Tom W. Blackburn, J. Frank Dobie, L. L. Foreman, William MacLeod Raine. [New York, Dell Publishing Company, Inc., c1956]

Cooks of Range and Trail: pp. [89]-107. At head of title: J. Frank Dobie.

1957

B102   Boatright, Mody C.; Hudson, Wilson M.; Maxwell, Allen, editors.

Mesquite and Willow. Dallas, Southern Methodist University Press [c1957]

Publication of the Texas Folklore Society . . . Number XXVII.
Br'er Rabbit Watches Out for Himself in Mexico [by] J. Frank Dobie: pp. 113-117.

B103   Cook, James H.

Fifty Years on the Old Frontier as Cowboy, Hunter, Guide, Scout, and Ranchman. Norman, University of Oklahoma Press [1957]

Copyright 1923. New edition copyright 1957.
Captain Cook's Place among Reminiscencers of the West. By J. Frank Dobie: pp. vii-xi.

B104   Gilfillan, Archer B.

Sheep, Life on the South Dakota Range. Minneapolis, University of Minnesota Press [c1957]

Illustrated by Kurt Wiese.
Foreword by J. Frank Dobie: pp. [i-viii]

1958

B105   The American Museum of Natural History.

The Illustrated Library of the Natural Sciences. New York, Simon and Schuster, 1958.

Editor: Edward M. Weyer, Jr.
Art Director: Frederick L. Hahn.
The Smart Coyote. By J. Frank Dobie: Vol. I, pp. 731-735. [Reprinted from Natural History, February 1942, Vol. XLIX, No. 2, pp. 70-75]

B106   Benthul, Herman F.

Literature of the Old Southwest. Dallas and New York, Noble and Noble, Publishers, Inc. [c1958]

The Mystery of the Palo Duro [by] J. Frank Dobie: pp. 43-50.
Tex Dorsey Sells a Herd of Cattle [by] J. Frank Dobie: pp. 302-306.

B107   Boatright, Mody C.; Hudson, Wilson M.; and Maxwell, Allen, editors.

Madstones and Twisters. Dallas, Southern Methodist University Press [c1958]

Publications of the Texas Folklore Society . . . Number XXVIII.
Madstones and Hydrophobia Skunks [by] J. Frank Dobie: pp. 3-17.

B108   Bourke, John G.

An Apache Campaign, in the Sierra Madre. New York, Charles Scribner's Sons [c1958]

Introduction by J. Frank Dobie.
Captain John G. Bourke as Soldier, Writer and Man, by J. Frank Dobie: pp. 5-16.
[A reprint of the 1886 edition without the illustrations]

B109a   Flanagan, John Theodore; and Hudson, Arthur Palmer, editors.

The American Folklore Reader; Folklore in American Literature. New York, A. S. Barnes & Co. [c1958]

Midas on a Goatskin, by J. Frank Dobie: pp. 227-234. Chapter VII of Coronado's Children (1930).

B109b   —— ——

Folklore in American Literature. White Plains, N. Y., Row, Peterson and Company [c1958]

B110   Hale, Jeanne and others, editors.

Adventures Here and There. Eau Claire, Wis., E. M. Hale and Company [c1958]

In a Wyoming Blizzard. By J. Frank Dobie. Illustrated by Lorence E. Bjorklund: pp. 189-191. [Race of Portuguese Phillips against a blizzard. From *On the Open Range*]

B111   Jenkins, John Holland.

Recollections of Early Texas. Austin, University of Texas Press [c1958]

Edited by John Holmes Jenkins, III.
Foreword: pp. [ix]-xiv. Signed: J. Frank Dobie.

B112   Nail, Olin Webster.

The First Hundred Years of the Southwest Texas Conference of the Methodist Church, 1858-1958. San Antonio, The Southwest Texas Conference [c1958]

On the Lord's Side. By J. Frank Dobie: pp. [78]-82.

B113   Natural Food Associates, Incorporated.

Natural Food and Farming Digest. Number Two. [Atlanta, Texas, Natural Food Associates, Inc. c1958]

A selection of articles from the monthly magazine.
Natural Taste for Natural Milk. By J. Frank Dobie: pp. 41-42.

1959

B114   Historical and Biographical Record of the Cattle Industry and the Cattlemen of Texas and Adjacent Territory. New York, Antiquarian Press, 1959.

Volume I, Historical. Volume II, Biographical.
With a New Introduction by J. Frank Dobie.
James Cox and His Cattle Industry, by J. Frank Dobie: Vol. I, pp. 1-6; and the same text repeated Vol. II, pp. 297A-297F.

B115   Jackson, Helen Hunt.

Ramona. Los Angeles, Printed for the Members of The Limited Editions Club at The Plantin Press, 1959.

Illustrations by Everett Gee Jackson.
Fifteen Hundred Copies Have been made . . .
Introduction: pp. vii. Signed: J. Frank Dobie.

B116   Nature Magazine

This Is Nature. Thirty Years of the Best from Nature Magazine. New York, Thomas Y. Crowell Company [c1959]

Selected and edited by Richard W. Westwood, editor, Nature Magazine.
Illustrated by Walter W. Ferguson.
Strange Animal Friendships [by] J. Frank Dobie: pp. 162-166.

1960

B117   Bedichek, Roy.

The Sense of Smell. Garden City, N. Y., Doubleday & Company, Inc., 1960.

Foreword: pp. 7-13. Signed: J. Frank Dobie.

B118   Downey, Fairfax Davis, editor.

My Kingdom for a Horse. Garden City, N. Y., Doubleday Company, Inc., 1960.

Illustrated by Matthew Kalmenoff.
Great Rides of the West, The Saga of the Saddle [by] J. Frank Dobie: pp. [140]-155.

1961

B119   Boatright, Mody C.; Hudson, Wilson M.; and Maxwell, Allen, editors.

Singers and Storytellers. Dallas, Southern Methodist University Press, [c1961]

Publication of the Texas Folklore Society. Number XXX.
Storytellers 1 Have Known [by] J. Frank Dobie: pp. 3-29.

B120   Jackson, Ralph Semmes.

Home of the Double Bayou; Memories of an East Texas Ranch. Austin, University of Texas Press [c1961]

Illustrated by Bubi Jessen.
Introduction: pp. [xv]-xviii. Signed: Frank Dobie.

B121   Kane, Harnett T., editor.

The Romantic South. New York, Coward-McCann, Inc. [c1961]

Edited, with Introduction and Commentary by Harnett T. Kane.

American Vista Series.
Jim Bowie and the Lost San Saba Mine [by] J. Frank Dobie: pp. 259-261.

B122   National Cystic Fibrosis Research Foundation.

The Celebrity Cook Book. New York, 1961.

Frank Dobie's Frijoles: p. 29.

B123   Outdoor Life.

Great Outdoor Adventures; Twenty-four of the Greatest True Action Stories Ever To Appear in Outdoor Life Magazine. New York, Outdoor Life ● E. P. Dutton & Co., Inc. [c1961]

Illustrated by Ray Pioch.
The Lonest Wolf, by J. Frank Dobie: pp. 51-60.

B124   Poe, Clarence; and Seymour, Betsy, editors.

True Tales of the South at War; How Soldiers Fought and Families Lived, 1861-1865. Chapel Hill, The University of North Carolina Press [c1961]

A Prodigal Soldier's Return . . . Dr. J. Frank Dobie: pp. 199-203. A version of this story in *The Longhorns*.

B125   Pooley, Robert Cecil; Lowers, Virginia Belle; Magdanz, Frances; and Niles, Olive S.

Vanguard. Chicago [etc.] Scott, Foresman and Company [c1961]

The Rider of Loma Escondida, by J. Frank Dobie: pp. [442]-449.

B126   Remington, Frederic.

Pony Tracks. Norman, University of Oklahoma Press [c1961]

Written and Illustrated by Frederic Remington.
The Western Frontier Library. Number 19.
A Summary Introduction to Frederic Remington. By J. Frank Dobie: pp. ix-xxi.

1962

B127   Branch, E. Douglas.

The Hunting of the Buffalo. Lincoln, University of Nebraska Press, 1962.

E. Douglas Branch, Singularisimo. By J. Frank Dobie: pp. v-xxix.

B128   Ford Motor Company, Publication Office.

The Ford Times Guide to Travel in U. S. A. Compiled from Articles Appearing in Ford Times through Courtesy of Ford Division and Ford Dealers throughout the United States. New York, Golden Press [c1962]

Painting by H. O. Kelly.
The Brush Country of Texas, by J. Frank Dobie: pp. 122-125.

B129   Sonnichsen, C. L., editor.

The Southwest in Life and Literature. New York, The Devin-Adair Company [1962]

Molded by Horn and Thorn [by] J. Frank Dobie: pp. [373]-382.

1963

B130   The Encyclopedia Americana. New York [etc.] Americana Corporation [c1963]

Houston, Samuel: Vol. XIV, pp. 449-450. Signed: J. Frank Dobie.

B131   Fuller, Edmund; and Kinnick, Jo, editors.

Adventures in American Literature. New York [etc.] Harcourt, Brace & World, Inc. [c1963]

The Heraldry of the Range: Vol. 2, pp. 20-29. At head of title: J. Frank Dobie.
From *On the Open Range.*

B132   Hourihane, H., compiler.

Mellifont Reader; Intermediate. Dublin, Mellifont [1963]

"Greatest of All the Comanches." pp. 62-65. Signed: J. Frank Dobie (Adapted) From *On the Open Range.*

B133   Hudson, W. H.; and Graham, R. B. Cunninghame.

Gauchos of the Pampas and Their Horses. Hanover, N. H., Westholm Publications, 1963.

Foreword by J. Frank Dobie.
The Gauchos and Horses of Hudson and Graham: pp. [11]-28. At head of title: J. Frank Dobie.

1964

B134   Boatright, Mody C.; Hudson, Wilson M.; and Maxwell, Allen, editors.

A Good Tale and a Bonnie Tune. Dallas, Southern Methodist University Press [1964]

Publication of the Texas Folklore Society, Number XXXII.
Two Treasure Tales [by] J. Frank Dobie: pp. 57-63.

Dobie, J. Frank, editor. Happy Hunting Ground. See B46.

—— ——Legends of Texas. See B3a.

1965

—— ——Coyote Wisdom. See B29b.

—— ——Man, Bird and Beast. See B11b.

—— ——Mustangs and Cow Horses. See B36b.

—— ——Rainbow in the Morning. See B5b.

—— ——Southwestern Lore. See B13b.

—— ——Tone the Bell Easy. See B15b.

*Magazine
Articles
And Stories*

1909

C1   Don Julian.

Southwestern University Magazine. Georgetown, Texas. April, 1909. Vol. 27, No. 7, pp. 389-391.

C2   Napoleon Bonaparte.

Southwestern University Magazine. Georgetown, Texas. February 1909. Vol. 27, No. 5, pp. 269-271.

1910

C3   Robert E. Lee.

Southwestern University Magazine. Georgetown, Texas. February 1910. Vol. 28, No. 5, pp. 203-205.

1917

C4   News of the Faculty.

The Alcalde. Austin, January-May, August 1917. Vol. V, No. 3, pp. [281]-282; No. 4, pp. [374]-378; No. 5, pp. [469]-471; No. 6, pp. [583]-587; No. 7, pp. [683]-687; No. 8, pp. [813]-815.

1919

C5   Anti-Angloism: Is It Justified?

The Trail Log. San Antonio, Texas, September 1919. Vol. I, No. 19, pp. [1], 7.

C6   Campus News.

> The Alcalde. Austin, December 1919. Vol. VII, No. 5, pp. 461-464.

C7   Generalization in Politics.

> The Trail Log. San Antonio, Texas, November 1919. Vol. I, No. 21, pp. [1]-2.

C8   The Seasonableness of Reading.

> The Texas Review. Austin, April 1919. Vol. IV, No. 3, pp. [252]-261.
> The Pump Room.

C9   "Words, Words, Words, My Lord."

> The English Journal. Chicago, January 1919. Vol. VIII, No. 1, pp. 8-15.

1920

C10   The Cowboy and His Songs.

> The Texas Review. Austin, January 1920. Vol. V, No. 2, pp. [163]-169.

C11   Faculty Facts and Fancies.

> The Alcalde. Austin, January-May, August 1920. Vol. VII, No. 6, pp. 550-557; No. 7, pp. 647-651; No. 8, pp. 738-745; No. 9, pp. 850-853; No. 10, pp. 970-973; No. 10 [sic] pp. 1058-1063.

C12   The Hour of Reading.

> The Texas Review. Austin, October 1920. Vol. VI, No. 1, pp. [80]-82.
> The Pump Room.

1922

C13   El [i.e. La] Cancion del Rancho de los Olmos.

> Journal of American Folk-lore. Philadelphia, April-June 1923. Vol. 36, No. 140, pp. 192-195.

C14   Folk-lore in Texas and the Texas Folk-lore Society.

> University of Texas Bulletin, No. 2245. The English Bulletin, No. 10. Austin, December 1, 1922. pp. [17]-27.

C15   Texas-Mexican Border Broadsides.

> Journal of American Folk-lore. Philadelphia, April-June 1923. Vol. 36, No. 140, pp. 185-191.

1924

C16   Folk-lore of the Southwest; What Is Being Done to Preserve It.

> Chronicles of Oklahoma. Oklahoma City, September 1924. Vol. II, No. 3, pp. [269]-284.

1925

C17   The Chisholm Trail.

> The Country Gentleman. Philadelphia, February 28, 1925. Vol. XC, No. 9, pp. 3, 22.

C18   Cowboy Songs.

> The Country Gentleman. Philadelphia, January 10, 1925. Vol. XC, No. 2, pp. 9, 38.

C19   Faculty Notes.

> The Alcalde. Austin, November 1925-July 1927. Vol. XIV, No. 1, pp. 51-52; No. 2, 134-137; No. 3, pp. 218-220; No. 4, pp. 297-298; No. 5, pp. 381-384; No. 6, pp. 456-457; No. 7, pp. 537-541; No. 8, pp. 618-620; Vol. XV, No. 1, pp. 40-42; No. 2, pp. 118-121; No. 3, pp. 199-201; No. 4, pp. 281-285; No. 5, pp. 340-343; No. 6, pp. 421-423; No. 7, pp. 496-500; No. 8, pp. 571-572.

C20   The Genius of Gusto.

> The South Atlantic Quarterly. Durham, N. C., April 1925. Vol. XXVI, No. 2, pp. [164]-178.

C21   Legends of the Southwest.

> The Country Gentleman. Philadelphia, November 1925. Vol. XC, No. 37, pp. 15-16, 103-105.
> Illustrated by Douglas Duer.

C22   The Old Trail Drivers.

> The Country Gentleman. Philadelphia, February 14, 1925. Vol. XC, No. 7, pp. 8, 28.
> See also C97.

1926

C23 a   Andy Adams, Cowboy Chronicler.

> Southwest Review. Dallas, January 1926. Vol. XI, No. 2, pp. [92]-101.

C23 b   —— ——

> The Cattleman. Fort Worth, February 1926. Vol. XII, No. 9, pp. 21-23, 25.
> [Reprinted] from The Southwest Review [January 1926]

C23 c   ———— ————

> The Alcalde. Austin, July 1926. Vol. XIV, No. 8, pp. 572-575.

C24   Buried Treasure in the Southwest.

> Our Boys (Curtis Publishing Company publicity organ) Philadelphia, January 1926. Vol. 19, No. 1-D, pp. 8-9.

Faculty Notes. See C19.

C25   Giants of the Southwest.

> The Country Gentleman. Philadelphia, August 1926. Vol. XCI, No. 8, pp. 11, 71-72.
> Illustrated by Douglas Duer.

C26   The Lost Nigger Gold Mine.

> The Country Gentleman. Philadelphia, March 1926. Vol. XCI, No. 3, pp. 16, 183-185.
> *Illustrated by Douglas Duer.*
> In *Coronado's Children.*

C27   Rattlesnakes.

> Holland's. Dallas, August 1926. Vol. 45, No. 8, pp. 52, 56.

C28   Romance in Local History Collections.

> News Notes, Bulletin of the Texas Library Association. El Paso, April, 1926. Vol. II, No. 2, pp. 3-4.

C29   Tales of the Mustang.

> The Country Gentleman. Philadelphia, October 1926. Vol. XCI, No. 10, pp. 9-10, 138, 141.
> Illustrated by Paul Bransom.
> Partly reprinted in *Tales of the Mustang* and in *The Mustangs.*

C30   The Texas Longhorn's Dying Bellow.

> The Cattleman. Fort Worth, March 1926. Vol. XII, No. 10, pp. 37, 143.
> In *The Longhorns.*

C31   Twenty-five Jack Loads of Spanish Gold.

> The Country Gentleman. Philadelphia, January 1926. Vol. XCI, No. 1, pp. 16, 117-119.
> Illustrated by Douglas Duer.
> In *Coronado's Children.*

1927

C32   Charles Goodnight — Trail Blazer

> The Country Gentleman. Philadelphia, March 1927. Vol. XCII, No. 3, pp. 26-27, 135-139.

C33   Detectives of the Cattle Range.

> The Country Gentleman. Philadelphia, February 1927.
> Vol. XCII, No. 2, pp. 30-31, 176-179.

Faculty Notes. See C19.

C34   Fifty Years of Battling for Interests of Range Cattlemen.

> The Cattleman. Fort Worth, March 1927. Vol. XIII, No. 10, pp. 16-23.

C35   Idea Might Be Embodied in an Existing Institution.

> Southwest Review. Dallas, April 1927. Vol. XII, No. 3, pp. 232-233.
> Pan-American University?

C36   Jim, Slim, and Bill. [Review of] Circus Parade, by Jim Tully.

> The Nation. New York, October 19, 1927. Vol. CXXV, No. 3250, pp. 429-430.

C37   The Mexican Vaquero of the Texas Border.

> The Southwestern Political and Social Science Quarterly. Austin, June 1927. Vol. VIII, No. 1, pp. [15]-26.

C38   "Old Charlie." [Review of] Riata and Spurs, by Charles A. Siringo.

> The Nation. New York, July 13, 1927. Vol. CXXV, No. 3236, p. 41.

C39   The Pacing White Mustang.

> The American Mercury. New York, December 1927. Vol. XII, No. 48, pp. 435-442.
> In *Tales of the Mustang,* and in *The Mustangs.*
> See also C48, C130, C176, C286, and C319.

C40   Swords and Saints of Six-guns.

> The Country Gentleman. Philadelphia, July 1927. Vol. XCII, No. 7, pp. 16, 42.
> Illustrated by Douglas Duer.
> The names that dot the Southwest record, a high tide of adventure.

C41   Where El Dorado Is.

> Southwest Review. Dallas, April 1927. Vol. XII, No. 3, pp. [163]-173.
> In *Coronado's Children.*

1928

C42   A Day With the Basques.

Southwest Review. Dallas, July 1928. Vol. XIII, No. 4, pp. [447]-458.

C43   "The Kid" and "Calamity." [Reviews of] The Authentic Life of Billy the Kid, by Pat F. Garrett [and of] Calamity Jane and the Lady Wildcats, by Duncan Aikman.

The Nation. New York, February 15, 1928. Vol. CXXVI, No. 3267, pp. 190-191.

C44   Kit Carson and Sam Houston. [Reviews of] Kit Carson, by Stanley Vestal [and of] Sam Houston, Colossus in Buckskin, by George Creel.

The Nation. New York, June 6, 1928. Vol. CXXVI, No. 3283, pp. 650, 652.

C45   Lion Markers.

The Country Gentleman. Philadelphia, May 1928. Vol. XCIII, No. 5, pp. 9-10, 111-115.
Illustrated by Paul Bransom.

C46   The Mystery of Lafitte's Treasure.

The Yale Review. New Haven, Conn., September 1928. N. S., Vol. XVIII, No. 1, pp. [116]-134.
In *Coronado's Children*.

C47   On the Trail of the Lost Tayopa.

The Country Gentleman. Philadelphia, August, September 1928. Vol. XCIII, No. 8, pp. 3-5, 41; No. 9, pp. 28, 30, 107-111.
In *Apache Gold and Yaqui Silver*.

C48   The Pacing White Mustang.

The Cattleman. Fort Worth, March 1928. Vol. XIV, No. 10, pp. 94-95, 97-103.
In *Tales of the Mustang* and in *The Mustangs*.
See also C39, C130, C177, C286, and C319.

C49 a   The Saga of the Saddle.

Southwest Review. Dallas, January 1928. Vol. XIII, No. 2, pp. [127]-148.
Partly reprinted in *On the Open Range;* partly in *The Flavor of Texas;* partly in *The Mustangs*.

C49 b —— ——

New York Herald Tribune Magazine. New York, July 5, 1931. pp. 8-9, 24-25.

Illustrations by Stockton Mulford.

Reprinting of The Sage of the Saddle in Southwest Review, January 1928.

C49 c —— ——

The Readers Digest. Pleasantville, N. Y., October 1931. Vol. 19, No. 114, pp. 544-546.

Condensed from New York Herald Tribune Magazine (July 5, '31)

C50   The Trailing Longhorns.

Frontier Stories. New York, May 1928. Vol. VIII, No. 2, pp. 56-62.

In *The Longhorns.*

C51   Western Literature Coming of Age. [Includes reviews of] Long Lance, by Chief Buffalo Child Long Lance; Cowboy, by Ross Santee; Custer, by Frazier Hunt [and of] Songs of the Open Range, by Ina Sires.

Southwest Review. Dallas, Autumn, 1928. Vol. XIV, No. 1, pp. v-xii.

1929

C52   The Biggest Ranch in America. [Review of] The X I T Ranch of Texas, by J. Evetts Haley.

The Nation. New York, September 4, 1929. Vol. 129, No. 3348. p. 254.

C53   Billy the Kid.

Southwest Review. Dallas, April 1929. Vol. XIV, No. 3, pp. [314]-320.

In *A Vaquero of the Brush Country.*

C54   Coronado's Children.

Holland's. Dallas, January, March 1929. Vol. 48, No. 1, pp. 34-35, 37; No. 3, pp. 52, 64-65.

Illustrations by G. Madden Jones.

In *Coronado's Children.*

C55   In the Brush Country.

Southwest Review. Dallas, January 1929. Vol. XIV, No. 2, pp. [119]-137.

Partly from the reminiscences of John Young.

In *A Vaquero of the Brush Country.*

C56   Midas on a Goatskin.

The American Mercury. New York, November 1929. Vol. XVIII, No. 71, pp. 271-277.
In *Coronado's Children*.

C57   The Razorbacks.

The Texas Monthly. Dallas, April 1929. Vol. III, No. 4, pp. [485]-495.

C58   A Tale of 44 Winchester.

The Southwestern Magazine. Georgetown, Tex., November 1929. Vol. XXXII, No. 1, pp. 7, 11.

C59   True Culture Is Eclectic, but Provincial.

Southwest Review. Dallas, July 1929. Vol. XIV, No. 4, pp. 482-483.
Points of View.

C60   West by South. [Reviews of books by William McLeod Raine; Frank C. Lockwood; Bill Smart; Frank W. McCarty; L. W. Payne and others; J. W. Madden, Holland Thompson, ed.; and of A. M. Fleming]

Southwest Review. Dallas, Summer 1929. Vol. XIV No. 4, pp. iii-v.

1930

C61   The Buried Gold at Fort Ramirez.

Southwest Review. Dallas, July 1930. Vol. XV, No. 4, pp. [434]-443.
In *Coronado's Children*.

C62   Cowboy Harris. [Review of] My Reminiscences as a Cowboy, by Frank Harris.

The Nation. New York, April 9, 1930. Vol. CXXX, No. 3379, pp. 425-426.

C63   Gold Is Where You Find It.

Holland's. Dallas, March-April 1930. Vol. 49, No. 3, pp. 15, 62-64; No. 4, pp. 11, 31, 33.
In *Coronado's Children*.

C64   The Heraldry of the Range.

The Saturday Evening Post. Philadelphia, December 20, 1930. Vol. 203, No. 25, pp. 10-11, 79-80.
In *On the Open Range*.

C65   Hunting Bighorns Below the Border.

The Country Gentleman. Philadelphia, April 1930. Vol. XCV, No. 4, pp. 22-23, 147-148.
Illustrated by Paul Bransom.

C66   "In Them Thar Hills."

The Texaco Star. Houston, March 1930. Vol. XVII, No. 3, pp. 21-25.
In *Coronado's Children.*

C67   Los Muertos No Hablan.

Southwest Review. Dallas, January 1930. Vol. XV, No. 2, pp. [177]-191.
In *Coronado's Children.*

C68   The Pecos Barricade.

The Alcalde. Austin, January 1930. Vol. XVIII, No. 4, pp. [139]-143.
In *Coronado's Children.*

C69   "Post Hole Bank" of Old Texas.

The Texaco Star. Houston, July-August 1930. Vol. XVII, No. 7, pp. 22-25.
In *Coronado's Children.*

C70   The Rider of Loma Escondida.

The Texaco Star. Houston, November 1930. Vol. XVII, No. 10, pp. 23-26, 32.
In *Coronado's Children.*

C71   A Son-of-a-Gun Stew. [Reviews of] John Marsh, Pioneer, by George D. Lyman; Conquest, by Jack O'Connor; Cattle, by William MacLeod Raine and Will C. Barnes; The Range Cattle Industry, by Edward Everett Dale; Frontier Trails, by Frank M. Canton edited by Edward Everett Dale; On the Old West Coast, by Major Horace Bell; Pioneer Life in Texas, by M. Krueger; Major Jim, by Fred Carey [and of] Pioneer Women in Texas, by Annie Doom Pickrell.

Southwest Review. Dallas, October 1930. Vol. 16, No. 1, pp. [iii]-vii.

C72   The Texan Part of Texas.

Nature Magazine. Baltimore, December 1930. Vol. 16, No. 6, pp. 343-346, 393, 395.

C73   West by South. [Review of] Uncle Sam's Camels, by Lewis Burt Lesley; A Frontier Doctor, by Henry F. Hoyt; Wild Men of the Wild West, by Edwin L. Sabin [and of] Memories and Viewpoints, by Captain Jason W. James.

Southwest Review. Dallas, Winter 1930. Vol. 15, No. 2, pp. [v]-viii.

C74   Western Stuff. [Review of] The Open Range and Bunk House Philosophy, by Oscar Rush; The Last Frontier, by Zack T. Sutley; The Last Rustler, by Lee Sage [and of] Six Horses, by Captain William Banning and George Hugh Banning.

> The Nation. New York, August 13, 1930. Vol. CXXXI, No. 3397, pp. 182-183.

1931

C75 a   Bowie and the Bowie Knife.

> Southwest Review. Dallas, April 1931. Vol. XVI, No. 3, pp. [351]-368.

C75 b   The Knife That Was Law.

> New York Herald Tribune Magazine. New York, August 2, 1931. pp. 4-5, 20-21, 23.
> Illustrations by Stockton Mulford.
> Most of this appeared as Bowie and the Bowie Knife in Southwest Review, April 1931.

C75 c   Jim Bowie's Knife.

> Frontier Stories. New York, Spring 1944. Vol. 15, No. 10, pp. 98-104.
> Mostly reprinted from Bowie and the Bowie Knife, Southwest Review, April 1931.

C76   But Was It an Onza?

> Holland's. Dallas, August 1931. Vol. 50, No. 8, pp. 11-12, 41.
> Illustrations by Alexander Hogue.
> In *Tongues of the Monte.*

C77   Captured by Indians.

> New York Herald Tribune Magazine. New York, October 11, 1931. pp. 16-17, 26.
> Paintings by W. R. Leigh.
> In *On the Open Range.*

C78   Coronado's Children Tell More Tales.

> New York Herald Tribune Magazine. New York, June 21, 1931. pp. 4-5, 25.
> With illustrations by Stockton Mulford.

C79   A Cowboy for to Be.

> New York Herald Tribune Magazine. New York, July 12, 1931. pp. 4-5.
> Illustrated by Stockton Mulford.
> In *On the Open Range.*

C80   Gusto and Legend.

Contempo. Chapel Hill, N. C., Mid-June 1931. Vol. I, No. 4, p. 1.

C81   How I Became a Hunter of Legends.

Wings. New York, February 1931. Vol. 5, No. 2, pp. 6-10.

The Knife That was Law. See C75b.

C82   Lost Gold of the Desert.

New York Herald Tribune Magazine. New York, January 18, 1931, pp. 4-5, 16, 24-25.
Illustrations by Stockton Mulford.
In *Coronado's Children*.

C83 a   "Not the Will of God."

New York Herald Tribune Magazine. New York, June 28, 1931. pp. 8-9, 23.
Illustrations by Stockton Mulford.
From *Apache Gold and Yaqui Silver*.

C83 b   —— ——

True West. Austin, Fall 1953. Vol. 1, No. 2, pp. 12-13, 48, 50.
Illustrated by Randy Steffen.

C83 c   —— ——

True West. Austin, January-February 1959, Vol. 6, No. 3, pp. 10-11, 36-37.
Illustrated by Randy Steffen.

C83 d   —— ——

Old West. Austin, Spring 1965. Vol. I, No. 3, pp. 22-23, 44.
Illustrated by Randy Steffen.

C84   The Pull of the Minometer.

New York Herald Tribune Magazine. New York, June 14, 1931. pp. 4-5, 28.
Illustrated by Stockton Mulford.

C85   Ranch Mexicans.

Survey Graphic. New York, May 1, 1931. Vol. XIX, No. 2, pp. 167-170.

The Saga of the Saddle. See C49b and C49c.

C86   Saving the Longhorn.

New York Herald Tribune Magazine. New York, July 26, 1931. pp. 14-16, 27.
Etchings by Henry Ziegler; painting by C. A. Russell.
In *The Longhorns*.

C87   Scalp Hunters' Ledge.

> New York Herald Tribune Magazine. New York, June 7,
> 1931. pp. [1]-3.
>> Illustrations by Stockton Mulford.
>> In *Apache Gold and Yaqui Silver*.

C88   Sealed with Blood.

> New York Herald Tribune Magazine. New York, Jan-
> uary 25, 1931. pp. 4-5, 23-25.
>> Illustrations by Stockton Mulford.
>> In *Coronado's Children*.

C89   A-Son-of-a-Gun Stew. [Reviews of] Lone Cowboy,
by Will James; Overland with Kit Carson, by George
Douglas Brewerton; Sixty Years in Southern California, by Harris Newmark; Giants of the Old West,
by Frederick R. Bechdolt; Alkali Trails, by William
Curry Holden; the Navajo Indians, by Mary Roberts Coolidge and Dane Coolidge; Lafitte the Pirate,
by Lyle Saxon; Folk-say, edited by B. A. Botkin;
Publications of the West Texas Historical and
Scientific Society, Number 3; Canticles of a Minis-
ter's Wife, by Gustine Courson Weaver; Santa's Cot-
ton Doll Farm, by Gustine Courson Weaver; Gun-
Shy, by Millie Moore Godbold [and of] Roadside,
by Lynn Riggs.

> Southwest Review. Dallas, January 1931. Vol. 16, No. 2,
> pp. [iii]-viii.

C90   A Son-of-a-Gun Stew. [Reviews of] The Cattle King,
by Edward F. Treadwell; Zuni Folk Tales, by Frank
Hamilton Cushing; Folk-Lore of Romantic Arkansas,
by Fred W. Allsopp; The Bloody Trail in Texas, by
J. Marvin Hunter; the History of Wichita Falls, by
Jonnie R. Morgan [and of] Debates in the Texas
Constitutional Convention of 1875, compiled by Seth
Shepard McKay.

> Southwest Review. Dallas, July 1931. Vol. 16, No. 4, pp.
> [iii]-iv, vi.

C91   Son-on-a-Gun-Stew. [Reviews of] Caballeros, by
Ruth Laughlin Barker; Wyatt Earp: Frontier Mar-
shall, by Stuart H. Lake; Gun Notches, by Thomas
H. Rynning, as told to Al Cohn and Joe Chisholm;
Big-Enough, by Will James; The Pooch, by Ross
Santee; Riata and Spurs, by Charles A. Siringo;
Outpost of Empire, by Herbert Eugene Bolton; The

Early Far West, by W. J. Ghent; Told at the Explorers' Club, by Roy Chapman Andrews, F. W. Hodge, Frederick S. Dellenbaugh, Warren K. Moorehead, and twenty-nine other modern explorers; Singing Cowboy, collected and edited by Margaret Larkin and arranged for the piano by Helen Black [and of] Devil's Ditties, by Jean Thomas.

> Southwest Review. Dallas, October 1931. Vol. 17, No. 1, pp. [iii]-x.

C92   The Southwest's Golden Fleece . . . The Los San Saba Mines.

> New York Herald Tribune Magazine. New York, February 1, 1931. pp. 10-12, 27.
> Illustrations by Stockton Mulford.
> In *Coronado's Children.*

C93   The Southwest's Lost Eldorado.

> New York Herald Tribune Magazine. New York, January 11, 1931. pp. 4-5, 24, 27.
> Illustrations by Stockton Mulford.
> In *Coronado's Children.*

C94   Tales and Trails.

> Current Literature. Columbus, Ohio, May 25-29, 1931. Vol. X, No. 17, pp. [67]-68.

C95   Tales of the Rattler.

> New York Herald Tribune Magazine. New York, August 23, 1931. pp. 10-11.
> Illustrations by Paul Bransom.

C96 a   A Trail Driver of the Fifties . . . W. W. Burton.

> New York Herald Tribune Magazine. New York, July 19, 1931. pp. 8-9, 16.
> Illustration b yStockton Mulford; photographs.

C96 b   Trail Driving a Hundred Years Ago.

> The Western Horseman. Colorado Springs, Colo., March 1950. Vol. XV, No. 3, pp. 6-7, 44-46.
> Illustrated by George Phippen.

C97   Veterans of Adventure.

> New York Herald Tribune Magazine. New York, November 8, 1931. pp. 10-11, 16.
> Painting by W. R. Leigh; photographs.
> Reissue with additions of The Old Trail Drivers.
> See also C22.

C98   The West's Vanishing "Varmints."

New York Herald Tribune Magazine. New York, August 16, 1931. pp. 6-7, 24.
Illustrations by Stockton Mulford.
Partly in *The Voice of the Coyote*.

C99   When the Grizzly Gave Battle.

New York Herald Tribune Magazine. New York, September 13, 1931. pp. 16-17, 27.
Painting by W. R. Leigh.

C100   When the Mustang Ranged the Plains.

New York Herald Tribune Magazine. New York, August 9, 1931. pp. 12-14, 21.
Paintings by W. R. Leigh.
In *The Mustangs*.

1932

C101 a   Brefogle's Gold in Death Valley.

The Texaco Star. Houston, November-December 1932. Vol. XIX, No. 6, pp. 9-10.
In *Apache Gold and Yaqui Silver*.

C101 b   —— ——

Exchange Quarterly. Sweetwater, Texas, Fall 1935. Vol. I, No. 2, pp. 1-2.

C102 a   Canine Cowboys.

New York Herald Tribune Magazine. New York, October 23, 1932. pp. 7, 21.

C102 b   —— ——

The Cattleman. Fort Worth, November 1934. Vol. XXI, No. 6, pp. 9-10.
In the New York Herald-Tribune Magazine.

C103   Diamonds in the Iron.

The Bright Scrawl. San Antonio, March 1932. Texas number, pp. 5, 22.

C104   Great Liars of the Golden West.

Vanity Fair. Greenwich, Conn., March 1932. Vol. 38, No. 1, pp. 30-31, 74.

C105 a   Hunting Cousin Sally.

New York Herald Tribune Magazine. New York, July 10, 1932. pp. 4-5, 17, 19.
Illustrations by J. Clinton Shepherd.
Concerns Ike Pryor.
See also C497.

C105 b   He Hunted Cousin Sally.

> Zane Grey's Western Magazine. New York, March 1953.
> Vol. 7, No. 1, pp. 85-95.

C106   I Don't Like——

> Southwest Review. Dallas, January 1932. Vol. XVII, No.
> 2, pp. [243]-245.
> Letters.

C107   Neighboring with Wolves, by C. B. Ruggles.

> The Saturday Evening Post. Philadelphia, January 9,
> 1932. Vol. 204, No. 28, pp. 16, 132-133.
> Rewritten by J. Frank Dobie before publication.

C108 a   The Outlaws of the Brush.

> The Saturday Evening Post. Philadelphia, December 10,
> 1932. Vol. 205, No. 24, pp. 8-9, 73-74, 76-77.
> In *The Longhorns*.

C108 b   —— ——

> True West. Austin, Summer 1953. Vol. 1, No. 1, pp. 10-11,
> 50-51.

C109   Silences. [Review of] Apache, by Will Levington Com-
          fort.

> Southwest Review. Dallas, January 1932. Vol. 17, No.
> 2, pp. [iii]-iv.

C110   Son-of-a-Gun Stew. [Reviews of] Narratives of the
          Trans-Mississippi Frontier, edited by Carl L. Can-
          non; Heel-Fly Time in Texas, by John Warren Hun-
          ter; Six Feet Six, by Bessie Rowland James and
          Marquis James; Texas Trails, by Harry Williams;
          Indian Wars of Idaho, by Ross Arnold; Black Elk
          Speaks, by John G. Neihardt; The Pony Express, by
          Arthur Chapman [and of] California Spanish and
          Indian Place Names, by Kelly McNary.

> Southwest Review. Dallas, April, 1932. Vol. 17, No. 3, pp.
> v-x, xii, xiv.

C111 a   Tom Gilroy's Fiddler.

> The Texaco Star. Houston, March-April 1932. Vol. XIX,
> No. 2, pp. 14-15.

C111 b   —— ——

> The University of Texas Longhorn, with which is com-
> bined Texas Ranger, Austin, May 1932. Vol. XVII, No. 8,
> pp. [8-9], 22-24.

C111 c   Frontier Fiddler.

> Ranch Romances. New York, June 18, 1943. Vol. 113, No. 3, pp. 95-97.

C111 d   Tom Gilroy's Fiddler.

> Frontier Times. Austin, Winter 1960. Vol. 35, No. 1, pp. 32-33.
> Illustrated by Al Martin Napoletano.

C112   Wanderlust of the Wild.

> Nature Magazine. Washington, D. C., October 1932. Vol. 20, No. 4, pp. 151-154.
> Illustrated by R. Bruce Horsfall.

C113   Western Books. [Reviews of] Gringo Builders, by J. L. Allhands [and of] Western Prose and Poetry, edited by Rufus A. Coleman.

> Southwest Review. Dallas, January 1932. Vol. 17, No. 2, pp. v-vi.

C114   With Spur and Winchester. [Reviews of] Buck Barry: Texas Ranger, edited by James K. Greer; Fighting Men of the West, by Dane Coolidge: Perilous Trails of Texas, by J. B. (Red John) Dunn; A Log of the Texas-California Cattle Trail, 1854, by James G. Bell, edited by J. Evetts Haley [and of] Financial History of the Public Lands of Texas, by Aldon S. Lang.

> Southwest Review. Dallas, July 1932. Vol. 17, No. 4, pp. [iii]-vi.

1933

C115   Colonel Abercrombie's Mole.

> Holland's. Dallas, February 1933. Vol. 52, No. 2, pp. 5-6, 38-39.
> By J. Frank Dobie and Will Dittrell.
> Illustrations by Ben Carlton Mead.

C116   George W. Saunders — My Friend.

> Frontier Times. Bandera, Texas, September 1933, Vol. 10, No. 12, pp. 538-541.

C117   Juan Oso, Bear Nights in Mexico.

> Southwest Review. Dallas, October 1933. Vol. XIX, No. 1, pp. [34]-64.
> A variant form of this was reprinted as Chapter IX of *Tongues of the Monte.*

C118   Son-of-a-Gun Stew. [Reviews of] The Phantom Bull, by Charles E. Perkins; The Gold Brick, by G. T. Bludworth; Scout and Ranger, by James Pike, with Introduction and Notes by Carl L. Cannon; Hall J. Kelley on Oregon, edited by Fred W. Powell; Scenery of the Plains, Mountains and Mines, by Franklin Langworthy, edited by Paul C. Phillips; The Emigrants' Guide to Oregon and California, by Lansford W. Hastings, with Historical Note and Bibliography by Charles H. Carey: Letters of an Early American Traveler: Mary Austin Holley, by Mattie Austin Hatcher; The Heroes of San Jacinto, by Sam Houston Dixon and Louis W. Kemp; A Dictionary of Spanish Terms in English, by Harold W. Bentley; New Mexico History and Civics, by Lansing B. Bloom and Thomas C. Donnelly [and of] Oklahoma Place Names, by Charles N. Gould.

Southwest Review. Dallas, October 1933. Vol. XIX, No. 1, pp. [13]-19.

C119   When I Was a Boy on the Ranch.

St. Nicholas Magazine. New York, October, 1933. Vol. LX, No. 12, pp. 570-571, 600-601.

1934

C120   Brush Country.

The Cattleman. Fort Worth, July 1934. Vol. XXI, No. 2, pp. 9, 11-12, 14-22.

By John Young, in collaboration with J. Frank Dobie.
From *A Vaquero of the Brush Country*.

Canine Cowboys. See 102b.

C121   In Texas or of Texas.

The Alcalde. Austin, April 1934. Vol. XXII, No. 7, pp. 149-150, 156.

C122 a   The Man of Goats

Southwest Review. Dallas, October 1934. Vol. XX, No. 1, pp. [35]-55.

Also published under the same title but in a variant form as Chapter XII of *Tongues of the Monte*.

C122 b   —— ——

The Southwestern Sheep and Goat Raiser. San Angelo, Tex., December 1942. Vol. 23, No. 3, pp. 24-25, 54-55, 58-59, 62-64.

Illustrated by Frank Anthony Stanush.
From the Book "Tongues of the Monte"

C123   Mexico's Mines Come Back.

> New York Herald Tribune Magazine. New York, March 11, 1934. pp. 14-15, 27.
> > Photographs by Anton Bruehl, from "Mexico."
> > Illustration by Stockton Mulford.

C124   Son-of-a-Gun Stew. [Reviews of] The Journey of the Flame, by Antonio de Fierro Blanco; From Texas to Mexico and the Court of Maximilian in 1865, by Alexander Watkins Terrell, edited by Fannie Ratchford; Riding the High Country, by Patrick T. Tucker, edited by Grace Stone Coats; The Trusty Knaves, by Eugene Manlove Rhodes; Advancing the Frontier, by Grant Foreman; Los Pastores, by Mary R. Van Stone; West of the Powder River, by Jack H. Lee; Texas Camel Trails, by Chris Emmett; The Hermit of the Cavern, translated and adapted by May E. Francis; Paradise in Texas, by W. B. Lewis [and of] Through Mexico on Horseback, by Joseph Carl Goodwin.

> Southwest Review. Dallas, April 1934. Vol. XIX, No. 3, pp. [1]-7 at end.

C125   Son-of-a-Gun Stew. [Reviews of] The Perote Prisoners, by Frederick C. Chabot; Traders to the Navajoes, by Frances Gillmor and Louisa Wade Wetherill; Early Days among the Cheyenne and Arapahoe Indians, by John H. Seger, edited by Stanley Vestal; The Cherokee Strip, by George Rainey; Frontier Fighter: The Autobiography of George W. Coe [and of] The Spur Ranch, by William Curry Holden.

> Southwest Review. Dallas, October 1934. Vol. XX, No. 1, pp. [1]-7 at end.

C126 a   Spanish Cow Pony.

> The Saturday Evening Post. Philadelphia, November 24, 1934. Vol. 207, No. 21, pp. 12-13, 64-66.

C126b   —— ——

> The Cattleman. Fort Worth, September 1943. Vol. XXX, No. 4, pp. 100, 102, 146-149.
> > Rprinted by special permission of The Saturday Evening Post, copyright 1934 by The Curtis Publishing Company.
> > Partly incorporated in *The Mustangs*.

1935

C127   Black Devil.

New Mexico. Santa Fe, September 1935. Vol. XIII, No. 9, pp. 16-17, 41-42.

Illustrations by Wilfred Stedman.

In *Mustangs and Cow Horses,* edited by J. Frank Dobie, and in *The Mustangs.*

Breyfogle's Gold in Death Valley. See 101b.

C128   Folk-lore and Literature.

Southwestern. Dallas, September 1935. Vol. I, No. 2, pp. 3-4.

C129   Juan Catorce.

New Mexico. Santa Fe, June 1935. Vol. XIII, No. 6, pp. 14-15, 43.

C130   The Phantom Stallion.

New Mexico. Santa Fe, August 1935. Vol. XIII, No. 8, pp. 14-15, 38-39.

Illustrated by Wilfred Stedman.

In *Tales of the Mustang* and *The Mustangs.*

See also C39, C48, C177, C286, and C319.

C131 a   A Question of Hides.

The Cattleman. Fort Worth, March 1935. Vol. XXI, No. 10, pp. 65-72.

C131 b   ⸺ ⸺

Ranch Romances. New York, November 6, 1942. Vol. 109 No. 3, pp. 101-109.

C132   Son-of-a-Gun Stew. [Reviews of] Legends and Dances of Old Mexico, by Norma Schwendener and Averil Tibbels; Fiesta in Mexico, by Erna Fergusson; Gringa, by Emma Lindsay Squier; Santa Anna, the Napoleon of the West, by Frank C. Hanighen; Latin-American Music, Past and Present, by Eleanor Hague; The Background of the Revolution for Mexican Independence, by Lilian Estelle Fisher; Rico, Bandit and Dictator, by Antonio de Fierro Blanco; The Diabolic Root, by Vincenzo Petrullo; Indian Justice, by John Howard Payne; Glamorous Days, by Frank H. Bushick; Saga of a Frontier Seaport, by Coleman McCampbell; The Log of an Arizona Trail Blazer, by John A. Rockfellow; Arizona in Literature, edited by Mary G. Boyer; Texas Ballads and Other Verse, by Paul Morgan [and of] Enchanted Windows, by Virginia Spates.

Southwest Review. Dallas, January 1935. Vol. XX, No. 2, pp. [23]-29.

C133   Son-of-a-Gun Stew. Books for the Texas Centennial—and Others. [Reviews of] The Alligator's Life History; Bird City; and Befo' De War Spirituals, by E. A. McIlhenny; Texas Legacy, compiled by Lois F. Boyla; Wild Life in the Southwest, by Oren Arnold; Indian Depredations in Texas, by J. W. Wilbarger; Thus they Lived, by Joseph W. Schmitz; Old Rough and Ready on the Rio Grande, by Florence Johnson Scott; Tall Men With Long Rifles, by James T. DeShields [and of] The Crow Indians, by Robert H. Lowie.

Southwest, Review. Dallas, July 1935. Vol. XX, No. 4, pp. 13-25.

C134   Son-of-a-Gun Stew. [Reviews of] Death on the Prairie, by Paul I. Wellman; Death in the Desert, by Paul I. Wellman: California Joe, by Joe E. Milner and Earle R. Forrest; Regional Dances of Mexico, by Edith Johnson; Pageants and Plays of Pioneers, by Jeston Dickey and Bessie Lee Dickey Roselle; The Daughter of Tehuan, by P. Alto Hoermann, translated from the German by Alois Braun; Wranglin' the Past, by Frank M. King [and of] A Tale of Men who Knew No Fear, by Gertrude Harrie.

Southwest Review. Dallas, October 1935. Vol. XXI, No. 1, pp. 115-119.

C135   Stories Made Up to Fit Sounds.

The Southwestern Magazine. Georgetown, Tex., December 1935. Vol. LIV, No. 2, pp. 35, 52-53.

C136   Two Southwestern Books. [Reviews of] Southwest, by Laura Adams Armer [and of] Pioneer Padre, by Rufus Kay Willys.

Southwest Review. Dallas, April 1935. Vol. XX, No. 3, pp. 28-29 at end.

1936

C137   Brother Coyote and the Lion.

The Announcer. Nederland, Tex., April 10, 1936. Vol. 7, No. 6, pp. [1], 15.
Mimeographed.
In *The Voice of the Coyote.*

C138   Buried Treasure!

This Week. New York, December 6, 1936. pp. 9, 19.
Illustrated by Walter M. Baumhofer.
[Original title: Old Man Chance and the Sans Saba
Bars]

C139   Down the Road to Mexico.

This Week. New York, March 22, 1936. pp. 14-15, 23.
Illustrated by O. F. Schmidt; photographs.

C140   The King of Cattlemen. [Review of] Charles Goodnight, Cowman and Plainsman, by J. Evetts Haley.

Southwest Review. Dallas, April 1936. Vol. XXI, No. 3,
pp. [355]-361.

C141   Meaning of the Texas Centennial.

Progressive Farmer and Southern Ruralist. Birmingham,
Ala., January 1936. Vol. 51, No. 1, pp. 6-7, 39.

C142   Mr. Dobie's Letter.

The Announcer. Nederland, Tex., April 10, 1936. Vol. 7,
No. 6, pp. [1], 15.
Mimeographed.

C143   The Old-Time Mexican Goat Herder.

The Southwestern Sheep and Goat Raiser. San Angelo,
Tex., December 1, 1936. Vol. 7, No. 5, pp. 17-20.
Partly from *Tongues of the Monte.*

C144   Son-of-a-Gun Stew. [Reviews of] Roemer's Texas,
translated by Oswald Mueller; Interwoven, by Sallie
Reynolds Matthews; They Die but Once, by James
B. O'Neil; Lane of the Llano, by T. M. Pearce; Cow-
boy Lingo, by Ramon F. Adams; Apache Agent: The
Story of John P. Clum, by Woodworth Clum; Sa-
tana, by Clarence R. Wharton: Bullets, Battles and
Gardenias, by Timothy G. Turner; Texas Prose Writ-
ings, by Sister Agatha; Early Texas Verse, edited
by Philip Graham; Bois d'Arc to Barbed Wire, by
James K. Greer; The Devil in Texas, by Frank
Goodwyn; Ghost Lore, by Henry Yelvington; Cowboy
Life, by Rufe O'Keefe [and of] Sam Bass, by Wayne
Gard.

Southwest Review. Dallas, July 1936. Vol. XXI, No. 4, pp.
441-452.

C145   Stories in Texas Names.

Southwest Review. Dallas, January, April, July, 1936.

Vol. XXI, No. 2, pp. [125]-136; No. 3, pp. [278]-294; No. 4, pp. [411]-417.

> No. 2: I. The Staked Plains. II. Cabeza de Vaca and Horsehead.
> No. 3: III. Downright Circumstantial Evidence.
> No. 4: IV. Prolonged Shadows.
> These articles are combined in *Straight Texas.*

C146   This Here Texas Tradition.

> Country Gentlemen. Philadelphia, June 1936. Vol. CVI No. 6, pp. 14-15, 80-81.
> Partly in Chapter I, *The Flavor of Texas.*

1937

C147   Billy Horses and Steel Dust.

> The Cattleman. Fort Worth, March 1937. Vol. XXIII, No. 10, pp. 25-26.

C148   Cunning Don Coyote.

> This Week. New York, August 22, 1937. pp. 10, 15.
> Illustrated by Jack Murray.
> In *The Voice of the Coyote.*

C149   Cures for Sale.

> This Week. New York, September 12, 1937. pp. 32.

C150   The Flavor of Texas.

> Acco Press. Houston, September 1937. Vol. XV, No. 9, pp. 8-11.
> From *The Flavor of Texas.*

C151   Ghost Lore, by Henry Yelvington. [A review]

> The Journal of American Folk-lore. Lancaster, Penn. and New York, January-March 1937. Vol. 50, No. 195. pp. 106-107.

C152   The Last of the Grizzly Hunters.

> The Saturday Evening Post. Philadelphia, December 11, 1937. Vol. 210, No. 24, pp. 14-15, 35, 38, 41.

C153   Smarter Than a Steel Trap.

> The Southwestern Sheep and Goat Raiser. San Angelo, Tex., December 1, 1937. Vol. 8, No. 5, pp. 14-15, 62-65.
> In *The Voice of the Coyote.*

C154   Some Books of Range Days. [Reviews of] The 101 Ranch, by Ellsworth Collings; The Chisholm Trail and Other Sketches, by T. U. Taylor; Life on the Range and on the Trail, by John Doak and R. J.

Lauderdale; My Foot's in the Stirrup, by W. S. Bartlett, edited by Mabel Major and Rebecca Smith [and of] History of Bell County, by George W. Tyler, edited by Charles W. Ramsdell.

Southwest Review. Dallas, April 1937. Vol. XXII, No. 3, pp. 309-313.

C155 "That Reminds Me —"

This Week. New York, February 7, 1937. pp. 27.

1938

C156 Border Patrol, by Mary Kidder Rak. [A review]

Southwest Review. Dallas, October 1938. Vol. XXIV, No. 1, pp. 95-97.

C157 Cowboy Songs and Other Frontier Ballads, collected by John A. Lomax. [A review]

Southwest Review. Dallas, October 1938. Vol. XXIV, No. 1, pp. 90-95.

C158 Mesquite.

The Southwestern Sheep and Goat Raiser. San Angelo, Tex., December 1, 1938. Vol. 9, No. 5, pp. 30-32, 59-63.

C159 On Being "First Class."

The Alcalde. Austin, April 1938. Vol. XXVI, No. 7, pp. [152]-154, 160.

C160 Pedro Loco.

Southwest Review. Dallas, July 1938. Vol. XXIII, No. 4, pp. 417-427.
In *Tongues of the Monte.*

C161 a The Texas Longhorn.

The Cattleman. Fort Worth, October 1938. Vol. XXV, No. 5, pp. 11-18, 20-23.
In *The Longhorns.*

C161 b The Texas Longhorn Made History.

Frontier Times. January, 1939. Bandera, Texas. Vol. 16, No. 4, pp. 166-176.

1939

C162 Escape from Goliad.

Southwest Review. Dallas, October 1939. Vol. XXV, No. 1, pp. [70]-74.

William Mason's narrative. Edited by J. Frank Dobie.
Notes on Texas History.
In *John C. Duval, First Texas Man of Letters.*

C163 a   The First Cattle in Texas and the Southwest.
genitors of the Longhorns.

The Southwestern Historical Quarterly. Austin, January
1939. Vol. XLII, No. 3, pp. [171]-197.

C163b   First Cattle in Texas and the Southwest.

The Cattleman. Fort Worth, March 1939. Vol. XXV, No.
10, pp. 33, 35-38, 40-42, 44-47, 49-51.
This is a reprint from the Southwestern Historical
Quarterly, Vol. XLII, No. 3, January, 1939.
In *The Longhorns.*

C164   The Hired Man on Horseback: My Story of Eugene
Manlove Rhodes, by May D. Rhodes. [A review]

Southwest Review. Dallas, January 1939. Vol. XXIV, No.
2, pp. [210]-216.

C165   John C. Duval: First Texas Man of Letters.

Southwest Review. Dallas, April 1939. Vol. XXIV, No. 3,
pp. [257]-281.
In *John C. Duval: First Texas Man of Letters.*

C166   The Longhorn Blood Call.

Southwest Review. Dallas, July 1939. Vol. XXIV, No. 4,
pp. [434]-452.
In *The Longhorns.*

C167   The Lost Mines of the Southwest.

The Missionary Catechist. Huntington, Ind., February
1939. Vol. 15, No. 3, pp. 5-6.

C168   Mavericks and Maverickers.

The Southwestern Sheep and Goat Raiser. San Angelo,
Tex., December 1939. Vol. 10, No. 3, pp. 16-17, 86-87.

C169   Old Prob's Visit to Texas, by John C. Duval.

Southwest Review. Dallas, April 1939. Vol. XXIV, No. 3,
pp. [282]-297.
Forenote, signed. J. Frank Dobie: pp. [282]-285.
In *John C. Duval: First Texas Man of Letters.*

C170 a   Rawhide.

Southwest Review. Dallas, October 1939. Vol. XXV, No.
1, pp. [15]-33.
In *The Longhorns.*

C170 b Rawhide Has Faithfully Served Texas.

> Frontier Times. Austin, January 1942. Vol. 19, No. 4, pp. 131-135.

C171 a The Roadrunner in Fact and Folklore.

> Natural History. New York, September 1939. Vol. XLIV, No. 2, pp. 74-82.
> Full article is in *In the Shadow of History*.

C171 b —— ——

> Texas Ornithological Society, Newsletter. Austin, May 1, 1956. Vol. IV, No. 4, pp. 1-14.
> This is a reprint of a reprint. The Texas Game, Fish, and Oyster Commission reprinted the article from the Texas Folk-Lore Society in 1939.
> Mimeographed.

C171 c —— ——

> Arizona Highways. Phoenix, May 1958. Vol. XXXIV, No. 5, pp. [2]-[11]
> Sketch: Ted Degrazia. Five sketches by C. M. Palmer, Jr. Photo: Texas Game and Fish Commission. Photographs by Jack Specht and Edgar Kincaid.

C171 d Paisano.

> Texas Game and Fish. Austin, October 1960. Vol. XVIII, No. 10, pp. 16-17, 28-29.

C171 e Paisano.

> Frontier Times. Austin, Fall 1961. Vol. 35, No. 4, pp. 35, 46-47.
> Ilustrated by Al Martin Napoletano.

C172 Stories, by John C. Duval.

> The Pure Juice of the Mustang Grape. Foreword by J. Frank Dobie. An Odorous Yarn. [Forenote by] J. F. D.
> Southwest Review. Dallas, October 1939. Vol. XXV, No. 1, pp. [34]-57.
> Edited by J. Frank Dobie, with Illustrations by Tom Lea.
> In *John C. Duval: First Texas Man of Letters*.

The Texas Longhorn Made History. See C161b.

C173 We Pointed Them North: Recollections of a Cowpuncher, by E. C. Abbott ("Teddy Blue") and Helena Huntington Smith. [A review]

> Southwest Review. Dallas, July 1939. Vol. XXIV, No. 4, pp. [490]-495.

1940

C174   As a Noted Texan Sees State Game Department.

Monthly Bulletin of the Texas Game, Fish and Oyster Commission. Austin, January 1940. Vol. 3, No. 2, pp. 3, 8.
Reprinted with the permission of the Dallas Morning News and The Houston Post.

C175 a   The Cowboy as a Courtier.

The Southwestern Magazine. Georgetown, Tex., September 1940. Vol. LVIX, No. 1, pp. 8-9.

C175 b   —— ——

Southwestern Magazine. Georgetown, Tex., November 1957. Vol. 76, pp. 8, 10.
[Reprinted from] The Southwestern Magazine 1940.

C176   Cows and Curiosity.

American Cattle Producer. Denver, November 1940. Vol. XXII, No. 6, pp. 5-9.
In *The Longhorns.*

C177   The Deathless Pacing White Mustang.

The Cattleman. Fort Worth, September 1940. Vol. XXVII, No. 4, pp. 113-115.
In *Tales of the Mustang* and *The Mustangs.*
See also C39, C48, C130, C286 and C319.

C178   Horns.

The Cattleman. Fort Worth, March 1940. Vol. XXVI, No. 10, pp. 21, 23-30.
This material is Chapter III of a book . . . on the Texas Longhorn [*The Longhorns*]

C179   Hot Irons: Heraldry of the Range, by Oren Arnold and John P. Hale. [A review]

Southwest Review. Dallas, July 1940. Vol. XXV, No. 4, pp. 386-489.

C180   Pitching Horse Is Still Range's Best Sport.

The Texas Prison Echo. Huntsville, Texas, September 1940. Vol. 12, No. 9, pp. [1]-2.

1941

C181 a   The Bawls and Lowings of the Longhorn.

American Cattle Producer. Denver, July 1941. Vol. XXIII, No. 2, pp. 3-4.
One of the many illustrations by Tom Lea from Dobie's "The Longhorn."
From *The Longhorns.*

C181 b   Bovine Sense of Smell.

> The Purebred. Chicago, February 1941. Vol. I, No. 2, pp.
> 7, 44-45.
>
> J. Frank Dobie in American Cattle Producer says old
> time Longhorns could smell water miles away.

C181 c   Smell and Thirst in Old-Time Texas Cattle.

> American Cattle Producer. Denver, January 1941. Vol.
> XXII, No. 8, pp. 5-8.

C182   Bob More, Man and Bird Man.

> Southwest Review. Dallas, Autumn, 1941. Vol. XXVIII,
> No. 1, pp. 135-155.

Bovine Sense of Smell. See C181b.

C183   E. L. Shettles, Man, Bookman and Friend.

> The Southwestern Historical Quarterly. Austin, January
> 1941. Vol. XLIV, No. 3, pp. 350-356.
>
> This essay, now slightly revised, was read by the
> author as a part of the funeral ceremonies.

C184 a   Mesquite.

> Arizona Highways. Phoenix, November 1941. Vol. XVII,
> No. 11, pp. 4-7, 44-45.
>
> Drawings . . . by Ross Santee.

C184 b   The Conquering Mesquite.

> Natural History. New York, May 1943. Vol. LI, No. 5,
> pp. [208]-217.
>
> All photos by the author unless otherwise indicated.
>
> Same material as Mesquite, Arizona Highways, No-
> vember 1941.

C184 c   ——— ———

> Southern Agriculturist. Nashville, Tenn., August 1947.
> Vol. LXXVII, No. 8, pp. 10-11.
>
> Mostly a rewrite from Mesquite, Arizona Highways, No-
> vember 1941.

C185   No Life for a Lady, by Agnes Morley Cleaveland.
[A review]

> Southwest Review. Dallas, Autumn 1941. Vol. XXVII,
> No. 1, pp. 161-163.

Smell and Thirst in Old-Time Texas Cattle. See C181c.

C186   Tracks on the Land.

> The Junior Historian. Austin, April 1941. Vol. I, No. 3,
> inside front cover.

1942

C187   The Alamo and La Bahia at San Jacinto.

Frontier Times. Bandera, Tex., September 1942. Vol. 19,
No. 12, pp. 406-408.
By J. Frank Dobie in the San Antonio Light.

C188   The Alamo's Immortalization of Words.

Southwest Review. Dallas, Summer 1942. Vol. XXVII,
No. 4, pp. 402-410.

C189   The Cowboy and the Judge.

Ranch Romances. New York, October 9, 1942. Vol. 109,
No. 1, pp. 112-114.

C190   Coyote Traits and Trails.

Arizona Highways. Phoenix, May 1942. Vol. XVIII, No. 5,
pp. 4-7, 40-42.
Drawings by Ross Santee, a photograph by Jack
Specht, San Antonio, Texas, 1934, and a black and white
reproduction by Luther Bookout.
In *The Voice of the Coyote.*

C191 a   Don Quixote of the Six-shooter.

New Mexico. Santa Fe, May 1942. Vol. 20, No. 5, pp. 19,
30-32.

C191 b   Clay Allison of the Washita.

Frontier Times. Bandera, Tex., February 1943. Vol. 20,
No. 5, pp. 82-85.

C191c   Gentleman Killer.

Frontier Times. Austin, Winter, 1957-'58. Vol. 32, No. 1,
New Series No. 1, pp. 12-13, 36.
Illustrated by William Loechel.

C192   A Genuine Cowboy Preacher and His Book.

The Cattleman. Fort Worth, October 1942. Vol. XXIX,
No. 5, pp. 88.

C193   Javeline Lore and Hunting.

Southwest Review. Dallas, Spring 1942. Vol. XXVII,
No. 3, pp. 304-319.

The Man of Goats. See C122b.

C194   Mister Ben Lilly—Bear Hunter East and West.

The Saturday Review of Literature. New York, May 16,
1942. Vol. XXV, No. 20, pp. 14-15.
In *The Ben Lilly Legend.*

A Question of Hides. See C131b.

Rawhide Has Faithfully Served Texas. See C170b.

C195   The Smart Coyote.

> Natural History. New York, February 1942. Vol. XLIX, No. 2, pp. 70-75.
> In *The Voice of the Coyote.*

C196   The Story Under the Grasses.

> Ranch Romances. New York, July 3, 1942. Vol. 107, No. 2, pp. 113-117.
> Story of the Ray Ranch.

C197   The Texas Bluebonnet.

> The Cattleman. Fort Worth, May 1942. Vol. XXVIII, No. 12, pp. 5-8.

1943

C198   The Art of Trailing.

> Ranch Romances. New York, February 12, 1943. Vol. 111, No. 2, pp. 108-110.
> Partly from *The Longhorns,* with additions.

C199   Ben Lilly of the Mountain.

> Arizona Highways. Phoenix, September-October 1943. Vol. XIX, No. 9-10, pp. 16-19.
> To be included in a book on Ben Lilly [*The Ben Lilly Legend*]

Clay Allison of the Washita. See C181b.

The Conquering Mesquite. See C184b.

C200   Cooks of Range and Trail.

> Ranch Romances. New York, July 16, 1943. Vol. 114, No. 1, pp. 102-106.

C201   The Cowboy's Philosophy.

> Frontier Times. Bandera, Tex., November 1943. Vol. 21, No. 2, pp. 78-80.

C202   Divided We Stand.

> Southwestern Railway Journal. Fort Worth, March 1943. Vol. XXXVII, No. 3, pp. [1]-2.

C203   Dobie Gives Us Texas.

> The Emancipator. Georgetown, Tex., June 1943, Vol. V, No. 10, pp. 30-[33]

C204 **a**   Domination of Education in Texas.

The Emancipator. Georgetown, Tex., November 1943. Vol. VI, No. 3, pp. 10-11.
The article . . . came out in the Texan and was copied in the Texas Outlook.

C204 b   —— ——

The Texas Outlook. Fort Worth, November 1943. Vol. 27, No. 11, p. 50.

Frontier Fiddle. See C111c.

C205   Frozen Inside a Buffalo Hide.

Ranch Romances. New York, April 23, 1943. Vol. 112, No. 3, pp. 100-102.

C206 **a**   Grizzly Hater.

New Mexico. Santa Fe, October 1943. Vol. 21, No. 10, pp. 14, 29-31.

C206 b   Bear Moore . . . Grizzly Hater.

Western Sportsman. Denver, May-June 1947. Vol. 7, No. 10, pp. 9, 26.
Illustrated by Walter J. Wilwerding.

C207   The Jeepy Jackrabbit.

Natural History. New York, January 1943. Vol. LI, No. 1, pp. 40-45.

C208   John Booth's Great Ride.

Ranch Romance. New York, August 1943. Vol. 114, No. 2, pp. 93-94.
From *The Flavor of Texas*.

C209   Life in Old Tucson, by Frank C. Lockwood. [A review]

Southwest Review. Dallas, Autumn 1943. Vol. XXIX, No. 1, p. 99.

C210 **a**   Old Bill.

The Atlantic. Boston, October 1943. Vol. 172, No. 4, pp. 113, 115, 117.
Accent on Living.

C210 b   Old Bill Cole and His Loot.

Frontier Times. Austin, Spring 1959. Vol. 33, No. 2, pp. 30-31, 63.
Illustrated by M. B. Cole.

C211   Rattlesnake-Guarded Treasure.

> Ranch Romances. New York, September 10, 1943. Vol. 115, No. 1, pp. 103-105.

C212   Rawhide Hobbles and the Code.

> Ranch Romances. New York, October 8, 1943. Vol. 115, No. 3, pp. 94-95.
>> As told to J. Frank Dobie by trail-driver John Tally.

The Spanish Cow Pony. See C126b.

C213   Stompedes.

> The Cattleman. Fort Worth, March 1943. Vol. XXIX, No. 10, pp. 113, 116-119, 121-122.
> This is Chapter 5 of "The Longhorns."

C214   Tales of the Panther.

> The Saturday Evening Post. Philadelphia, December 11, 1943. Vol. 216, No. 24, pp. 22-23, 57, 60-61.

C215   Texas.

> Transatlantic. London, November 1943. Vol. I, No. 3, pp. 21-26.

C216   Texas Folk-lore Society.

> Journal of American Folklore. Lancaster, Penn. and New York, July-September 1943. Vol. 56, No. 221, pp. 186-187.
> North American Folklore Societies. Compiled by Wayland D. Hand: pp. 161-191.

C217   When Cowman Bookkeeping Was Simple.

> The Cattleman. Fort Worth, July 1943. Vol. XXX, No. 2, pp. 34-35.

1944

C218   Among the Lincolnshire Reds in England.

> The Cattleman. Fort Worth, July 1944. Vol. XXXI, No. 2, pp. 20, 22, 24, 46-47.

C219   The Cold-Nosed Hounds.

> The Atlantic. Boston, January 1944. Vol. 173, No. 1, pp. 101, 103-104, 107.
> Accent on Living.

C220   Dobie on the Texas University Crisis.

> The Emancipator. Georgetown, Tex., December 1944. Vol. VII, No. 4, pp. [12]-14.
> From Associated Press dispatches.

C221   Greatest of All the Grizzlies.

California Folklore Quarterly. Berkeley and Los Angeles, January 1944. Vol. III, No. 1, pp. 12-15.

C222   Heather for Remembrance: Holiday in Scotland.

Southwest Review. Dallas, Summer 1944. Vol. XXIX, No. 4, pp. 512-524.
In *A Texan in England.*

C223 a   "How the Scoundrel Lied."

The Saturday Evening Post. Philadelphia, September 30, 1944. Vol. 217, No. 14, pp. 22-[23], 106-108.
In *A Texan in England.*

C223 b   —— ——

Britain. New York, November 1944. Vol. V, No. 1, pp. 59-67.
In *A Texan in England.*

Jim Bowie's Knife. See C75c.

C224   John W. Thomason.

Southwest Review. Dallas, Summer 1944. Vol. XXIX, No. 4, p. x.
Condensed in *A Texan in England.*

C225   Mister Ben Lilly in Louisiana.

Southwest Review. Dallas, Winter 1944. Vol. XXIX, No. 2, pp. 215-233.
In *The Ben Lilly Legend.*

C226   The Tom Paine Fortress over England.

The Freethinker. New York, July 1944. Vol. 8, No. 7, pp. [1]-2.

1945

C227   At the Anchor.

Southwest Review. Dallas, Winter 1945. Vol. XXX, No. 2, pp. 129-133.
From *A Texan in England.*

C228 a   A Boy and His Horse.

Esquire. Chicago, September 1945. Vol. XXIV, No. 3, pp. 88-89.
Illustration is a detail from a lithograph by Grant Wood.
In *The Mustangs.*

C228 b —— ——

The Cattleman. Fort Worth, September 1946. Vol. XXXIII, No. 4, pp. 208-210.

C229 Britain's American Invaders.

Leader. London, June 16, 1945. Vol. 2, No. 35, pp. 11-13.

C230 Bulls and the Blood Call.

The Cattleman. Fort Worth, March 1945. Vol. XXXI, No. 10, pp. 29-30, 117-119, 121-123.

This is chapter eight of "The Longhorns."

C231 England Remembers.

Southwest Review. Dallas, Spring 1945. Vol. XXX, No. 3, pp. 215-224.

A chapter from Mr. Dobie's forthcoming book, *A Texan in England.*

C232 The English Character.

The American Mercury. New York, April 1945. Vol. LX, No. 256, pp. 475-482.

In *A Texan in England.*

C233 Letter Home. London, to Austin, Texas.

The English-Speaking World. Rutherford, N. J., October-November 1945. Vol. XXVII, No. 6, pp. 377-380.

C234 Rendezvous with Destiny.

Accion Inter-Americana. Austin, July 1945. pp. 11, 20-22.

C235 The Right Medicine for Skunk Bite.

Ranch Romance. New York, March 23, 1945. Vol. 125, No. 1, pp. 80-82.

C236 a Strange Animal Friendships.

Nature Magazine. Baltimore, January 1945. Vol. 38, No. 1, pp. 9-12.

Illustrated by Prentice Phillips.

C236 b —— ——

The Reader's Digest. Pleasantville, N. Y., April 1945. Vol. 46, No. 276, pp. 123-124.

Condensed from Nature Magazine.

C236 c —— ——

Science Digest. Chicago, April 1945. Vol. 17, No. 4, pp. [35]-37.

Condensed from Nature Magazine.

C237   A Texan in England.

> The Saturday Review of Literature. New York, April 14, 1945. Vol. 28, No. 15, pp. 40, 44.
> This article is drawn from a forthcoming book by Mr. Dobie, *"A Texan in England."*

C238   Tranquility.

> The Emancipator. Georgetown, Tex., March 1945. Vol. VII, No. 7, pp. 16-19.

1946

A Boy and His Horse. See C228b.

C239   Bullsnake Men.

> Nature Magazine. Baltimore, March 1946. Vol. 39, No. 3, pp. 132-134.
> Illustrated by Russell O. Berg.

C240   Capsules.

> The Saturday Review of Literature. New York, January 5, 1946. Vol. XXIX, No. 1, p. 15.
> The Atomic Age.

C241   Dobie's Speech on Negro Education.

> The Texas Spectator. Austin, December 20, 1946. Vol. 2, No. 11, p. 5.

C242   English vs. American Newspapers.

> The American Mercury. New York, September 1946. Vol. LXIII, No. 273, pp. 304-312.

C243   J. Frank Dobie Talks About Recent Trends.

> The Texas Spectator. Austin, December 27, 1946. Vol. 2, No. 12, p. 2.
> Reprint of a recent article which was written for the Chicago Sun.
> Modern Trends in Texas Literature.

C244   Last of the Men on Horseback. [Buffalo Bill]

> The Saturday Review of Literature. New York, August 3, 1946. Vol. XXIX, No. 31, pp. 12-13.
> Strictly Personal.

C245   My Favorite Tree.

> American Forests. Washington, D. C., April 1946. Vol. 52, No. 4, p. [147]

C246   Painter to Force Tranquillity.

> The Texas Spectator. Austin, October 18, 1946. Vol. 2, No. 2, p. 3.

C247   Ranch-Style Beans.

> Sun-up. San Antonio, August 1946. Vol. 1, No. 6, p. 25.

C248   Samples of the Army Mind.

> Harpers Magazine. New York, December 1946. Vol. 193, No. 1159, pp. [529]-536.

C249   A Texan Teaches American History at Cambridge University.

> The National Geographic Magazine. Washington, D. C., April 1946. Vol. LXXXIX, No. 4, pp. [409]-441.
> With illustrations by staff photographer B. Anthony Stewart.
> Written after *A Texan in England* was published and contains new materials.

C250   Texas Needs Brains.

> Texas Ranger. Austin, October 1946. Vol. 59, No. 2, pp. 16-17, 25-26.

C251   Why I Am for Rainey.

> The Emancipator. Georgetown, Tex., August 1946. Vol. VIII, No. 12, pp. 21-27.

1947

Bear Moore—Grizzly Hater. See C206b.

The Conquering Mesquite. See C184c.

C252   Coyote, Hero-God and Trickster.

> Southwest Review. Dallas, Autumn 1947. Vol. XXXII, No. 4, pp. 336-344.
> In *The Voice of the Coyote*.

C253   Dobie on a Resignation.

> The Texas Spectator. Austin, April 7, 1947. Vol. 2, No. 26, pp. 7-8.

C254   Fabulous Little Plains Dweller.

> Western Sportsman. Denver, July-August 1947. Vol. 7, No. 11, p. 8.
> Illustrated by Geo. Phippen.
> In *The Voice of the Coyote*.

C255 a   In a Pit with a Grizzly.

> Western Sportsman. Denver, September-October 1947. Vol. 7, No. 12, pp. 12-13.
> Illustrated by Geo. Phippen.

C255 b —— ——

> Frontier Times. Austin, Winter 1959-60. Vol. 34, No. 1, pp. 20-21, 52.

C256   The Lost Gold Mine.

> Zane Grey's Western Magazine. New York, October 1947. Vol. 1, No. 8, pp. 143-158.

C257   Mr. Coyote, the Unpredictable.

> Country Gentleman. Philadelphia, November 1947. Vol. CXVII, No. 11, pp. 28, 149-152.
> Drawings by Robert Fink.
> In *The Voice of the Coyote*.

C258   Tall Tales of the Rattler.

> The Star Weekly. Toronto, March 15, 1947. p. 2.
> Illustrated by Paul Bransom.

C259   Texas Cowhand in England.

> The Rotarian. Chicago, June 1947. Vol. LXX, No. 6, pp. 11, 57-59.

C260 a   Trail-Driving Texas Horses.

> The Cattleman. Fort Worth, September 1947. Vol. XXXIV, No. 4, pp. 42, 78.

C260 b   Trailing Horse Herds.

> Ranch Romances. New York, April 2, 1948. Vol. 144, No. 4, pp. 96, 108.

C261   The Way of the Coyote with Sheep.

> Sheep and Goat Raiser. San Angelo, Texas, January 1947. Vol. 27, No. 4, p. 4.
> In *The Voice of the Coyote*.

C262   What I Saw Across the Rhine.

> The National Geographic Magazine. Washington, D. C. January 1947. Vol. XCI, No. 1, pp. 57-86.

1948

C263   Ab Blocker, Cowman.

> Ranch Romances. New York, September 3, 1948. Vol. 147, No. 3, pp. [46]-47.

C264   About Members.

> El Paisano. Austin, December 1948. Vol. 1, No. 1, pp. [1]-2.
> At the 1948 meeting, the Society took cognizance of the death of John A. Lomax by passing the following resolution by J. Frank Dobie.

C265   Architect of Annexation. [Review of] Anson Jones: the Last President of Texas, by Herbert Gambrell.

> The Saturday Review of Literature. New York, October 16, 1948. Vol. XXXI, No. 42, pp. 12, 38.

C266   Austin, the Capital of Texas.

> Holiday. Philadelphia, November 1948. Vol. IV, No. 5, pp. 104-[107], 129-131.
> By James Oak [pseudonym of J. Frank Dobie]

C267   Coyote Curiosity.

> Western Sportsman. Denver, May-June 1948. Vol. 8, No. 4, pp. 16, 21.
> In *The Voice of the Coyote.*

C268   The Coyote Is a Family Man.

> Southern Agriculturist. Nashville, Tenn., December 1948. Vol. LXXVII, No. 12, pp. 14, 23.
> In *The Voice of the Coyote.*

C269   The Coyote's Name in Human Speech.

> The New Mexico Quarterly Review. Albuquerque, Summer 1948. Vol. XVIII, No. 2, pp. 195-199.
> In *The Voice of the Coyote.*

C270   How Can We Meet the Challenge of Russia's Expansion in Europe?

> Town Meeting. New York, April 6, 1948. Vol. 13, No. 50, pp. 1-23.
> Moderator, George V. Denny, Jr. Speakers, Allen W. Dulles, Ellis Arnall, Robert St. John, James F. Dobie.
> Broadcast April 6, 1948, Town Meeting of the Air, American Broadcasting Company.

C271 a   How Low-down Is the Mangy Coyote?

> True. New York, September 1948. Vol. 23, No. 136, pp. 38-39, 86-88.
> In *The Voice of the Coyote.*

C271 b   —— ——

> Hunting Yearbook, published by True. Greenwich, Conn., 1949-1950 issue. pp. 20-21, 75-77.
> In *The Voice of the Coyote.*

C272   Hunger. [Personal experiences in getting hungry and eating]

> Western Sportsman. Denver, January-February 1948. Vol. 8, No. 2, p. 8.
> Illustrated by Geo. Phippen.

C273   The Magic of Don Coyote.

     Southwest Review. Dallas, Summer 1948. Vol. XXXIII, No. 3, pp. 243-250.

     In *The Voice of the Coyote*.

C274 a   The Monument of the Seven Mustangs.

     The Cattleman. Fort Worth, September 1948. Vol. XXXV, No. 4, pp. 46-[47], 193-197.

     Address delivered at unveiling of statue sculptured by A. Phimister Proctor in front of Memorial Museum, May 31, 1948.

C274 b   The Seven Mustangs . . . Sculptured by A. Phimister Proctor.

     Texas Literary Quarterly. Austin, Autumn 1948. Vol. I, No. 2, pp. [3]-8.

C275   Old Crip.

     Southwest Review. Dallas, Spring 1948. Vol. XXXIII, No. 2, pp. 125-129.

     In *The Voice of the Coyote*.

C276   A Range Horse of the Mexican Frontier.

     The Western Horseman. Colorado Springs, Colo., September-October 1948. Vol. XIII, No. 5, pp. 20-21, 61-62.

     Illustrated by Charles Paris.

     In *The Mustangs*.

C277   Road Runner.

     Western Sportsman. Denver, March-April 1948. Vol. 8, No. 3, pp. 10, 30.

     Partly from an article in *In the Shadow of History*.

The Seven Mustangs. See C274b.

C278   The Stranger of Sabine Pass.

     Southern Agriculturist. Nashville, Tenn., March 1948. Vol. LXXVII, No. 3, pp. 16, 61.

C279   Texas. An Explanation of the State and Its People.

     Holiday. Philadelphia, October-November 1948. Vol. 4, No. 4, pp. 34-37, 58-63, 93-96; No. 5, pp. 98-99, 116-124, 126-127.

     Part 1: illustrations by Robert Fawcett.

     Part II: illustrations by Geoffrey Biggs.

Trailing Horse Herds. See C260b.

C280   Valiant Horses in Violent Days.

     The Western Horseman. Colorado Springs, Colo., November-December 1948. Vol. XIII, No. 6, pp. 14-15, 38-41.

     Illustrated by Charles S. Paris.

     In *The Mustangs*.

C281   Wild Cunning.

> Western Sportsman. Denver, November-December 1948.
> Vol. 9, No. 1, pp. 15, 18.
>> Illustration by Walter J. Wilwerding.
>> In *The Voice of the Coyote.*

C282   Wildcatter.

> Holiday. Philadelphia, December 1948. Vol. 4, No. 6, pp.
> 106-[108], 133-136.
>> [Ed Bateman] plays the long shots for the world's
>> richest stakes—oil.

1949

C283   Coyotes Cooperate.

> Catholic Digest. St. Paul, Minn., August 1949. Vol. 13,
> No. 10, pp. 62-65.
>> Condensed chapter of . . . *The Voice of the Coyote.*

C284   Coyote * * * in Civilized Perspective.

> The Living Wilderness. Washington, D. C., Spring 1949.
> Vol. 14, No. 28, pp. [4]-9.
>> With illustrations by Claus J. Murie.
>> In *The Voice of the Coyote.*

C285   The Coyote: Trapper and Trapped.

> The Cambridge Review. Cambridge, Eng., November 12,
> 1949. Vol. LXXI, No. 1725, pp. 128-130.
>> Extract from . . . forthcoming book, The Voice of the
>> Coyote.

C286   The Deathless White Mustang.

> The Western Horseman. Colorado Springs, Colo., March-
> April 1949. Vol. XIV, No. 3, pp. 8-9, 30-31; No. 4, pp. 23,
> 28, 30-31.
>> Part 1: illustrated by Tom Lea.
>> Part II: illustrated by Joe Cisneros.
>> Remade from Tales of the Mustangs; and The Death-
>> less Pacing White Stallion (In *Mustangs and Cow
>> Horses*).
>> In *The Mustangs.*
>> See also C39, C48, C130, C177, and C319.

C287 a   Esau the Hunter.

> Southwest Review. Dallas, Winter 1949. Vol. XXXIV,
> No. 1, pp. 21-23.
>> In *The Ben Lilly Legend.*

C287 b   —— ——

> Together. Park Ridge, Ill., March 1962. Vol. VI, No. 3, pp. 28-29.
>
> Reprinted here by permission, it first appeared as the prologue in his book *The Ben Lilly Legend.*

C288   Gene Rhodes: Cowboy Novelist.

> The Atlantic. Boston, June 1949. Vol. 183, No. 6, pp. 75-77.
>
> Mainly from My Salute to Gene Rhodes, introduction to The Little World Waddies. Reprinted in The Best Novels and Stories of Eugene Manlove Rhodes. See B55 and B63.

How Low-down Is the Mangy Coyote? See C271b.

C289   Some Captive Coyotes.

> Sheep and Goat Raiser. San Angelo, Texas, December 1949. Vol. 30, No. 3, pp. 34-37.
>
> Illustrated by Frank Anthony Stanush.
>
> From *The Voice of the Coyote.*

C290   Tales of Don Coyote.

> The Pacific Spectator. Stanford, Calif., Spring 1949. Vol. III, No. 2, pp. 153-165.
>
> The tales here published from part of a volume, *The Voice of the Coyote,* to be issued by Little, Brown and Company in May.

C291   Tales of the Coyote.

> The American Mercury. New York, April 1949. Vol. LXVIII, No. 304, pp. 470-476.
>
> This article is based on material in . . . *The Voices of the Coyotes,* to be published soon.

C292   Tom Candy Ponting's Drive of Texas Cattle to Illinois.

> The Cattleman. Fort Worth, January 1949. Vol. XXXV, No. 8, pp. 34, 36, 38, 40, 42, 44-45.

C293   The Voice of the Coyote.

> The Saturday Evening Post. Philadelphia, February 19, 1949. Vol. 221, No. 34, pp. 30, 140-142.
>
> In *The Voice of the Coyote.*

C294   The War Against Aftosa.

> Country Gentleman. Philadelphia, March 1949. Vol. XCIX, No. 3, pp. 30, 136-140.

1950

C295   Brit Bailey of Bailey's Prairie.

Houston This Week. Houston, November 24, 1950. Vol. I, No. 1, p. 31.

C296   The Brush Country of Texas.

Lincoln-Mercury Times. Dearborn, Mich., November-December 1950. Vol. 2, No. 6, pp. 1-[4]
Paintings by H. O. Kelly.

C297   Cambridge.

Holiday. Philadelphia, June 1950. Vol. 7, No. 6, pp. 114-121, 143, 145-155.
Illustrations by Tom and Jean Hollyman.
See also C336.

C298   Earth and Metal. [Review of] Grant of Kingdom, by Harvey Fergusson.

Southwest Review. Dallas, Autumn 1950. Vol. XXXV, No. 4, pp. xviii-xxi.

C299   Figures of the Texas Earth: Sam Houston.

Houston This Week. Houston, December 1, 1950. Vol. I, No. 2, p. 31.

C300   Definition of a Texan.

Houston This Week. Houston, December 22, 1950. Vol. I, No. 4, p. 31.

C301   The Greatest Tracker of the West.

The Saturday Evening Post. Philadelphia, March 4, 1950. Vol. 222, No. 36, pp. [25], 87-90.
In *The Ben Lilly Legend*.

C302   Guilt by Rumor.

Southwest Review. Dallas, Summer 1950. Vol. XXV, No. 3, pp. 211-212.

C303   Indian Horses and Horsemanship.

Southwest Review. Dallas, Autumn 1950. Vol. XXXV, No. 4, pp. 265-275.
In *The Mustangs*.

C304   Of Men and Mounts. [Review of] The Horses of the Conquest, by R. B. Cunninghame Graham, edited by Robert Moorman Denhardt.

Southwest Review. Dallas, Spring 1950. Vol. XXXV, No. 2, pp. xv, 152.

C305   The Progenitor of the Mustang.

West Texas Historical Association Year Book.
Abilene, Tex., October 1950. Vol. XXVI, pp. [3]-19.
In *The Mustangs.*

C306   Reckless Breeds in Fact and Fiction. [Review of]
This Reckless Breed of Men, by Robert Class Cleland
[and of] The House of Beadle and Adams, by Albert
Johnnsen.

The Yale Review, New Haven, Conn., September 1950.
Vol. XL, No. 1, pp. 182-184.

C307   Silver Crossing.

Ranch Romances. New York, April 14, 1950. Vol. 158,
No. 1, pp. 38-39.

Trail Driving a Hundred Years Ago. See C96b.

C308   What Makes Texans Brag?

Houston This Week. Houston, December 8, 1950. Vol. I,
No. 3, p. 31.

C309 a   The Writer and His Region.

Southwest Review. Dallas, Spring 1950. Vol. XXXV, No.
2, pp. 81-87.
Incorporated in the new introduction to *Guide to Life
and Literature of the Southwest,* 1952.

C309 b   ——— ———

Sul Ross State College Bulletin. Alpine, Tex., June 1,
1953. Vol. XXXIII, No. 2, pp. 26-32.
Reprinted . . . from the spring 1950 issue of The Southwest Review.

1951

C310   Art of the Frontier. [Review of] The West of Alfred
Jacob Miller, notes by Alfred Jacob Miller and an
account by Marvin C. Ross.

The Saturday Review of Literature. New York, August
18, 1951. Vol. XXXIV, No. 33, pp. 16, 33.

C311 a   Books and Christmas.

Southwest Review. Dallas, Winter 1951. Vol. XXXVI,
No. 1, pp. 1-6.

C311 b   J. Frank Dobie's Christmas Card. Books and Christmas.

Frontier Times. Baird, Tex., January 1951. Vol. 28, No.
4, pp. 96-101.
Reprinted from the Winter 1951 issue of Southwest
Review.

C312 a   **The Comanches and Their Horses.**

Southwest Review. Dallas, Spring 1951. Vol. XXXVI, No. 2, pp. 99-103.

In *The Mustangs.*

C312 b   ―― ――

Frontier Times. Austin, Spring 1960. Vol. 34, No. 2, pp. 32-33, 45-46.

Illustrated by Randy Steffen.

C313   **Early Mustangers and Their Methods.**

The Cattleman. Fort Worth, September 1951. Vol. XXXVIII, No. 4, pp. 41-42, 88, 90, 92-94, 96, 98, 100.

This article . . . is a chapter from the forthcoming book, *"The Mustangs."*

C314   **How Wise Is the Owl??**

Cherokee Owl. Henderson, Tex., December 1951. Vol. I, No. 5, pp. 8-9.

C315   **Indians and Mustangs.**

The Western Horseman. Colorado Springs, Colo., June-July 1951. Vol. XVI, No. 6, pp. 10-11, 26, 28-29; No. 7, pp. 14-15, 40-45.

From the author's forthcoming book . . . on the mustangs [*The Mustangs*]

Illustrated by George Phippen.

J. Frank Dobie's Christmas Card. Books and Christmas. See C311b.

C316   **Living in the Open. [Review of] Karankaway Country, by Roy Bedichek.**

The Southwest Review. Dallas, Spring 1951. Vol. XXXVI, No. 2, pp. xii, xiv.

C317   **The Murderous Mustangs of the Plains.**

The Saturday Evening Post. Philadelphia, December 1, 1951. Vol. 224, No. 22, pp. 32-[33], 130, 132.

In *The Mustangs.*

C318   **Rising Interest in Religious Books.**

The Presbyterian Outlook. Richmond, Va., September 17, 1951. Vol. 133, No. 38, p. 18.

Dobie's reply to the question, Why rising interest in religion.

C319   **The Saga of the Pacing White Mustang.**

Zane Grey's Western Magazine. New York, December 1951. Vol. 5, No. 10, pp. 103-113.

In *The Mustangs.*

See also C39, C48, C130, C177, and C286.

C320   Shakespeare's Home Town.

>   Holiday. Philadelphia, July 1951. Vol. 10, No. 1, pp. 94-99, 125-126.
>   Photographs by Jean and Tom Hollyman.

C321   Techniques of Beef-Feeders. [Review of] Cowboys and Cattle Kings, by C. L. Sonnichsen.

>   The Saturday Review of Literature. New York, June 16, 1951. Vol. XXXIV, No. 24, pp. 44-45.

C322   Texas' Wild Flowers Having a Tough Time.

>   Wild Flower. Washington, D. C., April 1951. Vol. 27, No. 2, pp. [29]-31.
>   Reprinted by permission from Houston Post, April 16, 1950.

C323   Up the Trail to Wyoming.

>   The Western Horseman. Colorado Springs, Colo., March 1951. Vol. XVI, No. 3, pp. 8-9, 43-45.
>   Illustrated by Clarence Elsworth.
>   Largely extracted from *The Flavor of Texas.*
>   On Walter Billingsley.

C324   Wagon-Boss Independence.

>   Zane Grey's Western Magazine. New York, April 1951. Vol. 5, No. 2, pp. 125-128.

1952

C325   Blue Streak.

>   The Quarter Horse and the Quarter Horse Journal. Amarillo, July 1952. Vol. 4, No. 10, pp. 8-9, 24.
>   This story is from . . . *The Mustangs,* to be published soon.

C326 a   The Conservatism of Charles M. Russell.

>   The Montana Magazine of History. Helena, April 1952. Vol. II, No. 2, pp. 27-31.
>   A reprint of the introduction to Seven Drawings by Charles M. Russell, 1950.

C326 b   —— ——

>   Montana the Magazine of Western History. Helena, October 1958. Vol. 8, No. 4, pp. 57-63.

C327   Country Minded People.

>   The National Future Farmer. Mount Morris, Ill., Fall 1952. Vol. I, No. 1, pp. 17, 42-43.

C328   The Coyote of Song and Cunning.

> Texas Parade. Austin, November 1952. Vol. XIII, No. 6, pp. 12-14.
>> Photograph by Jack Specht; illustration by Dwain Kelley.
>> This is not from *The Voice of the Coyote*.

C329   A Deer Hunter's Camp.

> What's New. North Chicago, Christmas 1952. pp. [36]-37, 52, 54.

C330   Dr. M. W. Pickard and His Books.

> Southwest Review. Dallas, Spring 1952. Vol. XXXVII, No. 2, pp. 157-161.
>> The following words were set down to be read on Sunday, January 6, 1952, in the home of Miss Virginia Campbell at Kerrville, Texas, in memorialization of Dr. M. W. Pickard.
>> Points of view.

C331   I'll Never Forget That Better Remedy.

> The Alcalde. Austin, January 1952. Vol. XL, No. 4, p. 115.

C332   Knowledge Brings Understanding.

> The Press Woman. Kansas City, Mo., June 1952. Vol. 15, No. 6, p. 3.
>> Extracts from *A Texan in England*.

C333   The Lonest Wolf.

> Outdoor Life. New York, April 1952. Vol. 109, No. 2, pp. 36-37, 83-86.
>> Illustrated by Robert G. Doares.

C334   Mustang.

> Empire Magazine, The Denver Post. Denver, September 7, 1952. pp. 6-7.
>> Illustration by Richard Case.
>> In *The Mustangs*.

C335   My Horse Buck.

> The Atlantic. Boston, June 1952. Vol. 189, No. 6, pp. [25]-28.
>> In *The Mustangs*.

C336   The Mystery of Cricket.

> A. B. C. [i.e. American and British Commonwealth Association] London News-Letter. Reading, Eng., May 15, 1952. pp. 6-7.
>> Extracted from an article on Cambridge in Holiday Magazine.
>> See also C297.

C337   The Ride of His Life.

> The Western Horseman. Denver, May 1952. Vol. XVII,
> No. 5, pp. 12, 29-35.
>> Illustrated by George Phippen.
>> From J. Frank Dobie's forthcoming book *The Mus-
>> tangs,* to be published by Little, Brown and Co.

C338   The Sly Coyote.

> Empire Magazine, The Denver Post. Denver, March 2,
> 1952, pp. 6-7.
>> Illustration by H. Ray Baker.

C339   The Southwestern Scene. [Reviews of] The Desert
Year, by Joseph Wood Krutch; Southwest, by John
Houghton Allen; New Mexico: a Pageant of Three
People, by Erna Fergusson [and of] Trail Driving
Days, by Dee Brown and Martin F. Schmitt.

> The Yale Review. New Haven, Conn., Summer 1952. Vol.
> XLI, No. 4, pp. 611-613.

C340   That Better Remedy.

> The Alcalde. Austin, January 1952. Vol. XL, No. 4, p. 115.

C341   Treasure Tales of the Southwest.

> Read and Young American Magazine. Columbus, Ohio,
> December 1, 1952. Vol. II, No. 6, pp. 16-18.
> Reprinted from *Coronado's Children.*

C342   The Wild and Free Mustangs.

> Country Gentleman. Philadelphia, October 1952. Vol.
> CXXII, No. 10, pp. 34-35, 159-162.
>> Statue by Alex P. Proctor, Texas Memorial Museum,
>> photo by Betty Wallace. Illustrated by Harold Bugbee.
> From *The Mustangs.*

1953

C343   The Art of Discovery.

> Vogue. New York, March 1, 1953. Vol. 121, No. 4, pp.
> 140-141.
>> The fifteenth in Vogue's "Art of Living" series.

C344   The Artist Who Became a Cowboy. [Review of] Lost
Pony Tracks, by Ross Santee.

> New York Herald Tribune Book Review. New York, Sep-
> tember 27, 1953. Vol. 30, No. 7, pp. 1, 21.

C345   College Days.

> The Emancipator. San Antonio, February 1953. Vol. XV,
> No. 6, pp. 28-29.

C346   Come an' Get It, by Ramon F. Adams. [A review]

> Western Folklore. Berkeley, Calif., January 1953. Vol. XII, No. 1, pp. 67-68.

C347   Cowboys Don't Conform.

> Town-North. Dallas, December 1953. Vol. V, No. 7, pp. 12, 22.
> Illustrated by Howell Zinn.

C348   A Cowman and His Horse.

> The Quarter Horse Journal. Amarillo, December 1953. Vol. 6, No. 3, pp. 34-35.

C349   "Cowmen Dress Down."

> The Dude Wrangler. Bandera, Texas, April 1953. Vol. 5, No. 2, p. 31.

C350   The Cowman's Southwest: Being the Reminiscences of Oliver Nelson, edited by Angie Debo.

> Pacific Historical Review. Berkeley, Calif., August 1953. Vol. XXII, No. 3, pp. 294-296.

C351   Grass on the Ground and Grass in Big Talk.

> Soil and Water Magazine. Temple, Texas, April 1953. Vol. 2, No. 4, p. 13.

C352   The Greatest Hunter of Them All [Ben Lilly]

> Argosy. New York, September 1953. Vol. 337, No. 3, pp. 42-44, 68-70.
> Illustrated by Bob Kuhn.

He Hunted Cousin Sally. C105b.

C353   "How the Centipede Found Its Sting."

> Town-North. Dallas, October 1953. Vol. V, No. 6, pp. 16-17, 22.
> Illustrated by Howell Zinn.

C354   Lewis, Clark and a Vast, Young Land. [Review of] The Journals of Lewis and Clark, edited by Bernard De Voto.

> New York Herald Tribune Book Review. New York, November 15, 1953. Vol. 30, No. 14, p. 4.

C355   Limitless Lands & Longhorn Cattle — the Beginnings of Texas Real Estate.

> Texas Real Estate Magazine. Austin, August 1953. Vol. 1, No. 8, pp. 5, 21.
> From *The Longhorns*.

C356   Mexico City.

>   Holiday. Philadelphia, March 1953. Vol. 13, No. 3, pp. 34-[41] 87-88, 90, 92-93, 95, 97.

C357   The Mustang Men.

>   Empire Magazine, The Denver Post. Denver, March 22, 1953. p. 9.
>> Illustration by Richard Case.
>> From *The Mustangs*.

Not the Will of God. See C83b.

C358   Old Nelly, the Mustang Mare.

>   The Quarter Horse Journal. Amarillo, November 1953. Vol. 6, No. 2, p. 13.

The Outlaws of the Brush. See C108b.

C359 a   A Plot of Earth.

>   Southwest Review. Dallas, Spring 1953. Vol. XXXVIII, No. 2, pp. 89-100.

C359 b   —— ——

>   True West. Austin, July-August, 1962. Vol. 9, No. 6, pp. 12-17, 46.
>> Reprinted from the Southwest Review, Spring, 1953.

C360   Pop-eye, the Wood Rat.

>   Empire Magazine, The Denver Post. Denver, October 25, 1953, p. 11.

C361   The Proper Role of Learning. [Review of] The Changing Humanities, by David H. Stevens.

>   Saturday Review. New York, December 12, 1953. Vol. XXXVI, No. 50, p. 21.

C362   Roadrunner a Predator?

>   Texas Game and Fish Magazine. Austin, August 1953. Vol. XI, No. 9, pp. 30-31.
>> Letters to the Editor.

C363   The Roadrunner of the Southwest.

>   Texas Parade. Austin, October 1953. Vol. XIV, No. 4, pp. 38-40.

C364   This I Believe.

>   The Austin Unitarian. Austin, January 18, 1953. Vol. III, No. 34, pp. 1-3.
>> Mimeographed.

C365   Wisdom Is Where You Find It!

> Town-North. Dallas, November 1953. Vol. V, No. 7, pp. 12-13.
> Illustrated by Howell Zinn.

The Writer and His Region. See C309b.

1954

C366   Babicora.

> The American Hereford Journal. Kansas City, Mo., January 1, 1954. Vol. 44, No. 17, pp. 56-58, 60, 174-175.
> Personal recollections of a visit . . . to the late William Randolph Hearst's . . . ranch.

C367   Do You Understand Your Horse?

> The Quarter Horse Journal. Amarillo, December 1954. Vol. 7, No. 3, pp. 70-71.

C368   Good Coffee Is a State of Mind.

> Vogue. New York, April 1, 1954. Vol. 123, No. 6, pp. 173-175.

C369   Herodotus' Horse.

> The Quarter Horse Journal. Amarillo, April 1954. Vol. 6, No. 7, pp. 49-50.

C370   His Looks and My Ways Would Hang Any Man.

> Town-North. Dallas, January 1954. Vol. V, No. 8, pp. 9-10.
> See also C401.

C371   Home Is a Harbor.

> Perfect Home Magazine. Cedar Rapids, Iowa, June 1954. p. 3.

C372 a   Islands of Birds on the Texas Coast.

> Audubon Magazine. New York, September-October 1954. Vol. 56, No. 5, p. 225.
> Reprinted from Austin, Texas American Statesman, June 27, 1954.

C372 b   —— ——

> Texas Ornithological Society Newsletter. Austin, August 1, 1954. Vol. II, No. 7, pp. 2-4.
> Mimeographed.

C373   Knight of the Plains.

> The Elks Magazine. New York, June 1954. Vol. 33, No. 1, pp. [16-17], 52-54.
> Illustrated by Bob Kuhn.

C374   Looks That Kill.

> Outdoor Life. New York, July 1954. Vol. 114, No. 1, pp. 40-41, 104-106.
> Illustrated by Philip Ronfor.

C375   Mystery of the Lost Apache Mine.

> Mechanix Illustrated. New York, December 1954. pp. 66-68, 208-212.

C376   Night Horse.

> The Quarter Horse Journal. Amarillo, August 1954. Vol. 6, No. 11, p. 65.

C377   Payment in Full.

> Town-North. Dallas, February 1954. Vol. V, No. 9, pp. 11-12.
> Illustrated by Howell Zinn.

C378   Rattlesnake Guarded Treasure.

> Texas Parade. Austin, October 1954. Vol. XV, No. 5, pp. 43-45.

C379   Snowdrift, Lonest of All Lone Wolves.

> Montana Magazine of History. Helena, Summer 1954. Vol. 4, No. 3, pp. 10-16.

C380   Texas Jacks.

> Texas Parade. Austin, March 1954. Vol. XIV, No. 9, pp. 15-16.

C381   The Treasure Is Always There!

> True West. Austin, August-September 1954. Vol. 2, No. 1, pp. 14-15, 35-37.
> Illustrated by Randy Steffen.

C382   The Wrangler and His Horses.

> The Quarter Horse Journal. Amarillo, December 1954. Vol. 7, No. 3, pp. 32-33.

1955

C383   As the Moving Finger Writ.

> Southwest Review. Dallas, Autumn 1955. Vol. XL, No. 4, pp. 289-298.

C384 a   Between the Comanche and the Rattlesnake.

> Southwest Review. Dallas, Winter 1955. Vol. XL, No. 1, pp. 14-25.
> Drawings by Hal Story.

C384 b —— ——

> Frontier Times. Austin, Summer 1962. Vol. 36, No. 3, pp. 12-13, 36.
>> Illustrated by Al Martin Napoletano.
>> Photo from Ed Bartholomew.

C385 The Dream That Saved Wilbarger.

> True West. Tombstone, Ariz., August 1955. Vol. 2, No. 6, pp. 14-15, 41-42.
>> Illustrated by Randy Steffen.
>> In *Tales of Old Time Texas*.

C386 Madstone for Rabies.

> Texas Health Bulletin. Austin, November 1955. Vol. 8, No. 10, pp. 10-12.
>> This story first appeared in the Austin American-Statesman . . .

C387 Mi Querido San Antonio.

> Central America and Mexico. Houston, August 1955. Vol. III, No. 1, pp. 15-18.

C388 a The Robinhooding of Sam Bass.

> Montana the Magazine of Western History. Helena, Autumn 1955. Vol. 5, No. 4, pp. 34-41.
>> In *Tales of Old-Time Texas*.

C388 b —— ——

> True West. Austin, July-August 1958. Vol. 5, No. 6, pp. 8-10, 36.
>> Illustrated by Al Martin Napoletano.

C389 Wash Barker and the Rock Pens.

> True West. Austin, April 1955. Vol. 2, No. 4, pp. 27, 39.
>> Illustrated by Al Martin Napoletano.

C390 a The West's Greatest Ride.

> True. New York, June 1955. Vol. 35, No. 217, pp. 42-43, 86.
>> Illustrated by Paul Nonnast.
>> Story of the ride by Francois Xavier Aubry.

C390 b —— ——

> True Western Adventures. Greenwich, Conn., August [1959] No. 9, pp. 22-23, 67.

1956

C391 "Are Texans Justified in Their Bragging?"

> This Week Magazine. New York, February 5, 1956. p. 8.
>> 15 Tough Questions from This Week Readers: pp. 7-10.

C392   Bibliography of Texas, 1795-1845. Part I. Texas Imprints, by Thomas W. Streeter. [A review]

The Book Collector. London, Autumn 1956. Vol. 5, No. 3, pp. 283, 285.

C393   A Close Touch with Wild Turkeys.

Texas Ornithological Society Newsletter. Austin, November 29, 1956. Vol. IV, No. 10, pp. 4-6.
Mimeographed.

C394   Cock of the Walk. [Review of] Legend of Pancho Villa, by Haldeen Braddy.

Hispanic America Historical Review. Durham, N. C., pp. 297-298.

C395   Dobie: a Definition of Luck.

The Dallas Morning News Book Review. Dallas, November 24, 1956. p. 5.

C396   Dobie Unexpurgated.

The Texas Observer. Austin, February 15, 1956. Vol. 47, No. 43, p. 3.

C397   The Great Cattle Trails Out of Texas.

Ford Farming. Birmingham, Mich., Fall 1956. pp. 22-[25]

C398   Hard-Writing Cowhand. [Review of] A Bar Cross Man, by W. H. Hutchinson.

New York Times Book Review. July 29, 1956. p. 15.

C399   He Brags in Reverse.

Harry Oliver's Desert Rat Scrap Book. Thousand Palms, Calif. [1956?] p. 4.

C400   Hell-for-Leather Horse.

True. New York, March 1956. Vol. 36, No. 226, pp. 42-43, 65.
Photographed from TRUE by Sid Latham.

C401   "His Looks and My Ways Would Hang Any Man."

Southwest Review. Dallas, Summer 1956. Vol. XLI, No. 3, pp. 209-221.
See also C370.

C402   Of Gusto and the Modern Spirit.

The Dallas Morning News Book Review. Dallas, November 25, 1956. pp. 1, 6.

C403   The Planter Who Gambled His Bride.

The American Weekly. New York, June 10, 1956. p. 5.
Illustrated by Howard Nostrand.
From "Tales of Old-Time Texas."

C404   A Ranch on the Nueces.

> True West. Austin, July-August 1956. Vol. 3, No. 6, pp. 20-21, 35.
> Illustrated by B. D. Titsworth.
> Reprinted from Tales of Old-Time Texas.

C405a   The Ranchero's Secret Hoard.

> American Weekly Magazine. New York, May 27, 1956. pp. 10, 12-13.
> Illustrated by Howard Nostrand.
> Reprinted from *Tales of Old-Time Texas*.

C405 b   The Mezcla Man.

> True West. Austin, November-December 1957. Vol. 5, No. 2, pp. 10-11, 40.
> Illustrated by Clay McGaughy.

C406   Poetry and Prose at Georgetown: I-II.

> Southwest Review. Dallas, Winter 1956-Spring 1957. Vol. XLII, No. 1, pp. 1-10; No. 2, pp. 97-103.

The Roadrunner in Fact and Folk-Lore. See C171b.

C407 a   Tall Tales of Texas.

> Mechanix Illustrated. New York, November 1956. Vol. 52, No. 11, pp. 74-77.
> Illustrations signed: Harry Goff.
> From *Tales of Old-Time Texas*.

C407 b   Правдивые предания Тексаса.

> Америка. Washington, 1957. No. 12, pp. 8-9.
> Published for distribution in the Soviet Union by the United States Information Agency.

C407c   Opowieści Dawnego Teksasu.

> Ameryka. Washington [1959] No. 7, pp. 42-43.
> Illustrated by Ralph Rotinson.
> Published for distribution in Poland by Press and Publications Service, United States Information Agency.
> From *Tales of Old-Time Texas* — Newly Illustrated.

C408 a   Texas Longhorns Out of History.

> Ford Farming. Birmingham, Mich., Summer 1956. pp. 8-[11]
> [Rewritten on request]
> Illustrations by Tom Lea from J. Frank Dobie's book, "The Longhorns," published by Little, Brown and Company, Boston.

C408 b　—— ——

Old Trail Drivers Yearbook, Brush Country Edition. San Antonio, October 1960. pp. 4, 17-18.

1957

C409　Bibliography of Texas, 1795-1845. Part II. Mexican Imprints Relating to Texas, 1803-1945, by Thomas W. Streeter. [A review]

The Book Collector. London, Winter 1957. Vol. 6, No. 4, pp. 417-418.

The Cowboy as a Courtier. See C175b.

C410　The First Bookseller To Enrich My Life.

Antiquarian Booksellers Association of America, The Southern California Chapter. Van Nuys, Calif., Summer 1957. Bulletin Number Two, pp. [1]-3.
Article on Elijah Leroy Shettles.
See also C416.

C411 a　James Bowie, Big Dealer.

The Southwestern Historical Quarterly. Austin, January 1957. Vol. LX, No. 3, pp. [337]-357.

C411 b　Fabulous Frontiersman: Jim Bowie.

Montana, the Magazine of Western History. Helena, April 1959. Vol. 9, No. 2, pp. 43-55.

C412　The Lost Brayfogle Mine.

True West. Austin, May-June 1957. Vol. 4, No. 5, pp. 18-19, 38.
Illustrated by Randy Steffen.

The Mezcla Man. See C405b.
Poetry and Prose at Georgetown. See C406.
Правдивые предания Тексаса. See C407b.

C413　The Return of Old Sancho.

True West. Austin, September-October 1957. Vol. 5, No. 1, pp. 10-11, 31.
Illustrated by B. D. Titsworth.
From *The Longhorns*.

C414　The Right Remedy.

New Mexico Magazine. Santa Fe, January 1957. Vol. 35, No. 1, pp. 18, 41.

C415　Some Things Kept from College.

Southwestern University Ex-Students' Newsmagazine. Georgetown, Texas, May 1957. Series 57, No. 5, pp. [3, 14-15]

C416   Texas Book Dealer.

The Bookman's Bookfinder Specialist. Channelview,
Texas; June 10, 1957, pp. [2-3]; June 17, 1957, pp. [2-3]
Mimeographed.
Article on Elijah Leroy Shettles.
See also C410.

C417   Three Apache Women and a Lone White Man.

Arizona Highways. Phoenix, September 1957. Vol.
XXXIII, No. 9, pp. 8-[11]
Drawings by Ted de Grazia.

C418   The Unveiling of a Self-Portrait.

The New York Times Book Review. New York, September 1, 1957. Vol. LXII, No. 35, pp. [1], 15.

C419   Whiskey, Skunks and Rattlesnakes.

True West. Austin, July-August 1957. Vol. 4, No. 6, pp.
14-15.
Illustrated by Keith Soward.

1958

C420   Battle of the Beef. [Review of] The Cattlemen, by
Mari Sandoz.

Saturday Review. New York, June 28, 1958. Vol. XLI, No.
26, p. 30.

C421   Books on West and Southwest Suggested for High
School Libraries of the Area. Compiled by J. Frank
Dobie.

Heritage of Kansas. Emporia, Kan., November 1958. Vol.
2, No. 4, pp. 28-29.

C422   Captain John G. Bourke as Soldier, Writer, and Man.

Arizona Quarterly. Tucson, Autumn 1958. Vol. 14, No.
3, pp. [226]-233.
This essay [including a sentence omitted from the
book] . . . from the introduction to his edition of Burke's
An Apache Campaign.

C423   Charlie Acquires a Burro.

Texas Adventures. Houston, October 1958. Vol. 1, No. 1,
pp. 8-9.

The Conservatism of Charles M. Russell. See 326b.

C424   Fever for Gold.

> True West. Austin, November-December, 1958. Vol. 6,
> No. 2, pp. 14-15, 33-34.
>> Illustrated by Al Martin Napoletano.
>> The Lost Cabin Mine in the Big Horn Mountains . . .

Gentleman Killer. See C191c.

C425   A Great Race Horse. [Review of] The Dan Patch
Story, by Fred A. Sasse.

> Minnesota History. St. Paul, June 1958. Vol. 36, No. 2,
> pp. 65-66.

C426   He Didn't Hold to the Majority.

> Congressional Record, 85th Congress, Second Session.
> Washington, June 25, 1958. Vol. 104, No. 105, pp. A5776-
> A5777.
>> J. Frank Dobie. Extension of Remarks of Hon. Ralph
>> W. Yarborough of Texas in the Senate of the United
>> States. Wednesday, June 25, 1958: pp. A5776-A5777.
>> From the Austin (Tex.) American-Statesman of June
>> 22, 1958.

C427   How Jim Bowie Got His Silver.

> Frontier Times. Austin, Summer 1958. Vol. 32, No. 3,
> pp. 11, 32.

C428   Library Founders and Builders Due Eternal Gratitude
of Public.

> Congressional Record, 85th Congress, Second Session.
> Washington, March 21, 1958. Vol. 104, No. 46, p. A2692.
>> J. Frank Dobie's Salute to Libraries. Extension of Re-
>> marks of Hon. Ralph W. Yarborough of Texas in the
>> Senate of the United States. Friday, March 21, 1958:
>> pp. A2691-A2692.

C429   The Lost Apache Mine.

> True West. Austin, March-April 1958. Vol. 5, No. 4, pp.
> 8-9, 30-32.
>> Illustrated by Al Martin Napoletano.
>> Dr. Daniel B. McCall . . . This is his story.
>> For another story of this mine see *The Lost Nigger
>> Mine* in Coronado's Children.

C430 a   Madstones and Hydrophobia Skunks.

> Southwest Review. Dallas, Winter 1958. Vol. XLIII, No.
> 1, pp. 1-9.
>> The discussion on madstones herein . . . is to appear
>> a bit later in . . . "Madstones and Twisters"—p. iv.

C430 b —— ——

True West. Austin, March-April 1960. Vol. 7, No. 4, pp. 20-21, 46-48.

C431 Natural Taste for Natural Milk.

Natural Food and Farming. Atlanta, Texas, January 1958. Vol. 4, No. 10, p. 8.
[Reprinted from] The Houston Post, September 8, 1957.

C432 On the Trail in '66.

Frontier Times. Austin, Fall 1958. Vol. 32, No. 4, pp. 9, 40-41.
John Shepherd . . . recollections . . . of life on Texas ranges and on the trail.

C433 Religiosity and Palaver.

Time. New York, January 13, 1958. Vol. 71, No. 2, p. 63.

The Road Runner in Fact and Folklore. See C171c.

The Robinhooding of Sam Bass. See C388b.

C434 Schieffelin's Gold.

True West. Austin, September-October 1958. Vol. 6, No. 1, p. 13.
Photograph of Ed Schieffelin.

C435 Two Canyon Wrens and Three Books.

Audubon Magazine. New York, November-December 1958. Vol. 60, No. 6, pp. 256-257, 297, 304.

C436 What It Felt Like To Be There. [Review of] Fever in the Earth, by William A. Owens.

American Petroleum Institute Quarterly. New York, Spring 1958. pp. 42-43.

C437 What the Kid Said—Went!

Frontier Times. Austin, Winter 1958-59. Vol. 33, No. 5, pp. 9, 36.
Illustrated by Francis C. Hannon.
The most pleasant Billy the Kid anecdote . . . is in . . . book by R. B. Townsend entitled *The Tenderfoot in New Mexico*.

C438 Windows on the Southwest. [Review of] A Southwestern Century, by Lawrence Clark Powell.

Southwest Review. Dallas, Autumn 1958. Vol. XLIII, No. 4, pp. viii-ix.

1959

C439   Curious Coyotes.

> Frontier Times. Austin, Spring 1959. Vol. 33, No. 2, pp.
> 11, 36.
>> Photo courtesy E. P. Haddon, U. S. Fish and Wildlife
>> Service.

C440   Dakota Cowboy, by Ike Blasingame. [A review]

> The Westerners, New York Posse Brand Book. New York,
> 1959. Vol. 5, No. 4, pp. 92-93.

C441   Dog Ghosts, by J. Mason Brewer. [A review]

> Balance. Austin, March 12, 1959. p. 3.
> From Dobie's review in the Austin American.

C442   Don Espanol and the Four Skeletons.

> Frontier Times. Austin, Summer 1959. Vol. 33, No. 3, pp.
> 32-33.

Fabulous Frontiersman: Jim Bowie. See C411b.

C443   Helen Hunt Jackson and Ramona.

> Southwest Review. Dallas, Spring 1959. Vol. XLIV, No.
> 2, pp. 93-98.

C444   How Sam Houston Hill Killed Sam Bass.

> True West. Austin, July-August 1959. Vol. 6, No. 6, pp.
> 19, 34.
>> Through J. Frank Dobie by Bill Kittrell.

C445   "I Have Often Wondered About That Myself"

> Texas Adventures. Houston, January 1959. Vol. 2, No.
> 1, pp. 8-9.

In a Pit with a Grizzly. See C255b.

C446   The Meat That Caesar Fed Upon.

> Natural Food and Farming. Atlanta, Texas, December
> 1959. Vol. 6, No. 7, pp. 6, 24.

C447 a   Midnight, the Out-Pitchingest of All Pitchers.

> The Echo. Huntsville, Texas, October 1959. Vol. XXX,
> No. 11, p. 6.
> Revised from Sunday newspaper column.

C447 b   Midnight—Champion Bucking Horse of the World.

> The Texas Horseman. Cypress, Texas, April 1961. Vol.
> 5, No. 8, pp. 18-19.
>> Illustration signed: Bob Schoenke.
>> Photograph of the author.

C448   New Mexico's Royal Road, by Max L. Moorhead. [A review]

> Journal of Southern History. Houston, November 1959. Vol. 25, No. 4, pp. 539-540.

C449   No Help for the Alamo.

> True West. Austin, May-June 1959. Vol. 6, No. 5, pp. 6-9, 38-41.
> Photos courtesy Frontier Pictures.

Not the Will of God. See C83c.

Old Bill Cole and His Loot. See C210b.

Opowieści Dawnego Teksasu. See C407c.

C450   A Ram in the Thicket, by Frank C. Robertson. [A review]

> The Westerners, New York Posse Brand Book. New York, 1959. Vol. 6, No. 2, p. 47.

C451   Rattlesnake!

> Frontier Times. Austin, Fall 1959. Vol. 33, No. 4, pp. 18-19, 56-58.
> Texas Game & Fish Commission Photo.
> Reprinted from Do Rattlesnakes Swallow Their Young published by Texas Folklore Society.

C452 a   Roy Bedichek.

> The Texas Observer. Austin, June 27, 1959. Vol. 51, No. 12, pp. 1-3.

C452 b   —— ——

> Congressional Record, 86th Congress, First Session. Washington, July 28, 1959. Vol. 105, No. 127, pp. A6513-A6515.
>
> Roy Bedichek—A Tribute to the Philosopher-Naturalist of the Southwest. Extension of Remarks of Hon. Ralph W. Yarborough of Texas in the Senate of the United States. Tuesday, July 28, 1959: pp. A6512-A6516.

C453   She Sang, He Preached. [Review of] The Rainbow Sign, by Alan Lomax.

> New York Herald Tribune Book Review. New York, October 25, 1959. Vol. 36, No. 12, p. 6.

C454   Snowdrift—Lonest of the Lone.

> True West. Austin, September-October 1959. Vol. 7, No. 1, pp. [20]-[21], 48-50.
> Illustrated by Joe Grandee.

C455   The Way They Ran.

> The Cattleman. Fort Worth, March 1959. Vol. XLV, No.
> 10, pp. 52, 68, 70, 72, 74, 76, 78.
> This is Chapter VI of "The Longhorns."

The West's Greatest Ride. See C390b.

1960

C456   The Blue Egg of Silver and the Golden Hope.

> The Westerners, New York Posse Brand Book. New York,
> 1960. Vol. 7, No. 1, pp. 9-10.

C457   Caesar's Meat.

> The Atlantic. Boston, September 1960. Vol. 206, No. 3, pp.
> 98-[100]

The Comanches and Their Horses. See C312b.

C458   "Enlightened Is the Word for the Houston Post"

> Saturday Review. New York, January 30, 1960. Vol.
> XLIII, No. 5, inside front cover.
> Advertisement, with portrait of Dobie.

C459   Human Mind and Libraries.

> Congressional Record, 86th Congress, Second Session.
> Washington, April 11, 1960. Vol. 106, No. 66, pp. A3147-
> A3148.
>
> Frank Dobie on Librarians; a bold free mind com-
> ments on a facet of our culture. Extension of Remarks
> of Hon. Ralph W. Yarborough of Texas in the Senate of
> the United States. Monday, April 11, 1960: pp. A3147-
> A3148.

C460   James Cox and His Cattle Industry.

> Southwest Review. Dallas, Spring 1960. Vol. XLV, No.
> 2, pp. 136-142.
>
> The Antiquarian Press of New York is reprinting . . .
> Cox's Cattle Industry of Texas . . . an introduction.

Madstones and Hydrophobia Skunks. See C430b.

C461   Out of Regionalism, a Larger View.

> Saturday Review. New York, May 21, 1960. Vol. XLIII,
> No. 21, p. 17.

Paisano. See C171d.

C462   Some Taletellers I Have Known.

> The Dallas Morning News Book Review. Dallas, Novem-
> ber 27, 1960. p. 1.
>
> From essay, Singers and Storytellers, Texas Folklore
> Society Publication.

C463   Sundown.

> The Cattleman. Fort Worth, March 1960. Vol. XLVI,
> No. 10, pp. 45-46, 50.
> This is chapter XX of "The Longhorns."

Texas Longhorns Out of History. See C408b.

Tom Gilroy's Fiddler. See C111d.

1961

C464   Bibliography of Texas, 1795-1845. Part III: United
States and European Imprints Relating to Texas, by
Thomas W. Streeter. [A review]

> The Book Collector. London, Summer 1961. Vol. 10, No. 2,
> pp. 227-228.

C465   Dobie on First Classism.

> Texas Ranger. Austin, September 1961. pp. [16] 18, 41.
> Interview, Dave Crossley.
> Photography, Gilbert Qyrick.
> Art, Kerry O'Guinn.

C466   Foreword.

> Montana, the Magazine of Western History. Helena,
> October 1961. Vol. 11, No. 4, pp. 57-58.
> Up the Trail (and Back) in '82. Signed: Jack Potter:
> pp. 57-65.

C467 a   Gay Horse, Gay Rider!

> The Texas and Southwestern Horseman. Cypress, Texas,
> May 1961. Vol. 5, No. 9, pp. 21-22.
> Illustration signed: Bob Schoenke.

C467 b   —— ——

> The Westerners, New York Posse Brand Book. New York,
> 1961. Vol. 8, No. 4, p. 76.

C468   "Hoover Hogs"

> Frontier Times. Austin, Winter 1961. Vol. 36, No. 1, p. 32.
> Photograph from Texas Game and Fish Commission.
> On the armadillo.

C469   The Mad Mexican Millionaire.

> Frontier Times. Austin, Summer 1961. Vol. 35, No. 3, pp.
> [12]-13, 62-63.
> Illustrated by Ben Carlton Mead.
> On Pedro Alvarado.

C470   Memories of the Horse Age.

> True West. Austin, July-August 1961. Vol. 8, No. 6, pp.
> [12]-13, 47-48.
>> Photos from the Huffman Collection.

Midnight—Champion Bucking Horse of the World.
See C447b.

C471   The Mustang That Lost a "Fortune."

> True West. Austin, November-December 1961, Vol. 9, No.
> 2, pp. 41, 64.

"Of late, some people seem to consider that the chief
reason for advocating libraries and the reading of
books. See C475b.

Paisano. See C171e.

C472   Santa Anna's Gold.

> True West. Austin, May-June 1961. Vol. 8, No. 5, p. 29.

C473 a   Sheep.

> Southwest Review. Dallas, Summer 1961. Vol. XLVI, No.
> 1, pp. 181-188.

C473 b   —— ——

> Sheep and Goat Raiser. San Angelo, Texas, November
> 1961. Vol. 42, No. 2, pp. 24-27.
>> Courtesy of the Southwest Review.

C474   Storytellers I Have Known.

> Southwest Review. Dallas, Winter 1961. Vol. XLVI, No.
> 1, pp. 17-24.

C475 a   The Torch of the Mind . . . J. Frank Dobie . . .
comments . . .

> San Antonio Public Library. Monthly Staff Bulletin.
> San Antonio, April 1961. [2] p.

C475 b   "Of late, some people seem to consider that the chief
reason for advocating libraries and the reading of
books . . .

> ALA [American Library Association] Bulletin. Chicago,
> June 1961. Vol. 55, No. 6, front cover.
>> The quotation on this month's cover . . . appeared in
>> the monthly staff bulletin of the San Antonio Public
>> Library.
>> This quotation was reprinted in a great many news-
>> papers and periodicals.

C476   Tracks of Frederic Remington.

> Southwest Review. Dallas, Autumn 1961. Vol. XLVI, No. 4, pp. 280-285.
>
> This essay was written as an Introduction to the reprint of Remington's Pony Tracks being issued this fall by the University of Oklahoma Press.

C477   Why I Like Real Meat.

> The American Gun. Great Neck, N. Y., Summer 1961. Vol. 1, No. 3.

1962

C478   The Bear in the Hollow Cypress.

> Frontier Times. Austin, December-January 1963. Vol. 37, No. 1, pp. 45, 57-58.
>
> Illustrated by Al Martin Napoletano.

Between the Comanche and the Rattlesnake. See C384b.

C479   Censors & Satire.

> Bacchanal. Austin, March 1962. Vol. 1, No. 1, pp. 16-17, 55.

C480   E. Douglas Branch, Singularisimo.

> Southwest Review. Dallas, Spring 1962. Vol. XLVII, No. 2, pp. 109-118.

Esau the Hunter. See C287b.

C481   The Fire.

> Texas Game and Fish. Austin, June 1962. Vol. XX, No. 6, pp. 12-14.

C482   Inventor of the Bowie Knife?

> True West. Austin, November-December 1962. Vol. 10, No. 2, pp. 47, 56.
>
> According to Dan W. Jones, governor of Arkansas from 1897-1901, one James Black made the "genuine" Bowie knife.
>
> Reprinted from Tales of Old Time Texas.

A Plot of Earth. See C359b.

C483   Roy Bedichek: Fleas to Plato.

> Congressional Record, 87th Congress, Second Session. Washington, January 25, 1962. Vol. 108, No. 10, p. A546.
>
> Tributes to the Late Dr. Roy Bedichek, Texas Naturalist and Philosopher. Extension of Remarks of Hon. Ralph Yarborough of Texas in the Senate of the United States. Thursday, January 25, 1962: pp. A545-A547.
>
> From the Houston Post Sunday Magazine, Dec. 17, 1961.

C484   A Schoolteacher in Alpine.

Southwest Review. Dallas, Autumn 1962. Vol. XLVII,
No. 4, pp. 269-277.

C485   The Stallion and His Mares.

The Texas and Southwestern Horseman. Cypress, Texas,
November 1962. Vol. 7, No. 3, pp. 30-32, 34-35.
[Illustration] Drawn for The Texas Horseman by Bob
Schoenke.
Reprinted from *The Mustangs*.

C486   Talking Back to the Censors.

Southwest Review. Dallas, Summer 1962. Vol. XLVII,
No. 3, pp. 201-219.
Answers to the Texas Legislature's Textbook Investi-
gating Committee by John Edward Weems, J. Frank
Dobie and others.

C487   Thomas Gilcrease, 1890-1962.

American Scene. Tulsa, 1962. Vol. IV, No. 4, pp. 2-3.
Pencil sketch by Charles Banks Wilson.

1963

The Bear in the Hollow Cypress. See C478.

C488   Centipede Tales.

True West. Austin, September-October 1963. Vol. 11, No.
1, pp. 17, 71.
Illustration by Al Martin Napoletano.

C489   A Cowboy and His Polecats.

Frontier Times. Bandera, Texas, December-January 1964.
Vol. 38, No. 1, pp. 13, 67.

C490   The Coyote's Charm.

Audubon Magazine. New York, January-February 1963.
Vol. 65, No. 1, pp. 38-40.
Illustrations by Matthew Kalmenoff.

C491   The Deadly Reata.

True West. Austin, May-June 1963. Vol. 10, No. 5, pp.
38-39, 69-71.
Sketches from The Cowboy at Work, by Fay E. Ward,
courtesy Hastings House, Publishers, New York.

C492   Dobie: on Such as Writers.

Panorama, a Monthly Supplement of The Daily Texan.
Austin, May 12, 1963. Vol. 1, No. 7, pp. 6-7.

C493   Dobie: Webb in Thought Power.

Congressional Record, 88th Congress, First Session. Washington, December 20, 1963. Vol. 109, No. 211, p. 24099.
From the Daily Texan, Mar. 10, 1963.
Walter Prescott Webb: a Great American. Mr. Yarborough: pp. 24098-24114

C494 a   For Years We Three Sat Together.

The Texas Observer. Austin, July 26, 1963. Vol. 55, No. 17, pp. [2]-5.
Revised and enlarged from a newspaper column for this Walter Prescott Webb edition.

C494 b   —— ——

Congressional Record, 88th Congress, First Session. Washington, December 20, 1963. Vol. 109, No. 211, pp. 24104-24107.
Walter Prescott Webb: a Great American. Mr. Yarborough: pp. 24098-24114.

C495   Foreword.

True West. Austin, March-April 1963. Vol. 10, No. 4, p. 16.
Old Gran'pa, by Frank S. Hastings: pp. 16-18, 67-68.
Illustrated by Al Napoletano.

C496   Horse Race in a Cow Camp.

The Texas and Southwestern Horseman. Cypress, Texas, July 1963. Vol. 7, No. 11, pp. 7-8.

C497   Hunting Cousin Sally.

Southwest Review. Dallas, Summer 1963. Vol. XLVIII, No. 3, pp. 177-188.
See also C105.

C498   The Man Who Thought Like a Panther.

True West. Austin, November-December 1963. Vol. 11, No. 2, pp. 35, 60.

C499   A Mexico of Legend.

Frontier Times. Austin, October-November 1963. Vol. 37, No. 6, pp. 41, 56.
Nuggets: pp. 40-41, 56.

C500a   On My Friend, Walter Prescott Webb.

Great Plains Journal. Lawton, Okla., Spring 1963. Vol. 2, No. 2, pp. 37-41.
From the Houston Post, March 17, 1963.

C500 b   On My Friend, Walter Webb.

Texana. Waco, Texas, Spring 1963. Vol. I, No. 2, pp. [153]-161.

C500 c   On My Friend, Walter Webb.

Congressional Record, 88th Congress, First Session. Washington, December 20, 1963. Vol. 109, No. 211, pp. 24100-24101.

From the American-Statesman, Mar. 17, 1963.

Walter Prescott Webb: a Great American. Mr. Yarborough: pp. 24098-24114.

C501   Throwing Sunbonnets to Hungry Panthers.

Frontier Times. Austin, June-July 1963. Vol. 37, No. 4, pp. 37, 58.

Nuggets: pp. 36-37, 58.

From *Tales of Old-Time Texas.*

1964

C502   Cow Country Tempo.

The Texas Quarterly. Austin, Spring 1964. Vol. VII, No. 1, pp. 30-36.

A Cowboy and His Polecats. See C489.

Pamphlets, Reprints, Etc.

1923

DI   Dobie, J. Frank.

Texas-Mexican Border Broadsides. [Philadelphia, 1923]

Reprinted from The Journal of American Folk-lore, v.36, No. 140, April-June, 1923. pp.[185]-195.

El [i.e. La] Cancion del Rancho de Los Olmos. [By] J. Frank Dobie: pp. 192-195.

D2   —— ——

Weather Wisdom of the Texas-Mexican Border. [Austin, 1923]

cover-title, 13 pp.

Reprinted from Publications of the Texas Folk-lore Society, Number II, 1923.

1924

D3   —— ——

Folk-lore of the Southwest. What Is Being Done to Preserve It. [Oklahoma City, 1924]

cover-title, [269]-284 pp.

Reprinted from Chronicles of Oklahoma [Oklahoma City, September 1924. Vol. II, No. 3]

Bound in grey paper covers.

1925

D4   —— ——

The Genius of Gusto. [Durham, N. C., 1925]

Reprinted from the South Atlantic Quarterly, volume XXIV, number 2, April, 1925. pp. [1], [164]-178.

D5   —— ——

Versos of the Texas Vaqueros. Austin, Texas Folklore Society, 1925.

cover-title, 14 pp.
Reprinted from Publications of the Texas Folk-lore Society, Number IV, 1925.

1926

D6   —— ——

Andy Adams, Cowboy Chronicler. [Dallas, 1926]

12 pp.
Reprint from the Southwest Review, January, 1926.

1927

D7   —— ——

Ballads and Songs of the Frontier Folk. Austin, Texas Folk-lore Society, 1927.

cover-title, 63 pp.
Reprinted from Texas and Southwestern Lore (Publication number VI of the Texas Folk-lore Society, 1927)

D8   —— ——

The Mexican Vaquero of the Texas Border. Austin [1927]

cover-title, 12 pp.
Reprinted from The Southwestern Political and Social Science Quarterly, Vol. VIII, No. 1, June, 1927.

1928

D9   Atkinson, Mary Jourdan; and Dobie, J. Frank.

Pioneer Folk-Tales. Austin, Texas Folk-lore Society, 1928.

cover-title, 9 pp.
Reprinted from Publications of the Texas Folk-lore Society, Number VII, 1928.

D10   Dobie, J. Frank.

           More Ballads and Songs of the Frontier Folk. Aus-
           tin, Texas Folk-lore Society, 1928.

           cover-title, 26 pp.
           Reprinted from Publications of the Texas Folk-lore
           Society, Number VII, 1928.

1929

D11   Woodhull, Frost.

           Remedios [or Pharmacopeia Texana] San Antonio,
           Texas, [1929]

           Being a paper prepared for the Texas Folk-lore Society,
           April, 1929.
           Quotations signed: Frank Dobie: pp. 33, 40, 47, 48, 63,
           67, 78, and 89.

1932

D12   —— ——

           Mustang Gray: Fact, Tradition, and Song. Austin,
           Texas Folk-lore Society, 1932.

           cover-title, 15 pp.
           Reprinted from Publications of the Texas Folk-lore
           Society, Number X, 1932.

D13   Hastings, George E.

           "Hell in Texas." [Austin] Texas Folk-lore Society,
           1932.

           cover-title, 8 pp.
           Reprinted from Publications of the Texas Folk-lore So-
           ciety, Vol. IX, 1931.
           A Postscript by the Editor [J. Frank Dobie]: pp. 6-8.

D14 a   Dobie, J. Frank.

           Life and Literature of the Southwest. Austin, Uni-
           versity of Texas, 1932?

           Mimeographed.

D14 b   —— ——

           Life and Literature of the Southwest; an Incom-
           plete Guide to Books on Texas and the Southwest.
           Austin, University of Texas, 1936.

           28 numbered leaves.
           Mimeographed.

D14 c   —— ——

> 33 numbered leaves.
> Mimeographed.
> First mimeographed about 1932; revised 1936; revised 1938.

1933

D15   Dobie, J. Frank.

Juan Oso, Bear Nights in Mexico. [Dallas, Boyd Printing Company] 1933.

> 35, [1] pp.
> Reproduced from Southwest Review, Vol. XIX, No. 1.
> A variant form of this story appears as Chapter IX of *Tongues of the Monte* under title: Under the Sign of Ursa Major.
> Two hundred fifty copies of this edition have been printed. [Christmas greeting, 1933]

1935

D16   —— ——

Events in Texas History. [Dallas, Republic National Bank and Trust Company, 1935-36]

> 40 numbered leaves.
> Issued as single numbered sheets on heavy paper for weekly display in banks in the Southwest during the Texas Centennial year, 1936.
> Each a compressed account of some event in Texas, 1519-1936.
> Text by J. Frank Dobie; illustrated by Frank Calder.

D17   —— ——

The Hacienda of the Five Wounds. October 4th [1935]

> Folder with end sheets tipped in.
> End sheet pasted to verso of front cover has title above, Price, $3.00, and 2 paragraphs of advertising; end sheet pasted to recto of back cover is a reprint of p. 3, with running title, and text: *At this juncture three other vaqueros dashed . . .*
> Bound in yellow cloth.
> The book announced was published, 1935, with the title *Tongues of the Monte,* and later, *The Mexico I Like.*

D18   Texas. Commission of Control for Texas Centennial
       Celebrations. Advisory Board of Texas Historians.
       Minority Report . . . by J. Frank Dobie. Austin, 1935.

       32 numbered leaves.
       Mimeographed.

1936

D19   Dobie, J. Frank.

       Bigfoot Wallace and the Hickory Nuts. Austin,
       1936.

       7 pp.
       Three hundred copies . . . have been printed . . .
       On cover: The Merry Christmas Tale of Bigfoot Wallace
       and the Hickory Nuts.
       Christmas greeting, 1936.

D20   ⸺ ⸺

       J. C. Duval—First Texas Man of Letters. Dallas,
       Tardy Publishing Company [1936]

       [4], 9 pp.
       Reprinted from the October, 1936 issue of the Texas Out-
       look [sic]

       ⸺ ⸺ Life and Literature of the Southwest. See
       D14b.

1938

D21   ⸺ ⸺

       A Corner Forever Texas. [Austin, Whatley, 1938]

       8 pp.
       A plea for a Texas center in the University of Texas,
       with emphasis on the Texas collection of books and
       pamphlets . . . from The Alcalde, April, 1938.

       ⸺ ⸺ Life and Literature of the Southwest. See
       D14c.

D22   ⸺ ⸺

       Mesquite. [San Angelo, Texas, 1938]

       [4] pp.
       [Reprint from] The Southwestern Sheep & Goat Raiser
       —December 1, 1938.

D23   —— ——

The Texas Longhorn. [Fort Worth, 1938]

7 pp.
Reprinted from "The Cattleman," October, 1938.

1939

D24   —— ——

The First Cattle in Texas and the Southwest, Progenitors of the Longhorns. [Austin, 1939]

29 pp.
Reprint from The Southwestern Historical Quarterly, Vol. XLII, No. 3, January, 1939.
In *The Longhorns*.

D25   El Paso, Texas. Centennial Museum Gallery.

Exhibition of the Fifty Original Drawings by Tom Lea—Illustrating the new volume by J. Frank Dobie, Apache Gold & Silver—April 10 to 14, 1939, Centennial Museum Gallery. El Paso, Texas, Printed by C. Hertzog, 1939.

leaflet,
An introduction by J. Frank Dobie.

D26   Dobie, J. Frank.

The Roadrunner in Fact and Folk-lore. [Austin, 1939]

31 pp.
Reprint, 1939, for the Texas Game, Fish, and Oyster Commission from *In the Shadow of History,* the 1939 publication of the Texas Folk-lore Society. Austin, Texas.
This essay on the roadrunner appeared, somewhat abbreviated, in the Natural History Magazine, New York, September, 1939.
[Christmas greeting, 1939]

1940

D27   —— ——

Picthing [i.e. Pitching] Horses and Panthers. [Austin, 1940]

15 pp.
Reprinted from Mustangs and Cow Horses.
[Christmas greeting, 1940]

D28

The Passing of the Old West. The Picture. The
Artist. [Seattle, Frank McCaffrey, 1940?]

[4] pp.
The life of H. Wallace Caylor was sketched by J. Frank
Dobie in an article entitled "Texas Art and a Wagon
Sheet" which appeared in the Dallas Morning News,
March 11, 1940.

D29

Bob More, Man and Bird Man. [Dallas?] 1941.

23 pp.
Reproduced from Southwest Review, Volume XXVII,
number 1, Autumn, 1941.
Christmas greeting, 1941.

D30

Forty-four Range Country Books. [Austin?] 1941.

8 pp.
Mimeographed.
Topped out by J. Frank Dobie [an introduction] p. [1]

1942

D31   Dobie, Bertha McKee; and Dobie, J. Frank.

Old Alf, By Bertha McKee Dobie. The Alamo's Immortalization of Words, by J. Frank Dobie; as a
Christmas Remembrance [Austin] 1942.

cover-title, 15 pp.
Reprinted from Southwest Review [Dallas] Summer
1942.
The Alamo's Immortalization of Words: pp. 7-15.

D32   Dobie, J. Frank.

Over the Hump with O'Daniel. August 22. [Austin,
1942]

broadside.
A political handbill.

1943

D33

Divided We Stand. [n. p.] Oil Workers International Union—C.I.O. [1943?]
[4] pp.
A reprint of a newspaper article.

D34   —— ——

Old Bill, Confederate Ally. Austin, 1943.

leaflet.
Information about the Junior Historians on back of leaf.

1945

D35   —— ——

Cabeza de Vaca's Great Journey. Washington, D. C.,
Pan American Union, 1945.

15 pp.
Prepared with the cooperation of J. Frank Dobie.
Cover and Map by Dorothy Sweetser.

1946

D36   —— ——

Do Rattlesnakes Swallow Their Young? Austin,
1946.

24 pp.
Reprinted from Publications No. XXI of The Texas
Folklore Society.

1947

D37   —— ——

My Salute to Gene Rhodes. [El Paso, Carl Hertzog,
printer] 1947.

[1], 12, [2] pp.
A Christmas remembrance from Bertha and Frank
Dobie.

1948

D38   —— ——

My Mother—Ella Byler Dobie. [Beeville, Texas,
1948]

broadside.
Reprint of a newspaper article.

D39 a   —— ——

The Monument of the Seven Mustangs. [Fort
Worth, 1948]

[4] pp.
Reprint from The Cattleman, September, 1948.

D39 b   —— ——

The Seven Mustangs. [Austin, The Adams Publications] 1948.

1 leaf, 12 pp., 1 leaf.

A Christmas remembrance from Bertha and Frank Dobie.

A new printing of the address made at the unveiling of A. P. Procter's monument.

1949

D40   —— ——

A Christmas Lilt to You from Bertha and Frank Dobie, [Austin] 1949

[2] pp.

Drawing by Olaus J. Murie (*Voice of the Coyote*)

Quotation from Mary Austin.

Christmas greeting, 1949.

1950

D41   —— ——

Books and Christmas. [Dallas?, 1950]

cover-title, 8 pp.

Reprinted from the Winter, 1951 issue of Southwest Review, Dallas, Texas.

With wishes to you for a good Christmas and good books, Bertha and Frank Dobie, 1950.

Bound in light green paper covers lettered in dark green.

D42   —— ——

The Writer and His Region. Dallas, University Press, Southern Methodist University, 1950.

7 pp.

Reprinted from the Spring 1950 issue of Southwest Review.

Incorporated in the new introduction to Guide to Life and Literature of the Southwest, 1952.

Bound in green paper covers, lettered in black.

Russell, Charles M. Seven Drawings. See B74.

1951

D43   Dobie, J. Frank.

      Charm in Mexican Folktales. [Austin, 1951]

cover-title, 8 pp.
Reprinted from Texas Folklore Society Publication
XXIV. The Healer of Los Olmos and Other Mexican Lore
Dallas, 1951.
Cover-title: A Christmas Remembrance, Bertha and
Frank Dobie, 1951.
Bound in light green paper covers, lettered in dark
green.

D44   ——— ———

      The Comanches and Their Horses. [Dallas, 1951]

[Reprinted from] Southwest Review [Spring 1951, Vol.
XXXVI, No. 2] pp. 99-103.

1952

D45   [Baker and Taylor Catalogue]

      Books for Christmas. Main Book Shop. Kerrville,
Texas [1952]

Books and Christmas. By J. Frank Dobie: pp. 2-3.

D46   Dobie, J. Frank.

      The Conservatism of Charles M. Russell. [Helena,
1952]

Reprinted from The Montana Magazine of History.
Vol. II—April, 1952.

D47   ——— ———

      Wild and Free—illustration by Gutzon Borglum.
Austin, 1952.

cover title, 1 leaf 3 pp.
Text from *The Mustangs*.
Here's wishing one and all good hearts and free minds
at this Christmas Time! Bertha and Frank Dobie, 1952.
Bound in grey paper covers, stamped in black.

1953

D48   ——— ———

      Stories of Christmas and the Bowie Knife. Austin,
Texas, The Steck Company [c1953]

v, 65 pp.

Illustrated by Warren Hunter.

Christmas greeting for 1953 . . . one that is typically
Texan - [from] The Steck Company.

Most of the third story . . . about Tim Cude and the
oxen - first appeared in *The Longhorns* . . . "James
Bowie and the Bowie Knife" first appeared in the Southwest Review, Vol. XVI, April, 1931.

Bound in maroon buckram stamped in silver, in light
gray board case.

D49   —— ——

A Plot of Earth. [Dallas?, 1953]

cover-title, 1 leaf, 12 pp.

Reprinted from Southwest Review, Spring, 1953, Dallas,
Texas.

Bertha and Frank Dobie, Christmas, 1953.

Bound in buff paper covers, design simulating leather,
lettered in brown.

D50   —— ——

Two Kind of People. [Pasadena, California, 1953]

1 leaf.

This is Number Three of the Southwest Broadsides. The
text is from "The Writer and his Region," Southwest Review, Spring 1950, and is printed now by Grant Dahlstrom
at the Castle Press in Pasadena, 1953, for the friends of
Lawrence Clark Powell.

Lea, Tom. Tom Lea: a Portfolio of Six Paintings.
See B92.

1954

D51   Dobie, J. Frank.

Babicora. By J. Frank Dobie. [Kansas City, Mo.,
1954]

cover-title, [9] pp.

Babicora ranch . . . was owned by William Randolph
Hearst.

Reprinted from The American Hereford Journal, January 1, 1954. Kansas City, Mo.

D52   —— ——

The Mezcla Man, by J. Frank Dobie. El Paso Del
Norte: 1954.

2 leaves, 11 pp., 1 leaf.

Christmas 1954 . . . Bertha and Frank Dobie.

Carl Hertzog, El Paso, Texas [printer]

The cover design was obtained by making prints from an adobe . . . Mud, straw and pebbles create textural design. [Covers are light terra cotta paper, lettered in terra cotta]

1955

D53 —— ——

As the Moving Finger Writ. [Dallas? 1955]

cover-title, 12 pp.

Reprinted from Southwest Review, Autumn, 1955, Dallas, Texas.

Christmas 1955.

Bound in salmon paper covers lettered in brown.

D54 —— ——

Between the Comanche and the Rattlesnake. Dallas, Southern Methodist University Press [1955?]

cover title [12] pp.

Drawings by Hal Story.

A Reprint from Southwest Review, Volume XL, number 1, Winter, 1955, Published by Southern Methodist University Press, Dallas, Texas.

Bound in tan paper covers lettered in brown.

D55 —— ——

Trans Pecos. [El Paso, 1955]

[4] pp.

This extract from A Vaquero of the Brush Country by J. Frank Dobie was printed by Carl Hertzog at El Paso del Norte as Number Nine of the Southwest Broadsides for the friends of Lawrence Clark Powell in the year of our Lord 1955.

1956

D56 —— ——

Brush Country. [Pasadena, California, 1956]

broadside.

This extract from A Vaquero of the Brush Country by J. Frank Dobie was printed in 1956 by Grant Dahlstrom at the Castle Press in Pasadena as Number 10 of the Southwest Broadsides, for the friends of Lawrence Clark Powell.

D57 —— ——

"His Looks and My Ways Would Hang Any Man".
[Dallas? 1956]

cover-title, 15 pp.

Bertha and Frank Dobie. On Waller Creek, Austin, Texas, Christmas 1956.

Reprinted from Southwest Review, Summer, 1956, Dallas, Texas.

D58 —— ——

An Informal Hour with J. Frank Dobie, Stories of the Southwest. [A phonograph record] Spoken Arts 722 [1956]

2 sides. 12 in. 33⅓ rpm.

Informal Hour Series.

Read by the author.

Big-foot Wallace and the Hickory Nuts. The "Mezcla" Man. Sancho, the Long-horned Steer. Bears Are Intelligent People.

D59 The Southwest Conference. The Literature and Art of the Southwest and Mexico. Occidental College, Los Angeles, California, March 23-24, 1956.

[2] 45 numbered leaves.

Mimeographed.

Address on "The Desert in Southwest Literature" by J. Frank Dobie . . . pp. 8-15.

Panel Discussion on "The Southwest: Regional Character of Its Literature" . . . J. Frank Dobie . . . pp. 18-19.

Panel Discussion on "Geography and Southwest Literature" . . . J. Frank Dobie . . . pp. 31-32, 34.

D60 The Texas Institute of Letters.

A Brief History and Directory of The Texas Institute of Letters. 1936-1956. [Dallas, 1956]

1 leaf, [12] pp.

A Personal Foreword. Signed: J. Frank Dobie: pp. [1-2]

The publication of this brochure has been made possible through the courtesy of Cokesbury Book Store.

The Texas Institute of Letters Seal appearing on the [green paper] cover was designed and drawn by Miss Anne Toomey of The Dallas Morning News.

1957

D61 Dobie, J. Frank.

The Archives Wars of Texas. By J. Frank Dobie. [Austin, 1957]

[4] pp.

D62   —— ——

Charlie Acquires A Burro. [Austin, 1957]

broadside.
Reprinted from The American-Statesman, Austin, Sunday, Nov. 3, 1957, p. C-3.

D63   —— ——

James Bowie, Big Dealer. [Austin, 1957]

cover-title, 23 pp.
Bertha and Frank Dobie . . . Austin, Texas. Christmas 1957.
Reprinted from The Southwestern Historical Quarterly, Volume LX, No. 3, January 1957.
Bound in illustrated red paper covers stamped in black.

D64   Trigg-Russell Memorial Gallery, Great Falls, Montana.

Bronzes of Ch. Russell, On Exhibit Trigg-Russell Memorial Gallery, Great Falls, Montana, 1957.

cover-title, 24 pp.
An Appreciation. Signed J. Frank Dobie, Austin, Texas: p. 2.

1958

D65   Dobie, J. Frank.

Tom Gilroy's Fiddle. [Austin, 1958]

cover-title, 2 leaves, [8] pp.
. . . Merry Christmas! Bertha and Frank Dobie. On Waller Creek, Austin, Texas, 1958.
Designed by Jo Alys Downs.

D66   Jack Frost Ranches.

Bullmanac, 1958. [Dallas, 1958]

cover-title, 72 pp.
Jim Williams and Out Our Way, by J. Frank Dobie.
Reprinted from Cowboys Out Our Way . . . with permission of Charles Scribner's Sons: pp. 39-42.

D67   Natural Food and Farming Digest. Number Two. [Atlanta, Texas, c1958]

cover-title, [2], 5-146 pp.
Natural Taste for Natural Milk. By J. Frank Dobie: pp. 41-42.

D68   Reynolds, J. E., Bookseller.

The American West. Catalogue 50. Van Nuys, California, Fall 1958.

unpaged.
1381 items listed.
On Reading Book Catalogues, by J. Frank Dobie: [2] pp. at front.

D69   Smithsonian Institution. National Collection of Fine Arts.

Montana's Cowboy Artist. [Washington, 1958]

cover-title, 96 pp.
Official Program . . . October 12-November 2, 1958.
The Conservatism of Charles M. Russell, by J. Frank Dobie: pp. 57-63.

1959

D70   Dobie, J. Frank.

"When Work's All Done This Fall." Berkeley, Calif., University of California Press, 1959.

pp. 323-326.
Western Folklore a Reprint from volume XVIII, October, 1959, number 4, Berkeley and Los Angeles, Published for the California Folklore Society by the University of California Press.
Reprinted, with the permission of the Editor, from the San Antonio Light, June 28, 1959.
In tan paper covers.

D71   Powell, Lawrence Clark, editor.

The Southwest of the Bookman; Essays from Various Sources. Los Angeles, University of California Library, 1959.

[1] 60 leaves.
UCLA Library Occasional Paper Number 11, 1959.
Books and Christmas. J. Frank Dobie: pp. 40-45, Southwest Review, Winter, 1951.

1960

D72   The American Scene.

The Works of C. M. Russell in the Gilcrease Institute of American History, Tulsa, Oklahoma. [Tulsa, 1960]

27 pp.

Special issue of the American Scene, Vol. 3, No. 2, Summer, 1960.

The Art of Charles Russell, by J. Frank Dobie: p. 3.

D73   Antiquarian Press, Ltd.

Announces the republication of . . . The Cattle Industry of Texas. [New York, 1960]

cover title, 6 pp.

James Cox and His Cattle Industry, by J. Frank Dobie.

This printing of the introduction was distributed as an advertisement for the book, January, 1960.

Illustrated paper covers.

D74   Dobie, J. Frank.

Change, Change, Change. [Austin, 1960]

1 leaf.

Reprinted from The Texas Observer, v. 51, No. 40, Jan. 8, 1959 [i.e. 1960]

D75   —— ——

J. Frank Dobie Tells The Ghost Bull of the Mavericks and Other Tales. [A phonograph record] Domino Records [1960]

2 sides. 12-in. 33⅓ rpm.

Read by the author.

The Ghost Bull of the Mavericks. The Dream That Saved Wilbarger. Diamond Bill, Confederate Ally. Too Much Pepper. Drouthed Out.

D76   Reynolds, J. E., Bookseller.

Catalogue 58, June 1960; A Treasure Hunter's Catalogue Dedicated to C. P. E. Charles P. Everitt 1873-1951. With Reminiscences of Four Friends. Van Nuys, California [1960]

unpaged.

Charles P. Everitt, Bookman, by J. Frank Dobie: pp. [3-5]

1961

D77   Austin Public Library.

Notes and Anecdotes from the Austin Public Library to Its Friends, July 1, 1961. [Austin, 1961]

broadside.

The American Library Association . . . cover of its Bulletin . . . quotation from J. Frank Dobie . . . See also C475.

D78   Dobie, J. Frank.

Ella Byler Dobie and Christmas. [Austin, 1961]

broadside
[Reprinted from] The American-Statesman Sunday, Dec. 24, 1961.

D79   —— ——

Storytellers I Have Known. [Austin, 1961]

29 pp.
Reprinted from Singers and Storytellers, Texas Folklore Society Publication XXX: 1961, Southern Methodist University Press, Dallas, Texas.

Christmas . . . Bertha and Frank Dobie. On Waller Creek, Austin, Texas, 1961.

Bound in salmon paper covers, stamped in black and dark green.

D80   Reynolds, J. E., Bookseller.

The West of Ross Santee. Catalogue 66. Van Nuys, California, Fall 1961.

unpaged.
370 items listed.
Ross Santee — His "Cowboy", by J. Frank Dobie: pp. [6-7]

1962

D81   Dobie, J. Frank.

E. Douglas Branch, Singularisimo. [Dallas, 1962]

cover-title, [10] pp.
300 copies, reprinted from Southwest Review, Volume XLVII, Number 2, Spring, 1962.
Published by Southern Methodist University Press, Dallas, Texas.

D82   —— ——

A Schoolteacher in Alpine. [Austin?, 1962]

cover-title, 11 pp.
Reprinted from Southwest Review, Autumn, 1962, Dallas, Texas.
It's Christmas Time . . . Bertha and Frank Dobie. On Waller Creek, Austin, Texas, 1962.
Bound in green paper covers, lettered in dark green.

D83   International Bookfinders.

The Range Country, Literature of the American Cattle Trade. Catalogue Number 112. Beverly Hills, California [November 1962]

Range Life, Cowboys, Cattle and Sheep. By J. Frank Dobie: pp. [5-18]

1963

D84   Dobie, J. Frank.

Hunting Cousin Sally. [Austin, 1963]

cover-title, 14 pp.
Cover drawing by William D. Wittliff.
Reprinted from Southwest Review, Summer, 1963, Southern Methodist University Press, Dallas, Texas.
Bertha and Frank Dobie . . . Austin, Texas, Christmas, 1963.
Bound in blue paper covers, stamped in bright blue.

D85   —— ——

Out of Original Rock. [Denver, 1963]

10 pp.
Folded map of Southeast Texas following p. [2] photograph of the author p. [6]
Reprinted from the 1962 Brand Book of the Denver Posse of the Westerners, edited by John J. Lipsey, Denver, Colorado, 1963.
Bound in blue paper covers, lettered in black.

D86   Statewide Texas Salute to United States Senator Ralph W. Yarborough. [Municipal Auditorium, Austin, Texas, Saturday, October 19, 1963, Seven-thirty o'clock. Austin, 1963]

unpaged.
Caption title: Texas Salute, an Appreciation Dinner honoring United States Senator Ralph W. Yarborough, Program . . .
Illustrated by portraits and facsimiles.
Salute to Senator Ralph Yarborough: [1] p. Signed: J. Frank Dobie.
Bound in white paper covers, stamped in black, with a map of Texas across back and front covers.

The Humanities Research Center, The University of Texas

Russell Lee

Sunday Newspaper Column

The author's titles for the stories and articles printed, with varying titles, in the newspapers listed at the beginning of each year:

1939

Dallas Morning News.
Houston Post.

E1   Dying Ranchman's Wish-To-Hear
Texas Bull 'Beller' Down Canyon.   September 3, 1939
    In *The Longhorns.*

E2   Texas Longhorn and a
Shorthorn Library.   September 10, 1939

E3   Texas State Historical Association.   September 17, 1939

E4   Oxen Not "Dumb as an Ox"   September 24, 1939

E5   Haley's Proposed Texas
Range Museum.   October 1, 1939

E6   The Texian Kind of Neutrality.   October 8, 1939

E7   Alonzo Mitchell, of Lampasas,
Trail Driver.   October 15, 1939
    In *The Longhorns.*

E8   Roadrunner in Fact and Folklore.   October 22, 1939
    See also E97.

E9   The Word Maverick.   October 29, 1939
    In *The Longhorns.*

E10   The Maverick Branded Murder.   November 5, 1939
    In *The Longhorns.*

E11   Don Victoriana Chapa, Last of
the Longhorn Rancheros.   November 12, 1939
    In *The Longhorns.*

E12   Coppini's Alamo Monument.   November 19, 1939

E13   Essay on Folk-Lore.   November 26, 1939

E14   Texas Folk-Lore Society.   December 3, 1939

E15   Texas Game, Fish and Oyster
       Commission and Will Tucker.   December 10, 1939

E16   A Boot Full of Letters, on Coppini,
       Texan Flora, Rattlesnakes.   December 17, 1939

E17   John C. Duval, Texas Writer.   December 24, 1939
       In *John C. Duval: First Texas Man
       of Letters.*

E18   Outlaws of the Range.   December 31, 1939
       In *The Longhorns.*

1940

Austin Tribune, January 7-May 26, 1940.
Dallas Morning News.
Houston Post.
San Antonio Light.

E19   Sancho—the Returning Steer.   January 7, 1940
       In *The Longhorns.*

E20   "Pup," the Cow Dog.   January 14, 1940

E21   Strange Animals Roped in the Night
       [Yarns of Brush]   January 21, 1940
       In *The Longhorns.*

E22   God Loves a Cheerful Liar—
       Fendley Simpson.   January 28, 1940

E23   The Brush Country.   February 4, 1940
       In *The Longhorns.*

E24   Jack Thorp's Grizzly Story.   February 11, 1940

E25   Koss Barry and Other
       Bosque Co. Texians.   February 18, 1940

E26   Trapped by She-Bear
       [Frank Bryan story]   February 25, 1940

E27   Old Time Beef-Eating Texans.   March 3, 1940
       In *The Longhorns.*

E28   Texas Art and a Wagon Sheet
       [H. Wallace Caylor]   March 10, 1940

E29   Rawhide.   March 17, 1940

E30   Tending to Own Business—
       Code—Tally Story.   March 24, 1940

E31   The Line That Travis Drew.   March 31, 1940

E32	Hidden in a Drouth Crack [Treasure Story]	April 7, 1940
E33	Longhorn Bull Fight. In *The Longhorns.*	April 14, 1940
E34	San Jacinto Corn.	April 21, 1940
E35	El Paso and Ben Lilly. In *The Ben Lilly Legend.*	April 28, 1940
E36	Texas Culture— The Proposed Texas Center.	May 5, 1940
E37	Coyote Stories. In *The Voice of the Coyote.*	May 12, 1940
E38	Coyote Stories. In *The Voice of the Coyote.*	May 19, 1940
E39	Coyote Stories. In *The Voice of the Coyote.*	May 26, 1940
E40	Out of the Melting Pot Into the Fire.	June 2, 1940
E41	Coyote Stories. In *The Voice of the Coyote.*	June 9, 1940
E42	Coyote Stories. In *The Voice of the Coyote.*	June 16, 1940
E43	Morality in Killing.	June 23, 1940
E44	Pacing White Steed of Onion Creek. In *The Mustangs.*	June 30, 1940
E45	Pitching Horses of Range and Rodeo.	July 7, 1940
E46	What Horse Names Tell.	July 14, 1940
E47	The Old Menger Hotel.	July 21, 1940
E48	Mustangs That Preferred Death to Capture. In *The Mustangs.*	July 28, 1940
E49	O. Henry's Treasure Hunt.	August 4, 1940
E50	As Smart as a Cutting Horse.	August 11, 1940
E51	Clabe Robinson's Story of Horse. In *The Mustangs.*	August 18, 1940
E52	Traveling Over the Country— Jacksboro, Art in Amarillo.	August 25, 1940
E53	Man of Soil and His Apache Story [Peter Hurd's Ranch]	September 1, 1940
E54	Bear Moore, Grizzly Hater.	September 8, 1940
E55	The Road East from El Paso— Highway Civilization.	September 15, 1940

E56	Castles in Spain [Mexican folk tales] and Education.	September 22, 1940
E57	Roy Bean Stories.	September 29, 1940
E58	California Grizzly [Lewis B. Miller story]	October 6, 1940
E59	Texans Uphold Their Tradition as Fighters [Capt. Lee Hall]	October 13, 1940
E60	Texas Poetry-Being Reminded.	October 20, 1940
E61	Frank Bryan's Canebrake Story.	October 27, 1940
E62	Texas Christmas Cards.	November 3, 1940
E63	Northers and Norther Stories.	November 10, 1940
E64	A Texan in Montana [Marcus Snyder]	November 17, 1940
E65	Texas Historical Markers Hit.	November 24, 1940
E66	Good Cheer and Good Eating— Mogollon Mountain Hunger [A Hunter's Hunger]	December 1, 1940
E67	Old Blue, Goodnight's Lead Steer. In *The Longhorns*.	December 8, 1940
E68	The Cowboy as Courtier.	December 15, 1940
E69	The Christmas Coming of Tim Cude. In *The Longhorns*.	December 22, 1940
E70	New Year's and Old Cows.	December 29, 1940

1941

Beeville-Bee Picayune.
Dallas Morning News.
Houston Post.
San Antonio Light.

E71	The Art of Trailing. In *The Longhorns*.	January 5, 1941
E72	Talk Among the Folks at Home.	January 12, 1941
E73	Reading Sign. In *The Longhorns*.	January 19, 1941
E74	Old Time Circuit Riders. [John Wesley DeVilbiss]	January 26, 1941
E75	John W. Thomason's Lone Star Preacher.	February 2, 1941
E76	Mesquite.	February 9-16, 1941

E77	Tom Gilroy's Fiddler and Cowboy Dance.	February 23, 1941
E78	Davy Crockett and the Alamo.	March 2, 1941
E79	The Texas Bluebonnet.	March 9, 1941
E80	The Fiddler and the Wolves. In *On the Open Range*.	March 16, 1941
E81	Razorback Lore.	March 23, 1941
E82	Rain and Prayers for Rain.	March 30, 1941
E83	Southwestern Literature Enriches Home.	April 6, 1941
E84	Textbook Racket; Native Flora.	April 13, 1941
E85	Catfish Heroes.	April 20, 1941
E86	Texas Place Names.	April 27-May 4, 1941
E87	Razorback Heroes, Carlos Ashley's "Ballad of Cedar Mountain."	May 11, 1941
E88	Staked Plains: Origin and Power of Name.	May 18, 1941
E89	Pie Biter - Folk Hero.	May 25, 1941
E90	Jim Ballard's Smart Dogs.	June 1, 1941
E91	The Ferocious Javelina. From *Lazy E*. 342, 1941.	June 8, 1941
E92	Boyce House's Drama of Oil.	June 15, 1941
E93	Grandpa Didn't Sing Anthems.	June 22, 1941
E94	Rattlesnake-Guarded Treasure [Longworth legend]	June 29, 1941
E95	Texan Bragging in Reverse "Hell in Texas."	July 6, 1941
E96	Marques de Aguayo's Ride. In *Apache Gold and Yaqui Silver*.	July 13, 1941
E97	The Stranger of Sabine Pass [Longworth legend]	July 20, 1941
E98	Roadrunner, Our Fellow Citizen. See also E8.	July 27, 1941
E99	Tarantula Lore.	August 3, 1941
E100	The Fearful Leap. Ad Lawrence, Bender's Leap in Karnes County; Frank Mitchell's story from *The Longhorns*.	August 10, 1941

E101   Bears Are Very Intelligent People.   August 17, 1941
        Worth Ray's Bear story; Don Santiago
        Blanco in *Tongues of the Monte.*

E102   Buffalo Hunter and His Song
        [J. B. Freeman's Damned
        Old Buffalo Skinners]   August 24, 1941

E103   The Cowboy Who Befriended a Judge
        [Bob Castlebury's story]   August 31, 1941

E104   Patriots and Patriotism
        [with respects to Senator O'Daniel]   September 7, 1941

E105   Smart Coyote Shows
        His Smartness.   September 14, 1941
        Stories from Pete Gimson and Ernest
        Thompson Seton, etc. in
        The Voice of the Coyote.

E106   Brave Boys and Brave Men.   September 21, 1941

E107   Devil's Horse and Humming Bird.   September 28, 1941

E108   Mexican Morality Stories [Siete con
        un golpe; Frank Goodwyn's story]   October 5, 1941

E109   Texan Patriotism Yarns [From Pat
        Nixon, Frank Bryan, etc.]   October 12, 1941

E110   Bigfoot Wallace and Hickory Nuts.   October 19, 1941

E111   Andy Adams, Cowboy Chronicler.   October 26, 1941

E112   The Indian's Secret [J. D. Talley's story
        of San Marcos; Santa Fe trader]   November 2, 1941

E113   Clay Allison of the Washita.   November 9, 1941

E114   Crows.   November 16, 1941

E115   Rascal at His Worst.   November 23, 1941

E116   Frozen Inside Buffalo Hide.   November 30, 1941

E117   Wild Turkeys: Migrations of.   December 7, 1941

E118   After Pearl Harbor.   December 14, 1941

E119   "Daniel Boone," Great Wild Gobbler. December 21, 1941
        In *On the Ppen Range.*

E120   Amazing Gallantry for
        1942 Predicted.   December 28, 1941

1942

        Beeville-Bee Picayune.
        Dallas Morning News.
        Houston Post.
        San Antonio Light.

E121 In Defense of Polecats. January 4, 1942

E122 Ray Ranch, How It Was Founded. January 11, 1942

E123 Old Bostick's Horde of Gold. January 18, 1942

E124 Pablo Romero Roped Star Breast. January 25, 1942
In *On the Open Range.*

E125 Books for Army Camp Libraries. February 1, 1942

E126 Do Rattlers Swallow Their Young? February 8, 1942

E127 War Time. Wake Up. February 15, 1942

E128 How the People Look at War. February 22, 1942

E129 Snakes Do Swallow Their Young. March 1, 1942

E130 "Defense Will Not Win the War."
Let Us Shoot. March 8, 1942

E131 Time to Understand Russia
["Mission to Moscow"] March 15, 1942

E132 Shamefulness of O'Daniel Triviality.
Goliad Massacre. March 22, 1942

E133 Books in Camp; Franco in Mexico. March 29, 1942

E134 The Jeepy Jackrabbit. April 5, 1942

E135 Dale's Cowboy Yarns in Cow Country. April 12, 1942

E136 Remember the Alamo Battle Cry. April 19, 1942

E137 "Thermopylae Had Her
Messenger of Defeat." April 26, 1942

E138 Medicine Plant Garden at Austin. May 3, 1942

E139 Mothers of Fighting Men. May 10, 1942

E140 Gid Lincecum, Individualist. May 17, 1942

E141 Bee Hunters and Wild Honey. May 24, 1942

E142 Lost Honey Mines in Texas. May 31, 1942

E143 Traditions of Texas Gathered by
Women Students at Denton. June 7, 1942

E144 Honey in the Rock
[More Honey Mine Yarns] June 14, 1942

E145 We Fight Germany, Not Just Hitler:
O'Daniel Indifference. June 21, 1942

E146 The Mustang Grape. June 28, 1942

E147 John Booth's Great Ride. July 5, 1942
From *Flavor of Texas.*

E148   Fighting Tradition of Texas; O'Daniel;
        Bigfoot Wallace; Pleasanton Oak.   July 12, 1942

E149   Pet Coyote, by Nina Sue Taylor.   July 19, 1942
        In *The Voice of the Coyote.*

E150   Cuff, Ranch Dog
        [by Sol Wright in *My Rambles*]   July 26, 1942

E151   Fighting Texas Rangers
        [Life of Captain John R. Hughes]   August 2, 1942

E152   Cowboy Preacher [W. S. James and
        his *Cowboy Life in Texas*]   August 9, 1942

E153   Picture of Fascist in Texas
        [with Stanley Walker]   August 16, 1942

E154   The Mezcla Man.   August 23, 1942
        In *On the Open Range.*

E155   Snake Swallowing.   August 30, 1942

E156   Chuck Wagon [O. E. Brewster]   September 6, 1942

E157   Ab Blocker's Trail Cook
        [Frank Smith]   September 13, 1942

E158   Early Day Surgery.   September 20, 1942

E159   Ed Nichols Drove
        Horses to Kansas.   September 27, 1942

E160   Owl Wisdom - What He Says.
        See also E164 and E168.

E161   Total War.   October 11, 1942

E162   Mountain Sheep Extinction
        in Texas.   October 18, 1942

E163   Texan Pride and Patriotism.   October 25, 1942

E164   Owl Talk.   November 1, 1942
        See also E160 and E168.

E165   Fighting Men, Their Parents,
        O'Daniel.   November 8, 1942

E166   Cowboy Humor [J. E. McCauley's
        Story of pudding]   November 15, 1942

E167   The British and Their Empire
        [vs. Willkie]   November 22, 1942

E168   Owls, Men and Chickens.   November 29, 1942
        See also E160 and E168.

E169   What a Texas Seaman [Johnny
        Faulk] Saw in England.   December 6, 1942

E170   Deer Hunting - Luck vs. Skill.   December 13, 1942

| E171 | We People at Home - Steven's Promotion of Disunity. | December 20, 1942 |
| E172 | Panther as Friend of Man. | December 27, 1942 |

1943

Austin American-Statesman.
Dallas Morning News.
Houston Post.
San Antonio Light.

E173	1943 Taking Stock of Trust and Distrust ["He'll Do to Ride the River With"]	January 3, 1943
E174	Texas Norther 102 Years Ago.	January 10, 1943
E175	Northers to Brag About.	January 17, 1943
E176	Strange Friendships in Animal World.	January 24, 1943
E177	A Man's Bound To Think.	January 31, 1943
E178	The Tale of the Two Companions.	February 7, 1943
E179	Old Igo's Bookkeeping Was Simple.	February 14, 1943
E180	Divided We Stand.	February 21, 1943
E181	Cowboy Philosophy of Freedom.	February 28, 1943
E182	Loyalty of Comrades in Arms to Each Other.	March 7, 1943
E183	Greatest of All the Grizzlies.	March 14, 1943
E184	Dan Moody's Story of War.	March 21, 1943
E185	Old Bill, Confederate Ally.	March 28, 1943
E186	Take It but Don't Name It.	April 4, 1943
E187	Alligator Stories [Texans Who Have Associated Intimately with Alligators]	April 11, 1943
E188	A Boy, A Girl and Two Cows.	April 18, 1943
E189	Wild Turkey: "General Sam Houston"	April 25, 1943
E190	Long Lance's Story of Wolf Brother. Condensed in *The Voice of the Coyote.*	May 2, 1943
E191	Alligators Fight: Egged on by People of Goebbels Method.	May 9, 1943
E192	Authentic Liars.	May 16, 1943
E193	Nat Straw's Saddle Bear.	May 23, 1943
E194	Commencement Oration on Texas That Nobody Made.	May 30, 1943

E195   Out of the Books
[stories from current books]   June 6, 1943

E196   Sam Houston and
Sam Houston Stories.   June 13, 1943

E197   Ben Lilly in Texas.   June 20, 1943
In *The Ben Lilly Legend*.

E198   Sentry in the Night - - Headless Ghosts.   June 27, 1943

E199   Ben Lilly, Lion Hunter.   July 4, 1943
In *The Ben Lilly Legend*.

E200   Esau the Hunter.   July 11, 1943
In *The Ben Lilly Legend*.

E201   Ben Lilly—Philosopher-Hunter.   July 18, 1943
In *The Ben Lilly Legend*.

E202   Ben Lilly's Bear Story for Children.   July 25, 1943
In *The Ben Lilly Legend*.

E203   Regents Purging University of Texas.   August 1, 1943

E204   Ben Lilly—A Pretty Fair Shot.   August 8, 1943
In *The Ben Lilly Legend*.

E205   Colonel Calvert's Story of Bear
Dancing Partner.   August 15, 1943

E206   A Texas Seaman and His
Labor Union.   August 22, 1943

E207   Ben Lilly and Practical Jokes.   August 29, 1943
In *The Ben Lilly Legend*.

E208   Ben Lilly, Bear Killer.   September 5, 1943
In *The Ben Lilly Legend*.

E209   Ben Lilly, Keeper of Sabbath.   September 12, 1943
In *The Ben Lilly Legend*.

E210   Public Thoughts, out of Letters—
War and Politics.   September 19, 1943

E211   Davy Crockett's Rifle.   September 26, 1943

E212   Headless Rider in Oklahoma.   October 3, 1943
In *On the Open Range*.

E213   On Way to England
[from New York]   October 10, 1943

E214   Waiting for Plane with Grandpa
[New York]   October 17, 1943

E215   Panther Stories—Panther's Tail.   October 24, 1943

E216   Camp Cooks.   October 31, 1943

E217   Panther, Friend of Man.   November 7, 1943

E218 Plane Trip Across Ocean—
Landed in Ireland. November 14, 1943

E219 Wartime Encounters in
England—Snuff. November 21, 1943

E220 Dobie Wants Travel in Ireland,
Where Shannon River Flows, To
Be Close to Earth of Famous
Emerald Island. November 28, 1943

E221 Tom Paine and His Fortress. December 5, 1943

E222 Two Lords and a Dog. December 12, 1943
In *A Texan in England.*

E223 Glimpses of American Soldiers
in England. December 19, 1943

E224 Voices in the Dark. December 26, 1943
In *A Texan in England.*

1944

Austin American-Statesman.
Dallas Morning News.
Houston Post.
San Antonio Light.

Although released simultaneously, some of the papers
published the same article on different dates.

E225 Trafalgar Square, Girton College
Party, Brains Trust. January 2, 1944

E226 The Right Medicine for
Skunk Bite. January 9, 1944

E227 Kind Hearts [Christmas in
Cambridge] January 16, 1944

E228 Texans in England. January 23, 1944

E229 One of Ours—Bomber
Attack on London. January 30, 1944
In *A Texan in England.*

E230 Jeb Stuart and Another Soldier
and Gentleman. February 6, 1944

E231 General Ples Rogers and London. February 13, 1944

E232 Haircuts and Sergeants. February 20, 1944

E233 In the Country—Farming. February 27, 1944

E234 Americans in England. March 5, 1944

E235 College Life, English. March 12, 1944

E236 The Fens. March 19, 1944

E237	Youth Conferences— Thought in Democracy.	March 26, 1944
E238	Earthworms in the House of Lords.	April 2, 1944
E239	Bill Robinson and War on Home Front in America—Flak Happy.	April 9, 1944
E240	Mary the Rebel.	April 16, 1944
E241	The English and Their Soil— Reality in Discussions.	April 23, 1944
E242	Characteristics of English Character. In *A Texan in England*.	April 30, 1944
E243	Texas Soldiers on England and Closed Minds.	May 7, 1944
E244	In Wales. In *A Texan in England*	May 14, 1944
E245	Scotland. In *A Texan in England*.	May 21, 1944
E246	Edinburgh— Col. John W. Thomason.	May 28- June 4, 1944
E247	England in April. In *A Texan in England*.	June 11, 1944
E248	Cheshire.	June 18, 1944
E249	Newmarket Races and Other Features of the Week.	June 25, 1944
E250	D-Day: English Steadiness.	July 2, 1944
E251	Emancipated Minds—American Soldiers—Cambridge Ceremony.	July 9, 1944
E252	Summer Fireside Contemplation.	July 16, 1944
E253	British Remembrance. In *A Texan in England*.	July 23, 1944
E254	Sundials and the Sea.	July 30, 1944
E255	Kew in Pilotless-Bomber Time. In *A Texan in England*.	August 6, 1944
E256	Other Men's Flowers: Quotations from Letters.	August 13, 1944
E257	Forests—Nelson's Ship at Portsmouth.	August 20, 1944
E258	English Conservatism in Machines— Anglo-American Drumhead.	August 27, 1944
E259	Ban on Papers in American Bases.	September 3, 1944
E260	Gauchos in Hudson and Graham.	September 10, 1944

E261	American Soldier Views.	September 17, 1944
E262	Talk in Combination Room.	September 24, 1944
E263	English Remembrance of Their Dead.	October 1, 1944

In *A Texan in England.*

E264	Views on Russia.	October 8, 1944
E265	American Cemetery at Cambridge: Labor Views.	October 15, 1944
E266	Notes on What's in British Mind.	October 22, 1944
E267	Dim Lights Come On. Daily Occurences.	October 29, 1944
E268	English Pubs.	November 5, 1944

In *A Texan in England.*

E269	Winant; Tommy Atkins.	November 12, 1944
E270	Trip to Bristol.	November 19, 1944
E271	Trip Home on Queen Elizabeth.	November 26, 1944
E272	Back Home. Two Mysteries— Sinatra and Vs. Communism.	December 3, 1944
E273	Letters Quoted.	December 10, 1944
E274	Old Waddies and Academic Freedom.	December 17, 1944
E275	A Boy and His Horse [Christmas Story]	December 24, 1944

In *The Mustangs.*

| E276 | Elrich's Advice; Harmony
with Nature. | December 31, 1944 |

1945

Austin American-Statesman.
Brownsville Herald, January 7-May 27, 1945.
Dallas Morning News.
Houston Post.
San Antonio Light.
Valley Evening Monitor, McAllen, Texas.

E277	Port Isabel Unaware of Currents in History.	January 7, 1945
E278	Padre Island; Frank Norflet Stories.	January 14, 1945
E279	China Berries and Mistletoe Berries.	January 21, 1945
E280	Coyote Lore in Brownsville.	January 28, 1945

In *The Voice of the Coyote.*

E281	George Taylor's "Fox and Goose" Story; Coyote Analogue.	February 4, 1945
E282	Grey of Fallodon and W. H. Page on World War I.	February 11, 1945
E283	Letters from Soldiers and Other War Matters.	February 18, 1945
E284	"Tranquility in Texas," Regents Say.	February 25, 1945
E285	Five Touches of Nature: Cowmen, Panthers, Robins, Crows.	March 4, 1945
E286	Panther Attacks on Man; Panther Stories.	March 11, 1945
E287	Advance of Negroes.	March 18, 1945
E288	Panhandle Plains Historical Society Records, etc.	March 25, 1945
E289	Reaction in U. S.	April 1, 1945
E290	Trip to Zapata Country with Bob Snow: Rattlesnakes.	April 8-15, 1945
E291	Roosevelt Dead: "Rendezvous with Destiny."	April 22, 1945
E292	Miscellany from Letters— Jesse James Story.	April 29, 1945
E293	Mustang Cattle in Mustang, Texas.	May 6, 1945
E294	The Accents of History [against Trivial Banalities]	May 13, 1945
E295	The Sergeant Has Ideas. [Quoting Bob Jourdan]	May 20, 1945
E296	Review of Hart Stilwell's Border City.	May 27, 1945
E297	Out of England. Stories of Escaped Fliers, etc.	June 3, 1945
E298	The Sergeant Talks Mules. [Jack Whitehead in India]	June 10, 1945
E299	Rich in Time. [Tempo of Bell Ranch and Waller, Texas]	June 17, 1945
E300	Contemptible Fear of Russia.	June 24, 1945
E301	Bullsnake Pets.	July 1, 1945
E302	Signs of Awareness in Texas.	July 8, 1945

E303	The Charm of Bullbats, Swifts, Swallows.	July 15, 1945
E304	Greed; Nature's Healing.	July 22, 1945
E305	Idiotic Army Ways at New York Port of Embarkation.	July 29, 1945
E306	In New York Waiting To Go to England. Negro Folk Tale.	August 5, 1945
E307	Jack Thorp's Horse Stories. [Review of his *Pardner of Wind*] In *The Mustangs*.	August 12, 1945
E308	Aboard Queen Elizabeth: Lord Halifax on Texans, etc.	August 19, 1945
E309	GI University in England [Shrivenham]	August 26, 1945
E310	British Tommy; English Stories of American Geenerosity.	September 2, 1945
E311	Thanksgiving Services in St. Pauls, London.	September 9, 1945
E312	Shakespeare at Stratford and the Flower Show.	September 16, 1945
E313	America's Chance at Greatness.	September 23, 1945
E314	English Newspapers Reflect National Characteristics.	September 30, 1945
E315	Dogs and Sense of Smell [Montague Stevens' *Meet Mr. Grizzly*]	October 7, 1945
E316	Alert Minded GI Students.	October 14, 1945
E317	"Spiritual Content" [London]	October 21, 1945
E318	Reflections; Long Quotation from Lincolnshire Woman.	October 28, 1945
E319	English Pub Signs, Humor, Anecdotes.	November 4, 1945
E320	You Can't Build a Wall against Ideas; English Book Stores.	November 11, 1945
E321	Atomic Capsules.	November 18, 1945
E322	Miscellany of Stuff, English and American.	November 25, 1945
E323	"Silly Suffolk" Revisited— the Whitings.	December 2, 1945
E324	Fatal Embraces of the Wild.	December 9, 1945

E325	The Habit of Nobility— Eisenhower.	December 16, 1945
E326	English Fair Play, etc.	December 23, 1945
E327	Tolerance, etc. [Miscellany]	December 30, 1945

1946

Austin American-Statesman.
Dallas Morning News. Published the column
   only occasionally.
Houston Post.
San Antonio Light.
Valley Evening Monitor, McAllen, Texas.

E328	Sympathy for Nature Reflected in British Papers.	January 6, 1946
E329	Museum in London and Reflections on Texas.	January 13, 1946
E330	British Economy and the Proposed Loan to Britain.	January 20, 1946
E331	Cheerful England.	January 27, 1946
E332	Christmas in Paris	February 3, 1946
E333	Going to Germany with the Army.	February 10, 1946
E334	Frankfurt; German Life.	February 17, 1946
E335	Traveling in Germany, Heidelberg, Augsburg, Munich.	February 24, 1946
E336	Letter from Vienna.	March 3, 1946
E337	In Austria.	March 10, 1946
E338	"La Paloma" in Munich.	March 17, 1946
E339	German Military Spirit in Common Life [Munich]	March 24, 1946
E340	From Heidelberg; Dachau.	March 31, 1946
E341	Visit to German Prisoners. U. S. Army Not Educating Germany.	April 7, 1949
E342	In Berlin.	April 14-21, 1946
E343	Nuremberg and the Trials.	April 28, 1946
E344	From Wurzburg. German Politics and Schools; Catholic Church.	May 5, 1946
E345	In the Bremen Enclave.	May 12, 1946
E346	Not Rotten in Denmark.	May 19, 1946
E347	Train Riding in Germany.	May 26, 1946

E348	Visit to German Farms and Farm Area.	June 2, 1946
E349	France, after Germany, French Trees Seem Free.	June 9, 1946
E350	In England Again.	June 16, 1946
E351	Voyage to America from Le Havre. Color Brightness in New York.	June 23, 1946
E352	Notes on State of Civilization in Texas.	June 30, 1946
E353	Jack Rabbits.	July 7, 1946
E354	Cattle Brands and Horns. Stories from Hubbard in Cal. Pen.	July 14, 1946
E355	They All Want To Be Free [Mules, Turkeys, etc.] In *The Mustangs*.	July 21, 1946
E356	Buffalo Bill, Last of the Men on Horseback.	July 28, 1946
E357	Salty Sayings. Mody Boatright's Search for Them.	August 4, 1946
E358	Charlie Russell Didn't Want to Be Crowded.	August 11, 1946
E359	Charlie Russell, Individualist.	August 18, 1946
E360	Goldfinches in Iowa Corn.	August 25, 1946
E361	Notes on Minnesota.	September 1, 1946
E362	Denis Brogan in America.	September 8, 1946
E363	Balls of Rattlesnakes.	September 15, 1946
E364	I Heard the Owl a-Hooting.	September 22, 1946
E365	The Greedy Arab and the Old Physician [Mexican Folklore]	September 29, 1946
E366	UNESCO—Lets Try UNESCO.	October 6, 1946
E367	In America's Two Capitals [New York and Washington]	October 13, 1946
E368	The Old Peon's Story of Fidelity [from Parral, Chihuahua]	October 20, 1946
E369	On the Ranch Gallery—Book I'd like to Write. Rocky Reagan.	October 27, 1946
E370	Cat and Rattlesnake [Story from H. B. Parks]	November 3, 1946

E371   New Mexico Publishes
        on Wild Life.   November 10, 1946

E372   Mocking Birds and Rattlesnakes.   November 17, 1946

E373   When Coyotes Were
        Medicine Wolves.   November 24, 1946
            In *The Voice of the Coyote.*

E374   Eagle and Rattlesnake.   December 1, 1946
7375   Along the Deer-Hunting Way—
        Natures Aside.   December 8, 1946

E376   Visit to Luke Stillwill's Home.   December 15, 1946
            Trapper in *The Voice of the Coyote.*

E377   Christmas Letter: A Story;
        A hyme; A Thought.   December 22, 1946

E378   Is It a Fact? Queries on Nature
        Beliefs; Barnes' Story of Cottontail
        and Coach Whip Snake.   December 29, 1946

                        1947

        Austin American-Statesman.
        Dallas Morning News. Published the
            column only occasionally.
        San Antonio Light.
        Valley Evening Monitor, McAllen, Texas.

E379   Javalinas and Rattlesnakes.
        [from Herne, *Perils and Pleasures
        of a Hunter's Life*]   January 5, 1947

E380   Luke Stillwell [trapper] and Old
        Crip [coyote]   January 12, 1947
            In *The Voice of the Coyote.*

E381   Ranchmen Sentiment for Horses.   January 19, 1947

E382   Coyote Fluency [in voice]   January 26, 1947
            In *The Voice of the Coyote.*

E383   Sam Bass Stories.   February 2-9, 1947

E384   Life in Devils River Country.   February 16, 1947

E385   How Pecos Bill and Paul Bunyan
        Stories Started. [Jim Dan Hill]   February 23, 1947

E386   What the Coyote Says.   March 2, 1947
            In *The Voice of the Coyote.*

E387   English Spirit from Letters
        from England.   March 9, 1947

E388   Coyote and Badger.   March 16, 1947
            In *The Voice of the Coyote.*

E389	Coyote and Prairie Dogs. In *The Voice of the Coyote*.	March 23, 1947
E390	Brass Pegs on the Brazos [Belt's buried treasure story]	March 30, 1947
E391	UNESCO; First Mockingbird Spring Song in Washington; Diplomats.	April 6, 1947
E392	Ray Williams [Alpine], Wildlife Conservationist.	April 13, 1967
E393	Secret of the Guadalupes [Ben Sublett sequel]	April 20, 1967
E394	Game in Texas in 1868 and Now. Changed Attitudes. [quoted from Chas. A. Messiter's *Sport and Adventures Among North American Indians*]	April 27, 1947
E395	Ab Blocker, Cowman.	May 4, 1947
E396	Horse Stampedes: Trailing Horse Herds. In *The Mustangs*.	May 11, 1947
E397	Watching Armadillo at Kerrville.	May 18, 1947
E398	Coyotes and Rattlesnakes [also Bullsnakes] In *The Voice of the Coyote*.	May 25, 1947
E399	Armadillo [Kerrville]	June 1, 1947
E400	Grabbing at Park Lands by Private Interests.	June 8, 1947
E401	Coyote Cooperation. In *The Voice of the Coyote*.	June 15, 1947
E402	Coyote Cooperation on Antelopes. In *The Voice of the Coyote*.	June 22, 1947
E403	Lizards [King of Luling; Peter Ellis Bean]	June 29, 1947
E404	Cowboy Individualism— Wanted To Be Free.	July 6, 1947
E405	Frontier Funeral [Duplicate of "Wolfville's First Funeral"]	July 13, 1947
E406	Coyote Curiosity. In *The Voice of the Coyote*.	July 20, 1947
E407	Traveling West—Texas Plains; Denver.	July 27, 1947
E408	In the West - Phony Range War of Jackson Hole, Montana.	August 3, 1947

E409	Montana—Russell, etc.	August 10, 1947
E410	National Park Service Commended.	August 17, 1947
E411	On Upper Rio Grande in Colorado; National History Museum.	August 24, 1947
E412	Coming to Texas from West. Garrett's Native Flower Seeds.	August 31, 1947
E413	Pet Skunks.	September 7, 1947
E414	Miscellaneous Items out of Dog Days.	September 14, 1947
E415	UNESCO in Chicago.	September 21, 1947
E416	Horse Sentiment and American Loyalty [Commager]	September 28, 1947
E417	Bedichek's *Adventures with a Texas Naturalist.*	October 5, 1947
E418	Spain's "Indelible Mark" on Texas Culture.	October 12, 1947
E419	The Current of Texas Writing.	October 19, 1947
E420	Simple Justice and Simple Verdicts of Early JPs.	October 26, 1947
E421	Spots of Civilization in Texas.	November 2, 1947
E422	Nat Straw's Smart Bear.	November 9, 1947
E423	Rattling up Bucks.	November 16, 1947
E424	Nat Straw's Worst Panther.	November 23, 1947
E425	In and Out of the Air. From *Coronado's Children.*	November 30, 1947
E426	Edward Ayer and a Book [Ayer Collection]	December 7, 1947
E427	Wild Turkey Victory over Rattlesnake.	December 14, 1947
E428	My Father.	December 21, 1947
E429	Illusions and Delusions of 1947.	December 28, 1947

1948

Austin American-Statesman.
San Antonio Light..
Valley Evening Monitor, McAllen, Texas.

| E430 | Jim Ballard Talk. | January 4, 1948 |
| E431 | The Coyote's Name. In *The Voice of the Coyote.* | January 11, 1948 |

E432   Coyote's Name in Popular Speech.   January 18, 1948
        In *The Voice of the Coyote.*

E433   Relics in Uvalde: Skull of Him
        When He Was Baby.   January 25, 1948

E434   Romulus and Remus in Texas.   February 1, 1948

E435   Fort Davis and Pushing Population. February 8, 1948

E436   Repaying Good with Evil.
        Coyote folk tale in *The Voice of*
        the Coyote.   February 15, 1948

E437   From Lancaster, Pennsylvania.   February 22, 1948

E438   Letter from New York [Hobart
        Huson's book on Pythagoras]   February 29, 1948

E439   What on Travels Have Become a
        Part of Me [Nebraska]   March 7, 1948

E440   Old Dog and Coyote.   March 14, 1948
        Folk tale in *The Voice of the Coyote.*

E441   Man-Trailing Panther. [From Louis
        Slothower, Colorado Springs]   March 21, 1948

E442   Coyote and Fox Folk Tale.   March 28, 1948
        In *The Voice of the Coyote.*

E443   Coyote Meets Tar Baby.   April 4, 1948
        In *The Voice of the Coyote.*

E444   Sam Houston and Pamela Mann.   April 11, 1948

E445   Gid Graham's Pet Coyote.   April 18, 1948
        In *The Voice of the Coyote.*

E446   "Mr. Billy the Kid"
        [from R. B. Townshend]   April 25, 1948

E447   Billy the Kid as Robin Hood.
        [from Frank Applegate]   May 2, 1948

E448   "Why the Russians Behave Like
        Russians," by John Fischer.   May 9, 1948

E449   Drouth Stories.   May 16, 1948

E450   Letter from Bertha Dobie in England. May 23, 1948

E451   Critical Appraisal of Cowboy Life in
        Texas [John Alley of Oklahoma]   May 30, 1948

E452   Proctor's Mustang Monument.   June 6, 1948

E453   Audubon Camp at Kerrville.   June 13, 1948

E454   The Mustang That Became Mustanger. June 20, 1948
        In *The Mustangs.*

E455   Mary's Lamb—With the Dogs
        She Would Go.   June 27, 1948

E456   Letter from Bertha Dobie
        from England.   July 4, 1948

E457   Proud Man and His Horse.   July 11, 1948
        Arab story in *The Mustangs*.

E458   Phony Praise for Cowboy
        [Pat Neff] and Reality.   July 18, 1948

E459   Jayhawker Spirit—from Kansas.   July 25, 1948

E460   Art of Traveling in England
        [Bertha Dobie Letter]   August 1, 1948

E461   The Mystery of the Fireflies
        [from Alberto Guajardo]   August 8, 1948

E462   Panther Yarns from Ben Lilly.   August 15, 1948
        In *The Ben Lilly Legend*.

E463   Was It Snakes or Prayer that
        Brought Rain [Drouth]   August 22, 1948

E464   Esau the Hunter.   August 29, 1948
        Revised and reprinted. See also E200.
        In *The Ben Lilly Legend*.

E465   A Miscellany—Drouth Story,
        Isabel Maltsberger Verses.   September 5, 1948

E466   Mustang Intelligence.   September 12, 1948
        Don Alberto Guajardo story in *The Mustangs*.

E467   Fight Vs. Aftosa in Mexican
        Jungle Country.   September 19, 1948

E468   Little Things Happen in Mexico
        [Birthday Party]   September 26, 1948

E469   Tiempo de Dios in the Mexican
        Tempo.   October 3, 1948

E470   Crow Psychology vs. Coyote
        Psychology.   October 10, 1948
        In *The Voice of the Coyote*.

E471   Aunt Evelyn and a Cup of Tea—
        English Individualism.   October 17, 1948

E472   Old Time Ranch Drouths.   October 24, 1948

E473   Satire on Cowboy Serenading
        of Cattle.   October 31, 1948

E474   How Bigfoot Wallace Cowered
        the Dude.   November 7, 1948

E475   The Road to California.   November 14, 1948

E476   California and Water: Dixon
Wecter on Academic Freedom.   November 21, 1948

E477   Henry E. Huntington and
Huntington Library and
Art Gallery.   November 28, 1948

E478   Ella Byler Dobie.   December 5, 1948

E479   Notes in California.   December 12, 1948

E480   Children's Books—Remembrances.   December 19, 1948

E481   Conversation with a Year
Named 1948.   December 26, 1948

1949

Austin American-Statesman.
Fort Worth Star-Telegram. May 1, 1949-
San Antonio Light.
Valley Evening Monitor, McAllen, Texas.
January 2-September 25, 1949

E482   Joe Burdette's Story of Skinned Indian,
Book and Artist [Recollections]   January 2, 1949

E483   Jack Thorp's Story of Mexican
Mustangers.   January 9, 1949
     In *The Mustangs.*

E484   A Trip in Bajo California:
Below Tijuana.   January 16, 1949

E485   Brush Country of Texas;
Luis Berlandier's Diary, 1828.   January 23, 1949
     In *The Mustangs.*

E486   California Claims vs.
Texas Bragging.   January 30, 1949

E487   Wm. W. Arnett's Account of
Pioneer Texas, Green Peyton
and Texas Ideas.   February 6, 1949

E488   Frontier Non-Sympathy
for Animals.   February 13, 1949
     In *The Voice of the Coyote.*

E489   California Deserts and "The
Ultimate of Life"   February 20, 1949

E490   Household Rhymes—Collected by
Frances Alexander.   February 27, 1949

E491   Golden Age of California
Ranches—Spanish .   March 6, 1949

E492   Among the Redwood Trees
of California.   March 13, 1949

E493   Lost Mine Stories Heard at
Redwoods, California.   March 20, 1949

E494   Texas Viewed from California;
Some Texas Yarns.   March 27, 1949

E495   Coyotes and Other Influences from
Nature [Mrs. J. D. English]   April 3, 1949

E496   Jack Culley's *Cattle, Men and Horses*.   April 10, 1949

E497   Silver Ledge in the Colorado—
Legend of Lost Silver.   April 17, 1949

E498   Folk Wisdom and Freedom
to Disagree on Ideas.   April 24, 1949

E499   Wild Flowers in Live Oak County.   May 1, 1949

E500   Coyote and Dogs—
Arthur Woodward Story.   May 8, 1949

E501   On the Queen Elizabeth
Bound for England.   May 15, 1949

E502   London Since the War; Life Looks Up.   May 22, 1949

E503   Hyde Park Orators of London.   May 29, 1949

E504   Notes on Cambridge University.   June 5, 1949

E505   Cricket at Cambridge.   June 12, 1949

E506   A Trip to Devonshire.   June 19, 1949

E507   Food in England.   June 26, 1949

E508   Jack Barrett of The Anchor
at Cambridge.   July 3, 1949

E509   Stratford-upon-Avon.   July 10, 1949

E510   English Life Reflected in London
Newspapers: Nature.   July 17, 1949

E511   Dublin and the Irish.   July 24, 1949

E512   The Labor Government and the
Plight of Britain.   July 31, 1949

E513   "Old Juan Mora's Burro,"
by Frank Applegate.   August 7, 1949

E514   The West Still Walks in 7-League
Boots; Denver Red Rocks Theater;
Van Vleet Arabian Horses.   August 14, 1949

E515   Arabian Horses; from Davenport's
        My Quest of the Arabian.   August 21, 1949
        In *The Mustangs.*

E516   The Coyote Dun Horse; from
        The Blood of the Arab by Harris   August 28, 1949
        In *The Mustangs.*

E517   The Western Cult; Imitating
        Hollywood, etc.   September 4, 1949

E518   Charlie Russell; Story from E.M.
        Botsford, Littlefield, Texas.   September 11, 1949

E519   The Staked Plains of New Mexico
        and Texas.   September 18, 1949

E520   Anecdotes from Old Texas;
        Wayne Gard's *Frontier Justice,* etc. September 25, 1949

E521   Andy Adams; Man and Writer.   October 2, 1949

E522   Andy Adams' "Bear Sign" Story.   October 9, 1959

E523   The Right Words and the Right
        Tune—New Books Quoted.   October 16, 1949

E524   Ross Santee: *Cowboy.*   October 23, 1949

E525   The Power of the Panther's Tail.   October 30, 1949

E526   Panther Following People
        and Screaming.   November 6, 1949

E527   Panthers Baby Hungry
        [from *Back Yonder*]   November 13, 1949

E528   Panthers Lured by Motion.   November 20, 1949

E529   Boots Shined before Daylight
        [Beeville and Live Oak County]   November 27, 1949

E530   Mody Boatright's *Folk Laughter
        on American Frontier.*   December 4, 1949

E531   Remembrance of Childhood
        Christmas Books.   December 11, 1949

E532   Camp Fire on a Hunt.   December 18, 1949

E533   Christmasy Words and Deeds.   December 25, 1949

                            1950

        Austin American-Statesman.
        Fort Worth Star Telegram .
        San Antonio Light.

E534   Don't Let the Future Spoil
        the Present.   January 1, 1950

E535   Jeff Ake's Panther Story.   January 8, 1950

E536   Chas. A. Siringo [from Introduction
       to Siringo's *Texas Cowboy*]   January 15-22, 1950

E537   Batching on Devil's River Lake.   January 29, 1950

E538   Book Hunger on Open Range
       [from Introduction to Siringo's
       Texas Cowboy]   February 5-12, 1950

E539   Luck Is Being Ready for
       the Chance.   February 19, 1950

E540   Panther Ways.   February 26, 1950

E541   The Huisache—Proposed Lane of
       between Frio and Nueces.   March 5, 1950

E542   Travel: Kansas City, Stevens College,
       University of Oklahoma.   March 12, 1950

E543   The Runnable Fox: Fair Play.   March 19, 1950

E544   Authentic Lying: Hot Tamale Story. March 26, 1950

E545   Imitators of Bad Men—
       Frank James Revised.   April 2, 1950

E546   Earle Butler Story of Bad Men;
       Billy the Kid.   April 9, 1950

E547   Flower-Planting on Texas Highways. April 16, 1950

E548   Horse, Secret Atom Bomb
       of Spanish.   April 23, 1950
           In *The Mustangs.*

E549   Indian Horses Acquired
       from Spanish.   April 30, 1950
           In *The Mustangs.*

E550   Myth about Coronado Horse—
       Mustangs.   May 7, 1950
           In *The Mustangs.*

E551   Myth about De Soto Horse—
       Mustangs.   May 14, 1950
           In *The Mustangs.*

E552   Old World Origins of Some
       Texas Stories.   May 21, 1950

E553   Letters from Britishers Wanting
       to Come to U. S.   May 28, 1950

E554   Emerson Stringham of Keerville.   June 4, 1950

E555   Fox Story from James
       Willard Schulz Book.   June 11, 1950

E556 Writers Conferences and Journalism. June 18, 1950

E557 My Paisanos: Melton's "70 Years
in Saddle." June 25, 1950

E558 The Flavor of the Ozarks;
Travel in Arkansas. July 2, 1950

E559 Visit to Kansas: Manhattan; Writers'
Conference; Animal Talk. July 9, 1950

E560 Mr. Jim Dougherty and His Stories. July 16, 1950

E561 Independence of Old Time Wagon Boss. July 23, 1950

E562 Story of the Warrior and the
She-Grizzly. July 30, 1950

E563 Atomic and Other Indian Wisdom
[Catlin Story] August 6, 1950

E564 Indian Horses and Horsemanship. August 13, 1950
In *The Mustangs.*

E565 Indian Horsemanship. August 20, 1950
In *The Mustangs.*

E566 Early Indian Horses. August 27–
In *The Mustangs.* September 3, 1950

E567 Owl Lore. September 10, 1950

E568 Traveling Tales; Art in
Telling Them. September 17, 1950

E569 Blue Streak, the Mustang. September 24, 1950
In *The Mustangs.*

E570 Serenity and No Civilized Taverns
on Guadalupe River. October 1, 1950

E571 Indian Game of Horse-Stealing. October 8, 1950
In *The Mustangs.*

E572 Darwin's *Voyage of the Beagle;*
Pampas Life. October 15, 1950
In *The Mustangs.*

E573 Pacing White Stallion. October 22, 1950
Legend from Putnam's Magazine
in *The Mustangs.*

E574 Robert Frost Celebration;
His Poetry. October 29, 1950

E575 Carthage in East Texas. November 5, 1950

E576 Meat Too Fat—
Lean Meat Wanted. November 12, 1950

E577   Guri, Pet Coyote of Murie
Family in Wyoming.   November 19, 1950

E578   Ruxton of the Rockies.   November 26, 1950

E579   Sense of Smell in Horses.   December 3, 1950
In *The Mustangs.*

E580   Rattlesnake Bite Cured
Inferiority Complex.   December 10, 1950

E581   The Wisdom of Roy Bedichek
[Karankaway Country]   December 17, 1950

E582   Christmases of My Boyhood.   December 24, 1950

E583   Adventures with Little Things
on a Deer Hunt.   December 31, 1950

1951

Austin American-Statesman.
Fort Worth Star Telegram.
San Antonio Light.

E584   Time, Evolution, Ignorance.   January 7, 1951

E585   A Deer Hunt Down in
the Brush Country.   January 14, 1951

E586   The Lift of the Coyote's Tail [I]   January 21, 1951

E587   Drouths and Men of
Drouthy Land.   January 28, 1951

E588   The Comanches as Horse-Lifters.   February 4, 1951

E589   Comanches and Spanish Horses.   February 11, 1951

E590   The Life of the Coyote's Tail [II]   February 18, 1951

E591   The Greatest Philosopher on
Earth—The Fire.   February 25, 1951

E592   Horse-Eating Indians
and Frontiersmen.   March 4, 1951

E593   Harold Young and Abraham Lincoln
Fables on Conduct.   March 11, 1951

E594   Christiano—W. H. Hudson's Wild
Horse Story.   March 18, 1951

E595   Selling the Dobie Ranch in
Live Oak County.   March 25, 1951

E596   Burning Prickly Pear, Home-
Returning Horse, Panther.   April 1, 1951

E597   Bob Lemmons—The Mustanger Who
Turned Mustang.   April 8, 1951

E598	Saint Peter—Pulque Tale [from Mexico]	April 15, 1951
E599	Juan the Shoe-Shiner of Beeville and Jim Ballard's Tale.	April 22, 1951
E600	West Texas Winds and Tumbleweeds.	April 29, 1951
E601	How the Song of La Cucaracha Got Juan out of Paradise.	May 6, 1951
E602	Street Cries.	May 13, 1951
E603	Col. Crimmins' Trip through Santa Helena Canyon.	May 20, 1951
E604	W. B. Slaughter's Ride with a Gold Belt.	May 27, 1951
E605	Little Aubry's Ride.	June 3, 1951
E606	Chester Evans and His Horse Prince.	June 10, 1951
E607	Plagiarism in Texas Boasts.	June 17, 1951
E608	Cow Dogs.	June 24, 1951
E609	The Papago Indians Who Ran with Mustangs.	July 1, 1951
E610	Edith Long's Pet Skunk.	July 8, 1951
E611	The Gambler Who Gambled Away His Bride.	July 15, 1951
E612	Ellie Newman's Rides.	July 22, 1951
E613	Picture Window Architecture and Prayers Won't Bring Cool or Rain.	July 29, 1951
E614	Chinaco, Anti-Panther Horse.	August 5, 1951
E615	Drouth—Ramos Arizpe [biography by Nettie Lee Benton]	August 12, 1951
E616	Santa Anna's Gold; Terrapin and Snail.	August 19, 1951
E617	My Horse Buck.	August 26, 1951
E618	Visit to Saltillo, Mexico.	September 2, 1951
E619	Effects of Bull-Fighting on Mexicans.	September 9, 1951
E620	Another Juan Oso Story.	September 16, 1951
E621	Snowdrift the Lobo [Part 1-3]	September 23- October 7, 1951

E622   Sheepmen as Readers.
        Texas Sheepman by Robert Maudsley October 14, 1951

E623   Bowie Knife in New Books; P.
        Wellman's *The Iron Mistress.*   October 21, 1951

E624   Pageant of Life in Mexico City;
        Chapultepec Park.   October 28, 1951

E625   Sailfishing at Acapulco;
        Agricultural Experiment Station. November 4, 1951

E626   Changes and Charm in
        Mexico City.   November 11, 1951

E627   Carl Sandburg Looks
        Like an Author.   November 18, 1951

E628   Mustang, Civil War Cavalry   November 25-
        Horse [Part 1-3]   December 9, 1951

E629   How Br'er Rabbit
        Acted in Mexico.   December 16, 1951

E630   Margaret Hallett of Hallettsville. December 23, 1951

E631   Sun Time: El Tiempo de Dios.   December 30, 1951

1952

        Austin American-Statesman.
        Fort Worth Star-Telegram.
        San Antonio Light.

E632   And the Sly Coyote Trots
        Here and There.   January 6, 1952

E633   Know the Ways of the
        Cunning Coyote.   January 13, 1952

E634   How Is Your Belief About Ghosts? January 20, 1952

E635   Treasure through Window.   January 27, 1952

E636   Barbecues a Natural for
        Political Races.   February 3, 1952

E637   The Cooking and Selling
        of Barbecue.   February 10, 1952

E638   A Coyote's Way with the
        'Wise Serpent.'   February 17, 1952

E639   Museums Just Sprout in
        Oklahoma, It Would Seem.   February 24, 1952

E640   From 'Dixie' to 'The Eyes of Texas.' March 2, 1952

E641   Strange Voice of the Coyote
        Is Something Beyond Sound.   March 9, 1952

E662	Coyotes Recognized Cowboy as Their Friend.	August 3, 1952
E663	Books and Ideas Touching on Texas.	August 10, 1952
E664	Many City Dwellers Actually Are Country-Minded.	August 17, 1952
E665	More Wisdom Asked in Dealing with Wetbacks.	August 24, 1952
E666	Arrows Kept Secret of Yucatan Gold Nugget.	August 31, 1952
E667	Night Horse Ranked Highest with Cowhand.	September 7, 1952
E668	Two Cowmen Talk about Dry Weather.	September 14, 1952
E669	Mustang Cattle Were Free in the Old Days.	September 21, 1952
E670	Trail Driving from Texas Started before Civil War, Oldtimer Related.	September 28, 1952
E671	Law 100 Years Ago Was at Rope's End.	October 5, 1952
E672	Edna Ferber Gives Texas Myth Giant Boost.	October 12, 1952
E673	Transplanted Texans Buying Colorado Ranches.	October 19, 1952
E674	There's More to Autograph Parties Than Autographing.	October 26, 1952
E675	Individualism, Like Piety, Not Always Expressed in Words.	November 2, 1952
E676	Nobody Knows What His Memory Will Do.	November 9, 1952
E677	The Blue Darter That Missed His Mark.	November 16, 1952
E678	Chief Trait of Texas Deer: Curiosity.	November 23, 1952
E679	Animal Curiosity a Lot Like That of Men.	November 30, 1952
E680	South Texas Rancher Was Rugged, Yet Kind.	December 7, 1952
E681	Ira George Yates and the Yates Oil Field.	December 14, 1952

| E682 | Early '20's Rough Time for Cattlemen. | December 21, 1952 |
| E683 | Reflections beside a Hunter's Camp Fire. | December 28, 1952 |

1953

Austin American-Statesman.
Fort Worth Star-Telegram.
San Antonio Light.

E684	Blue Darter [Hawk] in Action [from Bill Turbiville]	January 4, 1953
E685	Throwing Sunbonnets to Hungry Panthers.	January 11, 1953
E686	Negro Folk-Talk: Uncle Beverley and Others.	January 18, 1953
E687	Panther Covers Sleeping Man with Leaves.	January 25, 1953
E688	Joe Evans of El Paso and His Stories.	February 1, 1953
E689	Grandpa Dubose and His Way of Dressing.	February 8, 1953
E690	On the Ranch Gallery [Uncle Jim]	February 15, 1953
E691	Roadrunner-Rattlesnake Fight.	February 22, 1953
E692	Paying for Favor with Information about Gold.	March 1, 1953
E693	Grass on the Ground and Grass in Oratory.	March 8, 1953
E694	Off-the-Trail Men of the Range: Individualism.	March 15, 1953
E695	The Traveling Anecdote.	March 22-April 5, 1953
E696	Immortality in Names: Mary Maverick's Memoirs.	April 12, 1953
E697	Nelly, Bill Turbiville's Mustang Mare.	April 19, 1953
E698	C. B. Ruggles Story of Blue Egg of Solid Silver.	April 26, 1953
E699	John Shepherd, Mavericker and Trail Driver of 1866.	May 3, 1953
E700	Shanghai Pierce.	May 10, 1953

E701   Apache Gold and the Lost Nigger
        Mine [Part 1-3]   May 17-31, 1953

E702   Cherry Springs.   June 7, 1953

E703   Wisdom and Tales from Jim
        Ballard of Beeville.   June 14, 1953

E704   Catfish, Lady Luck and
        Other Jim Ballard Tales.   June 21, 1953

E705   Tom Gilcrease and the
        "Earth of My Valley."   June 28, 1953

E706   Thomas Jefferson in Texas
        [C. P. Patterson's book]   July 5, 1953

E707   Pancho Robles Tales of Lost Mines
        and Enchanted Spring.   July 12, 1953

E708   What the Man Said to the Barkeep.   July 19, 1953

E709   Seven Quail and No Roadrunner.   July 26, 1953

E710   The Panhandle and Writers'
        Roundup at Canyon.   August 2 ,1953

E711   Taos, New Mexico.   August 9, 1953

E712   What Did I See on Travel to
        New Mexico and Back?   August 16, 1953

E713   Gauchos of Pampas and Literature.   August 23, 1953

E714   Incidents of Nature from Letters.   August 30, 1953

E715   The Pack Rat Named Pop-Eye.   September 6, 1953

E716   Sounds in the Night at Ranch
        of Long Ago.   September 13, 1953

E717   Centipede Lore.   September 20, 1953

E718   Goethe and Patriotism.   September 27, 1953

E719   Visit to the Babicora Ranch
        in Chihuahua [Part 1-4]   October 4-25, 1953

E720   The Savor of an Original Texas
        Cowman [Lee Moore, from Letters
        to Wyoming Stock Grower
        Association]   November 1, 1953

E721   The Lasso as a Weapon—
        Persia to Texas.   November 8, 1953

E722   Chuck Wagon Cooks of
        Range and Trail.   November 15, 1953

E723   Horses in Herodotus.   November 22, 1953

E742	By Their Wills You Shall Know Them.	April 25, 1954
E743	On Mexican Goats.	May 2, 1954
E744	The Lure of Treasure Destined Not To Be Found.	May 9-23, 1954
E745	Walter P. Webb's *More Water for Texas*.	May 30, 1954
E746	Treasure Hunters Scared Away by Phantom Panther.	June 6, 1954
E747	In Illinois. Old Negro's Breaking of Bad News.	June 13, 1954
E748	Country Quietness and Little Happenings.	June 20, 1954
E749	The Birds of Lydia Ann Island.	June 27, 1954
E750	My Mares Babe and Ginger.	July 4, 1954
E751	Traveling to Indiana through Homed Lands.	July 11, 1954
E752	Iowa, Minnesota, Wisconsin.	July 18, 1954
E753	Across Canada—Calgary Stampede, Moose, etc.	July 25, 1954
E754	Charlie Russell's Shadow over Montana.	August 1, 1954
E755	Cody, Wyoming.	August 8, 1954
E756	Traveling; Interesting People.	August 15, 1954
E757	Grass: Shade Helps It.	August 22, 1954
E758	Understanding Horses.	August 29, 1954
E759	Between Comanche and Rattlesnake..	September 5-19, 1954
E760	Jeff Turner the Indian Hater.	September 26-October 3, 1954
E761	The Girl of Capri and San Michele.	October 10, 1954
E762	The Headless Horseman of the Nueces. *In Tales of Old Time Texas*.	October 17-24, 1954
E763	About Johnson Grass.	October 31, 1954
E764	Bigfoot Wallace.	November 7-14, 1954
E765	Anecdotes about Eating.	November 21, 1954

| E766 | Gustav Dresel's Houston Journal—Old Texas. | November 28, 1954 |

| E767 | The Dream that Saved Scalped Wilbarger.
In *Tales of Old Time Texas.* | December 5-12, 1954 |

| E768 | To California and Larry Powell. | December 19, 1954 |

| E769 | A Crow Story. | December 26, 1954 |

1955

Austin American-Statesman.
Fort Worth Star-Telegram.
Houston Post.
San Antonio Light.

| E770 | After Christmas Thoughts. | January 2, 1955 |

| E771 | The Wild Woman of the Navidad.
In *Tales of Old Time Texas.* | January 9-30, 1955 |

| E772 | Ed Schieffelen's Lost Gold. | February 6, 1955 |

| E773 | The Reach of a Manacled Hand. | February 13, 1955 |

| E774 | "Man-Shy" Wild Cattle of Australia. | February 20, 1955 |

| E775 | Longworth's Vicey-Verscy Map.
In *Tales of Old-Time Texas.* | February 27-March 6, 1955 |

| E776 | The Robinhooding of Sam Bass.
In *Tales of Old-Time Texas.* | March 13-27, 1955 |

| E777 | Asa Jones's Cutting Horse. | April 3, 1955 |

| E778 | The Hawk and the Buzzard.
In *Tales of Old-Time Texas.* | April 10, 1955 |

| E779 | Toasts. | April 17, 1955 |

| E780 | Drouth Upon Land and Men. | April 24, 1955 |

| E781 | Folklore Anthology—*Texas Folk and Folklore.* | May 1, 1955 |

| E782 | English Teachers—Professor A. S. Pegues. | May 8, 1955 |

| E783 | Mi San Antonio Querido. | May 15, 1955 |

| E784 | Spring in Ohio. | May 22, 1955 |

| E785 | Davy Crockett Reconsidered. | May 29-June 5, 1955 |

| E786 | Heroization of Cowboys and Crockett. | June 12, 1955 |

E787	Trips to Nebraska and Corpus . Christi.	June 19, 1955
E788	The Leafy Month of June at Cherry Spirngs.	June 26, 1955
E789	Up the Trail to Modern Kansas.	July 3, 1955
E790	Bowie Knife Lore.	July 10-24, 1955
E791	Big Rattler and Ball of Rattlesnakes.	July 31, 1955
E792	Bowie's Authentic Duel with Bowie Knife. In *Tales of Old-Time Texas*.	August 7, 1955
E793	Pleasure in Little Things of Nature.	August 14, 1955
E794	Traveling Anecdotes about Santa Anna and Villa Weddings.	August 21, 1955
E795	Stories of Pet Crow and Pack Mule Artillery.	August 28, 1955
E796	Going Off to College.	September 4, 1955
E797	Jim Bowies' Gallantry. In *Tales of Old-Time Texas*.	September 11, 1955
E798	Letter from Hollywood.	September 18, 1955
E799	San Francisco and the Redwoods.	September 25, 1955
E800	Traveling and Being Reminded [California]	October 2, 1955
E801	Mad Stones, Mad People, Polecats.	October 9, 1955
E802	Mad Stone Lore.	October 16, 1055
E803	A Panther That Did Not Scare from Fire.	October 23, 1955
E804	An Old Hitchhiker's Yarns.	October 30, 1955
E805	More Mad Stone Lore.	November 6, 1955
E806	Tales of Blood-Thirsty Wildcats and Panthers.	November 13, 1955
E807	Marcus Snyder, Old-Style Texas Ranchman.	November 20, 1955
E808	Breyfogle's Gold.	November 27-December 4, 1955
E809	Tarantula Lore.	December 11, 1955
E810	Watching at the Tank.	December 18, 1955
E811	Clint Brown's Christmas Story from *You May Take the Witness*.	December 25, 1955

1956

Austin American-Statesman.
Fort Worth Star-Telegram.
Houston Post.
San Antonio Light.

E812	The Horns of an Outlaw Steer.	January 1, 1956
E813	Joseph J. Good's Biggest Rattlesnake.	January 8, 1956
E814	Anecdotes about Cattle Brands.	January 15, 1956
E815	"Admass" Texas According to J. B. Priestley's *Journey Down a Rainbow*.	January 22, 1956
E816	When Booger Red Rode the Man-Killer.	January 29, 1956
E817	Grandpa Dubose.	February 5-12, 1956
E818	In Alice High School.	February 19, 1956
E819	The Battle of the Alamo.	February 26-March 25, 1956
E820	Stories Not Factual: Lon C. Hill, etc.	April 1, 1956
E821	Definitions of the Southwest.	April 8, 1956
E822	Lost Mine of the Scorpions [Mexico]	April 15, 1956
E823	Tom Streeter's Bibliography of Texas.	April 22, 1956
E824	The Lost Cabin Mine.	April 29, 1956
E825	Characters and Anecdotes from Ohio.	May 6, 1956
E826	In New York.	May 13, 1956
E827	Witching for Water and Oil [George Ray]	May 20, 1956
E828	Uncle Frank Byler, Cowman.	May 27-June 3, 1956
E829	Evolution in Texas Writing [Sikes Johnson etc.]	June 10, 1956
E830	The Natural Born Orator.	June 17, 1956
E831	Monte Barrett Traveling in Scotland.	June 24, 1956
E832	Old Grandma and Other Cow Personalities.	July 1, 1956
E833	Chaucer's [The Pardoner's] Treasure Tale.	July 8, 1956
E834	One Spaniard, 4 Skeletons, 6 Greedy Men.	July 15, 1956

E835   A Cloud No Bigger than a
        Man's Hand.   July 22, 1956

E836   "How Sharp Your Teeth Are—
        How Long Your Claws." [Wm.
        Mowery's *Swift in the Night.*   July 29, 1956

E837   Trip Down into the Brush Country.   August 5, 1956

E838   New Stories and Old Puns.   August 12, 1956

E839   Ramirenia Creek and Other
        Water in Early Days.   August 19, 1956

E840   The Well-Digger [from Ruth Dodson]   August 26, 1956

E841   George McGehee
        Texian Individual.   September 2-9, 1956

E842   Gene Rhodes of the Bar Cross.   September 16, 1956

E843   "Jenny Kissed Me."   September 23, 1956

E844   Rattlesnakes and Suicide.   September 30, 1956

E845   Whiskey for Snakebite.   October 7, 1956

E846   What the Thrush Said
        [Frederick W. Hodge]   October 14, 1956

E847   Scorpions and Bull Snakes.   October 21, 1956

E848   Acorns, Deer, Silence.   October 28, 1956

E849   How Sam Bass Was Killed.
        [Bill Kittrell story]   November 4, 1956

E850   A Wolf in Imagination
        [from Barbara Clark Fogel]   November 11, 1956

E851   Dr. Allen of Southwestern
        University.   November 18, 1956

E852   Watching Wild Turkeys.   November 25, 1956

E853   Klauber's Great Work
        on Rattlesnakes.   December 2, 1956

E854   Frank Taulbee and Other
        Lawyers of Old Georgetown.   December 9, 1956

E855   Bob Slaughter of the Long S
        [from J. J. Good]   December 16, 1956

E856   A Christmasy Kind of Deed
        [by Ruth Dodson]   December 23, 1956

E857   Jim Dobie Ranch from George Parr
        to Duval County.   December 30, 1956

1957

Austin American-Statesman.

Fort Worth Star-Telegram.

Houston Post.

San Antonio Light.

E858	The Polkadot Pony [from Barbara Clark Fogel]	January 6, 1957
E859	Buzzards Against the Sky.	January 13, 1957
E860	Dr. Parr of Beeville Cultivated the Art of Being Odd.	January 20, 1957
E861	Midnight, Out-Pitchingest of all Pitching Horses.	January 27, 1957
E862	A Trip to New York.	February 3, 1957
E863	The Archives Wars of Texas.	February 10, 1957
E864	The Gleam That Led Captain Cooney.	February 17, 1957
E865	Several Sorts of People.	February 24, 1957
E866	Texas Independence Day and Socrates.	March 3, 1957
E867	A Pet Bull Calf Named Maxie.	March 10, 1957
E868	Three Apache Women and a Lone White Man [from Barbara Clark Fogel]	March 17-24, 1957
E869	Across the Sierra Madre with Pack Outfit.	March 31-May 5, 1957
E870	Archer B. Gilfillan, Philosopher, Shepherd and Author of *Sheep*.	May 12, 1957
E871	Ed. Shettles Gambler, Preacher Book Dealer.	May 19-26, 1957
E872	And the Rains Came.	June 2, 1957
E873	Sam Houston, Individual and Non-conformist.	June 9-16, 1957
E874	A Rabbit-Eating Pony.	June 23, 1957
E875	On a Cattle Ship [from Plimsoll's *Cattle Ships*]	June 30, 1957
E876	J. R. Williams, Saddest of Laughter-Makers.	July 7, 1957

E877	On Writing an Autobiography.	July 14, 1957
E878	July 4th in Kansas.	July 21, 1957
E879	A Madstone for Rabies.	July 28, 1957
E880	Silence and the Panther's Scream.	August 4, 1957
E881	The First Dobies in Texas.	August 11-18, 1957
E882	Hen Baker and the Six-Shooter Age.	August 25, 1957
E883	Individualism in the Six-Shooter Age.	September 1, 1957
E884	A Natural Taste for Natural Milk.	September 8, 1957
E885	Nat Straw's Worst Grizzly.	September 15, 1957
E886	Shanghai Pierce Flapjacks.	September 22, 1957
E887	Another Nat Straw Grizzly Bear Story.	September 29, 1957
E888	An Old Texian's Funeral Services for His Bear Dog.	October 6, 1957
E889	Talk with Roy Bedichek about Hot Tortillas etc.	October 13, 1957
E890	Talk with Roy Bedichek about Getting Rich on Rumor.	October 20, 1957
E891	Camping Under an Oxygen Tent.	October 27, 1957
E892	Charlie the Newsboy Acquires a Burro.	November 3, 1957
E893	Luck Is Being Ready for the Chance.	November 10, 1957
E894	How a Goatherder Changed My Life.	November 17, 1957
E895	Nelso Lee's *Three Years Among the Comanches.*	November 24, 1957
E896	Mature Minds and George Fuermann's *Reluctant Empire.*	December 1, 1957
E897	The Time of Books Is Here Again.	December 8, 1957
E898	Coyote Talk by a Winter Fire.	December 15, 1957
E899	Bounty at Christmas Time.	December 22, 1957
E900	An Interview with Myself at the End of 1957.	December 29, 1957

1958

Austin American-Statesman.
Fort Worth Star-Telegram.
Houston Post.
San Antonio Light.

E901	Wade Hampton, Killer of Bears.	January 5, 1958
E902	Centipede Lore	January 12, 1958
E903	How Jim Bowie Got His Silver.	January 19, 1958
E904	How Does Mr. Coyote Detect a Gun?	January 26, 1958
E905	Along the Way in Texas.	February 2, 1958
E906	More Centipede Lore.	February 9, 1958
E907	Clay Allison, Most Eccentric of Gunmen.	February 16, 1958
E908	Out of the Postman's Bag.	February 23, 1958
E909	Frank Goodwyn's *The Black Bull* and Other Vaquero Lore.	March 2, 1958
E910	Where the Elm and the Gourd Shaded the Ground.	March 9, 1958
E911	Salute to Libraries and Books.	March 16, 1958
E912	Pet Bobcat That Made a Duster Flow Oil.	March 23, 1958
E913	Two Pet Crows and their Patrons.	March 30, 1958
E914	Douglas Rigby's *Desert Happy* [Story of Gambrel's Quail]	April 6, 1958
E915	The Ghosts of Two Texas Books That Never Were.	April 13, 1958
E916	Mockingbird Takes Care of Itself.	April 20, 1958
E917	Johnny Faulk's Prize Liar Named Bill and His Yarns.	April 27, 1958
E918	Bill's Constructive Memory on the Great Cyclone of Austin.	May 4, 1958
E919	A Selection of Communications.	May 11, 1958
E920	The Old Spaniard and His Map of Pirate Gold.	May 18, 1958
E921	Neville Hutto's Story of a Fierce Doe.	May 25, 1958

E922	From Mayhaw Jelly to Mustang Grape Cobbler.	June 1, 1958
E923	Two Canyon Wrens and Three .Books.	June 8, 1958
E924	Joe Small's Texian Yarns.	June 15, 1958
E925	On Staying Outside the Majority Group.	June 22, 1958
E926	Blowing the Horn for Dinner.	June 29, 1958
E927	Notes Along the Way of Life.	July 6, 1958
E928	Spanish Treasure in the Money Hole—East Texas.	July 13, 1958
E929	They Just Ain't Dug Deep Enough.	July 20, 1958
E930	On *A Bride Goes West,* by Nannie T. Alderson and Helena Huntington Smith.	July 27, 1958
E931	Code of the West.	August 3, 1958
E932	Old-Time Confederate Anecdotes.	August 10, 1958
E933	Galveston: Ain't Nobody in No Hurry Round Here."	August 17, 1958
E934	*Interwoven*: A Ranchwoman Looks at Life.	August 24, 1958
E935	Observations on Lizards.	August 31, 1958
E936	Circumstantial Evidence in Live Oak County and in The Black Hills.	September 7, 1958
E937	Bill Cole of the Monterrey Loot Legend, Part I[-II]	September 14-21, 1958
E938	Bill Cole and Harry Warren.	September 28, 1958
E939	When the Rio Grande Was Bloodstained [from Jesse Sumpter of Eagle Pass]	October 5, 1958
E940	My Boyhood Experience in Farming.	October 12, 1958
E941	Watermelons and Cabbage Growing on Our Ranch.	October 19, 1958
E942	Lone Wild Horse in Search of Company.	October 26, 1958
E943	Joe Small's Story: "I've Often Wondered About That Myself."	November 2, 1958
E944	Ike Blazingame's *Dakota Cowboy and His Horses.*	November 9, 1958

E945	Armadillo Lore.	November 16, 1958
E946	Bucks with Locked Horns.	November 23, 1958
E947	Memories of Camps That Were Home.	November 30, 1958
E948	Dog Ghosts and Other Negro Folk Tales by J. Mason Brewer.	December 7, 1958
E949	Rattlesnakes in the Brush Country During Deer Season.	December 14, 1958
E950	Merry Christmas, Hot Peppers and Old Times.	December 21, 1958
E951	A Horse's Instinct for Direction.	December 28, 1958

1959

Austin American-Statesman.
Fort Worth Star-Telegram.
Houston Post.
San Antonio Light.

E952	The Drama of Death in Literature and Elsewhere.	January 4, 1959
E953	A Gaucho Knife Duel [from *Don Segundo Sombra*]	January 11, 1959
E954	The Music of Cattle Bawling [from *Peter Lecky, by Himself*]	January 18, 1959
E955	The West, Land of Imagined Freedom.	January 25, 1959
E956	A Sandhill Crane Named Tim.	February 1, 1959
E957	Zippe, a Coyote Hunter.	February 8, 1959
E958	Vanished Pampas Life [*Pampas Grass*, by Geo. Harkness Newbery]	February 15, 1959
E959	The Artist Keeps His Independence [talk with Lynwood Giacomini]	February 22, 1959
E960	Wild Australian Bulls [from *Wild Life and Adventre in the Australian Bush*, by Arthur Nicols]	March 1, 1959
E961	Appetite—with Eyes Bigger Than Stomach.	March 8, 1959
E962	Flavor in County Histories [J. C. Terrell's *Reminiscences of the Early Days in Fort Worth*, and other books]	March 15, 1959

E963   Bowie Knife Duel in Dark Room
        [from Palmer Cox's *Frontier Humor*]   March 22, 1959

E964   Geo. W. Kendall, Sheep Rancher
        [based on Kendall's *Letters from a
        Texas Sheep Ranch to Henry
        Stephens Randall*]   March 29, 1959

E965   Of Far Away and Long Ago
        [from *A Thousand Miles' Walk
        Across South America*
        by Nathaniel H. Bishop]   April 5, 1959

E966   Panther Stories [from *The Big Texas
        Ranches*, by W. S. Willis]   April 12, 1959

E967   The Rawhide [from *Arizona Nights*
        by Stewart Edward White]   April 19, 1959

E968   Mysterious Dave Mather and
        Professionals in Piety.   April 26, 1959

E969   Charles Goodnight Independent.   May 3, 1959

E970   Sam Houston Anecdotes.   May 10-17, 1959

E971   I Remember Supper at Chata's.   May 24, 1959

E972   The Western Gambler in Reality
        and Romance [partly from *Long John
        Dunn of Taos*, by Max Evans]   May 31, 1959

E973   Snake Yarns in Lucan's *Pharsalia*:
        Dramatic Episodes of the Civil Wars,
        translated by Robert Graves.   June 7, 1959

E974   Brother Coyote's Defenders.   June 14, 1959

E975   Lots of Snakes in Corn Patch.   June 21, 1959

E976   The Origin of "When Work's All
        Done This Fall."   June 28, 1959

E977   My Friend Bedichek.   July 5, 1959

E978   Reasoning or Instinct? [From J. B.
        Blackwell of Pear Burner Fame]   July 12, 1959

E979   The Lobo as Remembered by
        Bob Castlebury.   July 19, 1959

E980   Santa Fe in Books [Gregg's *Commerce
        of the Prairies and Santa Fe, the
        Autobiography of a Southwestern Town*,
        compiled by Oliver LaFarge]   July 26, 1959

E981   Individualism among English Women:
        Lady Hester Lucy Stanhope.   August 2, 1959

E982	Paisanos of the Brush Country.	August 9, 1959
E983	The Legend of Spanish Gold and Silver and the Poverty of Reality as Set Down in *The Letters of Antonio Martinez, Last Spanish Governor of Texas,* 1817-1822, translated by Virginia H. Taylor.	August 16, 1959
E984	Effortlessness in Nature: "Drive on your Cart."	August 23, 1959
E985	Pancho Villa Stories.	August 30-September 6, 1959
E986	The Paisano, Our Fellow Countryman.	September 13, 1959
E987	Rattlesnake Stories [from J. B. Blackwell of Pear Burner Fame]	September 20, 1959
E988	Peter the Great and the Vigor of the Earth: Khrushchev in America.	September 27, 1959
E989	Horseback Travel in the Argentine *Two Thousand Miles' Ride through the Argentine Provinces,* by Wm. McCann]	October 4, 1959
E990	Charlie Everitt, Bookseller and Friend.	October 11, 1959
E991	With the National Guard in World War I.	October 18, 1959
E992	Treasure Hunting in France in World War I, from Fred Curry.	October 25, 1959
E993	"Furniture Books" and Beautiful Books.	November 1, 1959
E994	Mi San Antonio Querido: *San Antonio, a Historical and Pictorial Guide,* by Charles Ramsdell.	November 8, 1959
E995	The Meat That Caesar Fed On.	November 15, 1959
E996	A Butcher [John Rainey] and His Meat.	November 22, 1959
E997	The Real Thing: Young Bell's Lead Steer in 64 *Years in the Cow Business in Texas.*	November 29, 1959

E998   The Dominguez Bandits of the Big
          Bend [from *The Way I Heard It*,
          by Walter Fulcher, edited
          by Elton Miles]   December 6, 1959

E999   Johnson of San Felipe Springs Was
          a Character [from *Reminiscences*
          in manuscript by Zenos R. Bliss]   December 13, 1959

E1000   Bears and Russian Gypsies [from
          The Book of the Bear, by
          Harrison and Mirrless]   December 20, 1959

E1001   A Nugget of Gold in a Pine Root,
          told by Victor Lieb.   December 27, 1959

                        1960

          Austin American-Statesman.
          Fort Worth Star-Telegram.
          Houston Post.
          San Antonio Light.

E1002   Despite King Canute's Swan Song,
          People Are No Worse.   January 3, 1960

E1003   The Sage Brush Colt in Boller's
          *Among the Indians—Eight Years
          in the Far West.*   January 10, 1960

E1004   The Llaneros of Venezuela.   January 17, 1960

E1005   Beside the Campfire
          [Memorable Campfires]   January 24, 1960

E1006   Fires by Which I Have
          Written in Happiness.   January 31, 1960

E1007   Hero Folk Tales of Tinland and
          Auracanian Indians of Chile. February 7, 1960

E1008   Smuggling a Man Out of Mexico. February 14, 1960

E1009   Hobert Hudson's *History of
          Refugio County, Texas.*   February 21, 1960

E1010   Domesticating the Buffalo.   February 28, 1960

E1011   Godmother Death.   March 6-20, 1960
          From *Tongues of the Monte.*

E1012   A Sheepherder and His Tales [from
          W. C. Minor's *Footprints in the Trail*]   March 27, 1960

E1013   My Salute to Public Libraries
          and Their Librarians.   April 3, 1960

E1014   Curiosity in Horses
         [from W. H. Hudson]   April 10, 1960

E1015   Grasses and Grass Growers.   April 17, 1960

E1016   Thomas Bewick's Wood Cuts
         Make Me Happy.   April 24, 1960

E1017   Blend of Action and Thought:
         The Scottish Chiefs, University
         of Oklahoma Press.   May 1, 1960

E1018   The Tumblebug of Brains and
         Other Fables.   May 8, 1960

E1019   Ranchero People of Texas and
         California [The Chapas of Live Oak
         County; Bill Sterling's Don Eusebio
         Garcia; Don Diego Olivera of Dana's
         The Blonde Ranchero.   May 15, 1960

E1020   Independent, and Honest.   May 22, 1960

E1021   In the Shadow of Jim Bowie.   May 29, 1960

E1022   The Burning of Sir Richard
         Burton by his Wife.   June 5, 1960

E1023   Ranch Horses of My Boyhood.   June 12, 1960

E1024   Ranch Horses of My Boyhood.   June 19, 1960

E1025   Pretense Research—High School
         Pupils Who Devil Writers.   June 26, 1960

E1026   A Fourth of July Kind of
         Independence, 1960.   July 3, 1960

E1027   "Never Marry a Horse"; Runaway
         Horses and Runaway Mules.   July 10, 1960

E1028   Wyatt Earp: Hero Out of a Sow's Ear.   July 17, 1960

E1029   A Wild Ride That Wasn't Glorious
         [by John C. Myers]   July 24, 1960

E1030   On Being Casual with Rattlesnakes.   July 31, 1960

E1031   Preparing for the Future [based on
         Walter Webb's story]   August 7, 1960

E1032   The Coyote That Led Distressed
         Indian Woman to Safety [from
         George Bird Grinnell]   August 14, 1960

E1033   Pedro Alvarado: Shard of Reality.   August 21-28, 1960

E1034   The Old Mexico of Legend
         and Lore.   September 4, 1960

E1035   Story Tellers I've Known.
        [Part I-II]   September 11-18, 1960

E1036   Folk Anecdotes from Benjamin
        Butler Harris of *The Gila
        Trail* and other sources.   September 25, 1960

E1037   Two Philosophers: Another
        Burro and I.   October 2, 1960

E1038   John Graves and His
        Goodbye to a River.   October 9, 1960

E1039   Nat Straw of the Adams Diggins
        Gold and of Grizzlies.   October 16, 1960

E1040   Snake-Killing Cats and Dogs.   October 23, 1960

E1041   Mule Lore: Must the Mule Lift
        Its Tail To Bray?   October 30, 1960

E1042   Railroad Smith, John Rigby and
        Other Story Tellers I've Known.   November 6, 1960

E1043   Shooting My First Deer.   November 13, 1960

E1044   Hunt for Wild Turkeys on the
        Canadian River in the Indian
        Territory, 1878.   November 20, 1960

E1045   Lassoing Mustangs on the
        Steppes of Russia.   November 27, 1960

E1046   Being Master of Time;
        Cattle in Ireland.   December 4, 1960

E1047   Waiting in a Blind for
        Turkeys and Deer.   December 11, 1960

E1048   Silver Christmas Trees and
        Christmases of Long Ago.   December 18, 1960

E1049   Wild Turkeys and Wild
        Turkey Shooting.   December 25, 1960

1961
Austin American-Statesman.
Fort Worth Star-Telegram.
Houston Post.
San Antonio Light.

E1050   Belle Starr in Bed under Disguise.   January 1, 1961

E1051   Old-Time Texas Longhorns.   January 8, 1961

E1052   General Beale on Camels and
        Kit Carson.   January 15, 1961

E1053   Cold, Wet, Hungry—Then Food.   January 22, 1961

E1054   On Dave Garroway's "Today" Show.   January 29, 1961

E1055   Civil War Stories.   February 5, 1961

E1056   Old Mr. Flood, by Joseph
Michell: Food.   February 12, 1961

E1057   Uncle Beverly, Ex-Slave Preacher.   February 19, 1961

E1058   On Thomas Jefferson,   February 26-
Part 1 [-III]   March 12, 1961

E1059   On Rattlesnakes
[from John C. Myers]   March 19, 1961

E1060   Old-Time Cowman Talk.   March 26, 1961

E1061   Woman in the Bloody
Bucket Saloon.   April 2, 1961

E1062   A Pet Fox [from *My Life as an
Indian*, by Schultz]   April 9, 1961

E1063   Rescue of a Wild Swan in Scotland.   April 16, 1961

E1064   Horse Intelligence in Frost's "Stopping
by a Woods on a Snowy Evening."   April 23, 1961

E1065   Textbook Publishers as Stiflers
of Human Minds.   April 30, 1961

E1066   Two Foxes, One Jackrabbit,
Milch Cows on Our Ranch in
Live Oak County.   May 7, 1961

E1067   Milking Cows Another Way.   May 14, 1961

E1068   Education Courses vs. Civilized Living.   May 21, 1961

E1069   Cattle Stampeder and
Thief in Australia.   May 28, 1961

E1070   Florence Merriam's Charming Horses.   June 4, 1961

E1071   Animals and People Out of
Ralph Jackson's *Home on the
Double Bayou.*   June 11, 1961

E1072   Ideas from Letter Writers.   June 18, 1961

E1073   Frederic Remington, Artist of the West.   June 25, 1961

E1074   Paul Revere's Own Accounts of his Ride.   July 2, 1961

E1075   Remington and Russell,
Western Artists.   July 9, 1961

E1076	Sheep Walks in Old Spain.	July 16, 1961
E1077	Rattlesnakes Swimming in Water.	July 23, 1961
E1078	*The Queen's Necklace,* by Frances Mossiker.	July 30, 1961
E1079	The Missing Head of Pancho Villa.	August 6, 1961
E1080	Out of Boswell's Life of Dr. Johnson.	August 13, 1961
E1081	John Aubrey's *Brief Lives* for Humanity.	August 20, 1961
E1082	The Juice of Life in John Aubrey's Anecdotes.	August 27, 1961
E1083	Friendly Feelings for Friendly Rattlesnakes.	September 3, 1961
E1084	Caballeros and Cargadores in Mexico.	September 10, 1961
E1085	Old Brother Hog-Nosed Skunk.	September 17, 1961
E1086	Horse-Charmer of the Trans-Pecos.	September 24, 1961
E1087	Jim Ballard's Stories and Philosophy.	October 1, 1961
E1088	The Grey Wolf in Stories.	October 8, 1961
E1089	A Whisperer to Horses, by George Borrow.	October 15, 1961
E1090	Folk Tales on Husbands and Wives.	October 22, 1961
E1091	Lyndon Johnson's Camel Driver; the Censors.	October 29, 1961
E1092	Rattlesnake Tales of Horror.	November 5, 1961
E1093	Some Ranch People of Live Oak County.	November 12, 1961
E1094	On a Number of Things.	November 19, 1961
E1095	Possessed by Books.	November 26, 1961
E1096	The Blunts and Other Eccentrics.	December 3, 1961
E1097	From Bedichek to Plato.	December 10, 1961
E1098	Hunting White-Tailed Deer from a Blind.	December 17, 1961
E1099	Ella Byler Dobie and Christmas.	December 24, 1961
E1100	The Thinkers [in verse]	December 31, 1961

1962

Austin American-Statesman.
Fort Worth Star-Telegram.
Houston Post.
San Antonio Light.

E1101	Notes on Life in Texas for 1961.	January 7, 1962
E1102	From Aesop to Sandburg.	January 14, 1962
E1103	A Wild Goose and Her Gander.	January 21, 1962
E1104	On the Sheepiness of Sheep, Part I[-II]	January 28-February 4, 1962
E1105	A Pet Lobo and a Man [from James Willard Schultz]	February 11, 1962
E1106	The Sheepiness of Sheep, Part III.	February 18, 1962
E1107	Ab Blocker, Cowman.	February 25, 1962
E1108	Sheep: Marys Littl'e Lamb.	March 4, 1962
E1109	A Ballad and Wordsworth's "The Daffodils."	March 11, 1962
E1110	Lying about Snakes: Their Power To Charm.	March 18, 1962
E1111	A Night of Terror in Cambridge.	March 25, 1962
E1112	A Man Down in a Bear Den.	April 1, 1962
E1113	Libraries and Books.	April 8, 1962
E1114	King of the Condors.	April 5, 1962
E1115	A Dance Hall Singer of Aspen.	April 22, 1962
E1116	When a Mile Was a Mile: Tempo of the Horse Age.	April 29, 1962
E1117	Shadows of Life: Thomas Bewick.	May 6, 1962
E1118	Rattlesnakes I Have Known.	May 13, 1962
E1119	Rattlesnakes, Smelling Them, Bedichek.	May 20, 1962
E1120	Ideas for a Graduation Talk.	May 27, 1962
E1121	Rattlesnakes. Trapping Them.	June 3, 1962
E1122	Some Good Thing Out of Pecos, Texas: Young Bell.	June 10, 1962
E1123	Silent Dog and Silent Ghost.	June 17, 1962
E1124	The Bull Who Ate Pancakes.	June 24, 1962
E1125	John Adams and Two July 4ths.	July 1, 1962

E1126	Rattlesnakes: The Smell of, etc.	July 8, 1962
E1127	Ralph Yarborough's Story of Stallion and Confederate Officer.	July 15, 1962
E1128	Stories about Praying, by Captain Molesworth and Wilson Hudson.	July 22, 1962
E1129	Two Pet Roadrunners.	July 29, 1962
E1130	Rattlesnakes: Roping Them and Other Rope Stretching.	August 5, 1962
E1131	Books Enriched by Association.	August 12, 1962
E1132	Rattlesnakes and Other People.	August 19, 1962
E1133	Teaching School at Alpine, Texas [I-II]	August 26- September 2, 1962
E1134	Roadrunners Encouraged by Uvalde Rancher.	September 9, 1962
E1135	Rattlesnakes and a Treasure Hunter.	September 16, 1962
E1136	A Roadrunner and a Lost Girl.	September 23, 1962
E1137	Brother Coyote: The Charm of	September 30, 1962
E1138	Joe Wolfe and Martin Dodson, Old-Time Cowmen.	October 7, 1962
E1139	Cows with Special Appetites [by John C. Myers]	October 14, 1962
E1140	Movers, Mules and Old Rawhide.	October 21, 1962
E1141	Coyote—Its Haunting Voice in the Night.	October 28, 1962
E1142	Some Gatherings Along the Way.	November 4, 1962
E1143	The Sense of Direction in Some People.	November 11, 1962
E1144	Civil War Stories and Politicians.	November 18, 1962
E1145	Findley Simpson: Yarn Teller, Part [I-II]	November 25- December 2, 1962
E1146	After My Car Wreck of November 2, 1962.	December 9, 1962
E1147	W. H. Hudson of the Pampas.	December 16, 1962
E1148	Live Oak County People I Knew at the Ranch.	December 23, 1962
E1149	J. M. Shannon, San Angelo Character.	December 30, 1962

1963

Austin American-Statesman.
Fort Worth Star-Telegram.
Houston Post.
San Antonio Light.

E1150	John Chism and No Soup. In *Cow People.*	January 6, 1963
E1151	Stanley Walker's Outlook on Life.	January 13, 1963
E1152	Stanley Walker Observations.	January 20, 1963
E1153	Reminiscences of Frank Graham [Part 1-2]	January 27- February 3, 1963
E1154	Robert Frost of the Vermont Farm.	February 10, 1963
E1155	Bernal Diaz of the Conquest.	February 17, 1963
E1156	Censorship and Enlightened Minds.	February 24, 1963
E1157	The Two Minnies of Old Fort Worth. In *Cow People.*	March 3, 1963
E1158	Chuck Wagon Cook on the 101 Ranch. In *Cow People.*	March 10, 1963
E1159	My Friend, Walter Prescott Webb.	March 17, 1963
E1160	Memoirs of Henry Flipper.	March 24, 1963
E1161	"Almost Persuaded": Tales from Wilson Hudson.	March 31, 1963
E1162	An Essay on "Faces of Israel."	April 7, 1963
E1163	Don't Wed Yourself to a Horse. In *Cow People.*	April 14, 1963
E1164	The Hired Man on Horseback. In *Cow People.*	April 21, 1963
E1165	He Can't Come: He Has To Die. In *Cow People.*	April 28, 1963
E1166	Variations in Nature.	May 5, 1963
E1167	Barbecue on LBJ Ranch for UN Representatives.	May 12, 1963
E1168	Hill People in "Wimberley's Legacy."	May 19, 1963
E1169	Sheep on Earth and Sheep in Heaven.	May 26, 1963
E1170	A Horse Race in a Cow Camp.	June 2, 1963

E1171	How Smart Is a Smart Horse? Part in *Cow People*.	June 9, 1963
E1172	Cowman Doesn't Waste Words. In *Cow People*.	June 16, 1963
E1173	"I Guess He Needed Killing." In *Cow People*.	June 23, 1963
E1174	Recollections of Rattlesnakes.	June 30, 1963
E1175	Horses of the Argentine [from W. H. Hudson]	July 7, 1963
E1176	A Stingy Man and His Horse. In *Cow People*.	July 14, 1963
E1177	A Variety of Horse Lovers. In *Cow People*.	July 21, 1963
E1178	How Far Can a Horse Think? In *Cow People*.	July 28, 1963
E1179	Roy Bedichek and the Coffee Pot.	August 4, 1963
E1180	Rodney Kidd's Trip with Roy Bedichek.	August 11, 1963
E1181	A Colt-Killer Panther of the Brush Country.	August 18, 1963
E1182	A Horse Trader from Erasmus.	August 25, 1963
E1183	Certain People Out of the Earth.	September 1, 1963
E1184	Causes, Questions, Solicitations of the Day.	September 8, 1963
E1185	Cows in the Drouth of 1916-17 [Part 1-2]	September 15- 22, 1963
E1186	The Bedouin and His Famous Mare.	September 29, 1963
E1187	Talk and Silence in Old-Time Cow People. In *Cow People*.	October 6, 1963
E1188	Old-Time Cow People Talk. In *Cow People*.	October 13, 1963
E1189	Hen Baker and the Coyotes. In *Cow People*.	October 20, 1963
E1190	As Gay as a Grig.	October 27, 1963
E1191	Meeting the Sting of Death.	November 3, 1963
E1192	Charles M. Russell: Painter and Man.	November 10, 1963
E1193	Robert Frost's Letters.	November 17, 1963
E1194	Happenings in Old-Time Mexico.	November 24, 1963

E1195	The Sowers and the Reapers of Hate.	December 1, 1963
E1196	Mody Boatright's Oil Lore.	December 8, 1963
E1197	Cactus Bucks and Antlers.	December 15, 1963
E1198	The Instinct for Association.	December 22, 1963
E1199	John Fitzgerald Kennedy: The Summing Up.	December 29, 1963

1964

Austin American-Statesman.
Fort Worth Star-Telegram.
Houston Post.
San Antonio Light.

E1200	Drouthed People.	January 5, 1964
E1201	Terrazas of Chihuahua.	January 12, 1964
E1202	Drouths.	January 19, 1964
E1203	Civilized West.	January 26, 1964
E1204	Civilized Rancher.	February 2, 1964
E1205	Storytellers.	February 9-16, 1964
E1206	The Drouth and Prayer.	February 23, 1964
E1207	Jane Long of Aloneness and Love.	March 1, 1964
E1208	Teddy Roosevelt as a Cowman.	March 8, 1964
E1209	Jack Potter's First Train Ride.	March 15, 1964
E1210	With Kindness to Horse and Ox	March 22, 1964
E1211	Hidden Clay Pot of Gold	March 29, 1964
E1212	Storytellers.	April 5, 1964
E1213	Books, Humans Are Interwoven.	April 12, 1964
E1214	Shakespeare Is Personal to Me.	April 19, 1964
E1215	Lomax True Story Teller.	April 26, 1964
E1216	Of John A. Lomax.	May 3, 1964
E1217	Being a Guest in the White House.	May 10, 1964
E1218	Hash and Humanity in White House.	May 17, 1964
E1219	Monsters.	May 24, 1964
E1220	In New York City Half Century Ago.	May 31, 1964
E1221	Columbia University Personalities.	June 7 ,1964
E1222	Sermons I Remember Hearing.	June 14, 1964

E1223	Ideas, Newspapers and People.	June 21, 1964
E1224	The Rattling of a Rattlesnake.	June 28, 1964
E1225	My Questioning Cousin Dick.	July 5, 1964
E1226	Burton of 'The Arabian Nights'	July 12, 1964
E1227	A Parrot Smuggled Across Rio.	July 19, 1964
E1228	Responses to Letter-writers.	July 26, 1964
E1229	Ancient Fiddler of Memories.	August 2, 1964
E1230	Roadrunner Killing Rattlesnake.	August 9, 1964
E1231	Drouth Miseries Recalled.	August 16, 1964
E1232	Young Ike Pryor's Hunt for Cousin Sally.	August 23-September 6, 1964
E1233	A Champion Trapper of Lions.	September 13, 1964
E1234	Mark Twain Called Lincoln of US Literature.	September 20, 1964

Index

Guy Gillette

American Museum of Natural
History...B105
American Peoples
Encyclopedia Yearbook...B85
American Petroleum Institute
Quarterly...C436
American Scene...C487, D72
American Soldier Views...E261
American Statesman...C372a,
C386, C426, C441, D78
American Weekly
Magazine...C403, C405a
American West...D68
Americans in England...E234
America's Chance at
Greatness...E313
Америка. [i.e. Amerika]...C407b
Ameryka...C407c
Among the Lincolnshire Reds
in England...C218
Among the Redwood Trees of
California...E492
Ancient Fiddler of
Memories...E1229
And the Rains Came...E872
And the Shy Coyote Trots
Here and There...E632
Andy Adams, Cowboy
Chronicler...C23, D6, E111
Andy Adams: "Bear Sign"
Story...E522
Andy Adams: Man and
Writer...E521
Anecdotes about Cattle
Brands...E814
Anecdotes about Eating...E765
Anecdotes from Old Texas...E520
Animal Curiosity a Lot Like
That of Man...E679
Animal Tales of the
Southwest...B64
Animals and People...E1071
Announcements...B13
Announcer...C137, C142
Announces the Republication
of...Cattle Industry...D73
Another Juan Oso Story...E620
Another Nat Straw Grizzly Bear
Story...E887
Anti-Angloism:Is It
Justified?...C5
Antiquarian Booksellers
Association of America...C410
Antiquarian Press, ltd....D73
Antonetta's Leap...B3
Apache and His Secret...B71
Apache Campaign...B108, C422

Apache Gold and the Lost
Nigger Mine...E701
Apache Gold and Yaqui
Silver...A7, B33, C47, C83,
C87, C101, D25, E96
Appetite...E961
Appreciation...D64
Arabian Horses...E515
Archer B. Gilfillan...E870
Architects of Annexation...C265
Archive Wars of
Texas...D61, E863
"Are Texans Justified in Their
Bragging?"...C391
Argosy...C352
Arizona Highways...C171c,
C184a, C190, C199, C417
Arizona Quarterly...C422
"Arkansas Traveler"...B35
Armadillo...E399
Armadillo Lore...E945
Arnall, Ellis...C270
Arnold, Oren...B26
Arrows Kept Secret of Yucatan
Gold Nugget...E666
Art of Charles Russell...D72
Art of Discovery...B96, C343
Art of Living...C343
Art of the Frontier...C310
Art of Trailing...C198, E71
Art of Traveling in
England...E460
Artist Keeps His
Independence...E959
Artist Who Became a
Cowboy...C344
Arts of Living...B96
As a Noted Texan Sees State
Game Department...C174
As Gay As a Grig...E1190
As Smart As a Cutting
Horse...B36, E50
As the Moving Finger
Writ...C383, D53
Asa Jones' Cutting Horse...E777
At the Anchor...C227
Athletic Association of
Southwestern University...B1
Atkinson, Mary Jourdan...B7, D9
Atlantic..B60, C210a, C219,
C288, C335, C457
Atomic Age...C240
Atomic and Other Indian
Wisdom...E563
Atomic Capsules...E321
Aubry, Francois Xaxier...C390
Audubon Camp at Kerrville..E453

The text of this book is composed on the Linotype in 8 and 10 point Ionic Roman and Italics. Display lines are set in 24 point Century Nova Italic.

Composed and Printed by Colorgraphics, Oklahoma City, Oklahoma.

Designed by John A. Bridges, Paul E. Tate and Marvin E. Tong, Jr.

Paper, Sulgrave Ivory Antique Laid Text, manufactured by Standard Paper Manufacturing Co.

Bound by Becktold Company, St. Louis, Missouri.

Cloth for cover is Interlaken Bookcloth, manufactured by Arkwright-Interlaken Inc.